ENLIGHTENMENT AND THE GASPING CITY

ENLIGHTENMENT AND THE GASPING CITY

Mongolian Buddhism at a Time of Environmental Disarray

SASKIA ABRAHMS-KAVUNENKO

CORNELL UNIVERSITY PRESS
ITHACA AND LONDON

First published 2019 by Cornell University Press

Library of Congress Cataloging-in-Publication Data

Names: Abrahms-Kavunenko, Saskia, author.
Title: Enlightenment and the gasping city : Mongolian Buddhism at a
    time of environmental disarray / Saskia Abrahms-Kavunenko.
Description: Ithaca : Cornell University Press, 2019. | Includes biblio-
    graphical references and index.
Identifiers: LCCN 2018047981 (print) | LCCN 2018050327 (ebook) |
    ISBN 9781501737664 (pdf) | ISBN 9781501737671 (epub/mobi)
    | ISBN 9781501737640 | ISBN 9781501737640 (cloth) | ISBN
    9781501737657 (pbk.)
Subjects: LCSH: Buddhism—Mongolia—Ulaanbaatar. | Air—
    Pollution—Mongolia—Ulaanbaatar. | Human ecology—Mongolia—
    Ulaanbaatar. | Human ecology—Religious aspects—Buddhism. |
    Ethnology—Mongolia—Ulaanbaatar.
Classification: LCC BQ599.U43 (ebook) | LCC BQ599.U43 A27 2019
    (print) | DDC 294.309517/3—dc23
LC record available at https://lccn.loc.gov/2018047981

To the incredible, strong, and tenacious people of Ulaanbaatar

Contents

Acknowledgments

There are many people that I would like to thank for their help with this book. Without them, I could not have completed or likely even begun this manuscript.

First, I would like to thank all of my Mongolian friends and acquaintances who made time to chat with me about their lives, were a part of formal interviews, traveled with me, and allowed me to participate in ritual activities.

I am grateful to all of my students, teachers, friends, and acquaintances at Jampa Ling. Without your help I would not have been able to carry out my initial research. I am endlessly grateful to Zorigt Ganbold, whose weekly classes on Buddhism were always a pleasure and whose friendship warmed even the coldest of winter days. Many thanks to Baasansuren Enkhtungalag for being a great friend and a patient translator. Thank you also to Munguntsetseg Natsagdorj, Pürevsükh Urtnasan, and Otgonchimeg Tsendjav for always making us feel welcome at Jampa Ling and to Tsevlee Ongio for your delicious cups of *süütei tsai* and to your family for their ongoing warmth. Thanks to Delgermaa for teaching us how to make *buuz* and *khuushuur* and worrying that we couldn't take care of ourselves, even though we were twice your age. My gratitude to Caitriona Ni Threasaigh and to Amber Cripps for introducing Shultz and me to Jampa Ling and for being marvelous humans. Many thanks also to Panchen Ötrul Rinpoche and Geshe Lhawang Gyaltsen for supporting my research.

Thanks to all those from the Foundation for the Preservation of the Mahāyāna Tradition who supported my research. Special thanks to Thubten Gyalmo (Glenda Lee), whose generosity of spirit and deep calm contributes so much to the lives of lay Buddhists in Ulaanbaatar. Thanks also to Ani Thubten Samten and Ani Tenzin Tsultram.

Many thanks to all of those who made us feel welcome in Mongolia, including, but not limited to, those with whom we chatted, sang, traveled for hours in minivans, and ate. Many thanks go to Marc and Tuya, Ankha, Turuu, Oyuka, Enkhjargal, Shirmen, Dawaa, and Boloroo.

I am grateful to Altanzaya Dorjderem for enlivening my research and for your help with introductions and translations. Thanks also to your family: Nominjin for your help with translations and joyous karaoke singing and Robert Cater for many a spicy discussion. Many thanks go also to Soyombo and Oyunomin for greeting us with ever boundless warmth.

I am grateful to the American Center for Mongolian Studies. Special thanks to Baigalmaa Begzsuren, Tsermaa Tomorbaatar, and Marc Tasse.

Thanks to all the people who helped me during my research as research assistants and with transcriptions and translations, in particular, Munkhsoyol Bayardalai, Zolzaya Sukhbaatar, Altantsetseg Genden, Selenge Baatartsogt, Munkerdene Gantulga, Hishgue Tumurbaatar, Chimegsaikhan Munkhbayar, and Tian Tian Wedgwood Young.

I am appreciative of the feedback I received about my ideas and writing from the Max Planck Institute for Social Anthropology. Thanks so much to the research group Buddhist Temple Economies in Urban Asia, specifically to Christoph Brumann, Beata Switek, Hannah Klepeis, and Kristina Jonutyte. I loved sharing ideas with you all and participating in our weekly meetings. Thanks also to all those who participated in the rich intellectual life at the Max Planck Institute during my research fellowship. Thanks to Jutta Turner for her help with mapping. Many thanks to Chris Hann and to all of the talented scholars who were a part of the Department of Resilience and Transformation in Eurasia.

Thanks to my wonderful doctoral supervisors Victoria Burbank and Debra McDougall for providing such penetrating and balanced critiques of my work and for your unflagging support. Thanks to everyone from the Department of Anthropology and Sociology at the University of Western Australia. Thanks also to Vesna Wallace and Caroline Humphrey, who took the time to examine my dissertation, and to the two anonymous peer reviewers who took the time to review this manuscript.

Many thanks to the University of Western Australia and the Max Planck Institute for Social Anthropology for funding this research. Many thanks to Taylor and Francis (www.tandfonline.com) for allowing me to reprint portions of my article "The Blossoming of Ignorance: Uncertainty, Power and Syncretism amongst Mongolian Buddhists," originally published in *Ethnos: Journal of Anthropology*.

I am grateful to the Mongolian Studies Department at Eötvös Loránd University and Ágnes Birtalan for their research and for facilitating many insightful conferences. Special thanks go to Krisztina Teleki and Zsuzsa Majer for carrying out such excellent research without which I would have been completely lost and for being great company in Mongolia.

Thanks also to the Emerging Subjects of the New Economy research group at University College London for providing me with excellent feedback about my research. Thanks specifically to Rebekah Plueckhahn (it was great to have you in the field throughout my research), Rebecca Empson, Uranchimeg Ujeed, Lauren Bonilla, Hedwig Waters, Liz Fox, and Joseph Bristley for their feedback about some of the ideas that have become part of this book.

I am grateful to Brian Baumann for your feedback about my PhD and for hiking and tall tales. Many thanks to Marissa Smith for your feedback. Thanks to Jessica Madison-Pískatá for keeping it sparkling. Many thanks also to Bumochir Dulam and Lhagvademchig Jadamba from the National University of Mongolia.

A colossus of thanks to Emma Browne for your invaluable friendship and for introducing me to so many people. Thanks to Lama Karma Chimé Shore for sharing the tales of Buddhists in the Baikal region that first inspired us to travel to Mongolia and for introducing me to Buddhism in the first place.

Thanks to my parents, Mike and Helen, for supporting me throughout my doctoral research and beyond.

Thanks to James Marshall for all the adventures, inspiration, and continuing support.

And my boundless gratitude to my husband, Shultz, for talking to me about these ideas for years, for adventuring with me to Mongolia and on and on, and for editing this book with thoroughness and care.

Note on Transliteration and Terms

The transliteration of Mongolian, Sanskrit, Tibetan, and Chinese words are noted by the use of italics. Unless otherwise indicated, foreign words in italics are Mongolian. Mongolian terms generally follow contemporary Cyrillic spellings, rather than the classical script (see table below). When proper names have a common transcription in English, such as Khan rather than Khaan and Tuya instead of Tuyaa, the typical spelling is used to assist comprehension. Tibetan transliterations follow the Wylie system. Where possible, to avoid complicated transliterations that are difficult for the nonspecialist, common spellings of religious terms, such as "Gelugpa" for *dGe lugs pa* and "Rinpoche" for *Rin po che*, are used where either Mongolian or Tibetan transliterations could have been used. Likewise, where Sanskrit is commonly used to express Buddhist terms, such as *sūtra*, the Sanskrit term is used rather than its Mongolian counterpart. The use of Sanskrit is marked by "Sans." Tibetan is marked by "Tib." For Chinese terms, I have used "Ch." If disambiguation is required, the Mongolian terms are marked by "Mong." To avoid confusion, an *s* has been added to the singular form of non-English terms to indicate the plural.

Transliterations for Mongolian used in this book:

А: a	Ё: yo	Л: l	Р: r	Х: kh	Ы: i
Б: b	Ж: j	М: m	С: s	Ц: ts	Ь: i
В: v	З: z	Н: n	Т: t	Ч: ch	Э: e
Г: g	И: i	О: o	У: u	Ш: sh	Ю: yu/yü
Д: d	Й: i	Ө: ö	Ү: ü	Щ: shch	Я: ya
Е: ye/yö	К: k	П: p	Ф: f	Ъ: i	

The term "lama" rather than "monk" or "priest" is used throughout the book to indicate the monastic community. This reflects the local usage of the term *lam*. Unlike the term's usage elsewhere, this term is used for all male Buddhist religious specialists that wear robes and is not specifically reserved for high lamas.

ENLIGHTENMENT AND THE GASPING CITY

Introduction

It's early 2010 in Ulaanbaatar, Mongolia's capital city, and the winter is brutally cold, with temperatures plunging to minus 40°C and below. This winter there is a terrible *zud*[1] with conditions so bad that by the end of the winter over 8.5 million animals, almost 20 percent of the national herd, will have died (UNDP 2010, 2). The only animals I have seen for the last few months, except humans, are the city's imperturbable sparrows and the stray dogs that huddle in the city's open rubbish-collection points for warmth. It has been well below zero since early October, and by January even the pine trees have lost their needles. It is evening and I have decided to brave the nighttime temperatures to go see the film *Avatar*, the global hype around which having enveloped Ulaanbaatar too. Some friends pick me up, and we arrive, a little late, to a packed cinema. In the movie we are transported to an intensely colorful world with luminescent forests and the explicit interspecies connections of an imaginary, utopic iteration of our planet. Humans are the foes, waging war on an alien world to meet their own energy needs.

In the end they lose the battle and are sent back to their "dying world," our earth. The film finishes and we shuffle out, a little dazed, in search of my friend's car. The shock devastates; to walk out from technicolor immersion to the dark, freezing city choked in smog. As the frigid air hits my exposed upper face I feel the temperature as sharp, then numbing pain. This sensation is accompanied by the strongly acrid smell of burning coal and the near vertigo that comes with walking on a thick layer of ice, ever on the verge. The audio landscape is saturated with humming engines and car horns as drivers haphazardly navigate the overcrowded, deteriorating streets. The population of the Soviet-planned capital has more than doubled since the end of the socialist period, and the city is buckling under the pressure.

Ulaanbaatar's air pollution is worst in the *ger* (nomadic felt tents) areas that are located to the north, west, and east. Not reached by the city's coal-fired, Soviet-built central heating systems that heat the capital's centrally located apartment blocks, these ger neighborhoods must provision themselves with inefficient cast-iron stoves burning coal from Mongolia's coal mines. Because the temperatures are below zero for most of the year these stoves must run day and night to keep ger-area dwellers from freezing. The ger districts' built environment, consisting of gers and small cheaply built concrete buildings arranged inside wood-fenced compounds (*khashaa*) that are connected by unpaved roads, provides little protection for residents from the outside air. These neighborhoods house Ulaanbaatar's poorer inhabitants, and the worsening air pollution is a tangible consequence and correlate of growing social inequalities.

My apartment is an old, blue-gray five-story Soviet building in the center of the city, a bus or taxi ride away from one of my main field sites, Jampa Ling, a newly built Dharma Center[2] located at the edge of the western ger areas. On a particularly bad day in November 2009, the air outside of Jampa Ling is thick with smog, and it feels distressingly like being in a house fire. The atmosphere is so saturated with particulates that I cannot see across the street. In these conditions the effects are immediate: the smoke burns my eyes and lungs, and I contract a heaving cough from being outside for not much more than ten minutes. Mongolian friends tell me that it is just my lungs trying to clear out the bad air and that after a while they will stop trying and adapt to the air pollution. They are right. Within a month my cough has stopped. My frequent dreams of drowning, from which I wake up gasping for air, continue.

As in most cities affected by chronic problems, life in the polluted winter months continues as usual. Though the city is insinuated by a shrouding of dark smoke, people go to work, children attend school, and those living in the ger areas continue to burn coal as their only source of heating. My friend Tuya tells me in 2015 that her friends and acquaintances make jokes about their own air pollution amnesia. It is too cold to fix infrastructure in the winter, so problems need to be repaired in summer when it is warm enough. But everyone forgets about the pollution, she says, as soon as the air is clear again in the warmer months.

During the winter I, just like everyone else, continue my work as usual. I travel around the city to talk to lay Buddhists who are regular students at Dharma Centers and those that occasionally visit local temples. I attend ritual activities at temples, Buddhist centers and sacred sites. I discuss Buddhism with taxi drivers, friends, and acquaintances. Inside the newly built, colorfully decorated Dharma Centers, inattentive of the outside pollution, I sit on the carpeted floor and learn meditation with other lay Buddhists. The teacher tells us to imagine that our mind is like a clear blue sky and that our thoughts are like passing clouds. The students are told to perceive the thoughts like the clouds, letting them pass, rather than engaging or clinging to them. The clarity and brightness of the sky is symbolically linked to the ideal qualities of the mind.

Landlocked between China and Russia, Mongolia's landscape consists of steppe, desert, mountains, lakes, and some forest in the north. The sky (*tenger*) is wide and unobstructed. It plays a key role in the country's national imagination and has a long history of being worshipped. Mongolia's sky, as many a proud Mongol tells me, is clear for an average of 250 days a year. Buddhist prayer scarves are commonly colored bright blue (*tsenkher*) symbolizing reverence for the sky and its qualities. *Ovoos*, sacred rock cairns, are scattered all across the country and connect the mountaintops in veneration to the heavens. On *ovoos*, poles are mounted, from which prayer flags wave, catching the air in order to multiply blessings. The clarity of the sky and the light that it bestows are frequently discussed in Buddhist *sūtras*[3] (*sudar*). It is present in Buddhist iconography and utilized metonymically in teachings to lay Buddhists and religious specialists. At Dharma Centers bright light and clear skies are explicitly linked to purification (*ariutgal*) practices that are thought to help individuals reach enlightenment. Purification, along with light and clarity, are closely connected to enlightenment, both in its association with the seventeenth-century Enlightenment movement within Europe and its meanings within Buddhist soteriology (Sneath 2009).

In a country where the clear sky is so revered, and a city where the heavens routinely recede behind veiling smog, this book will explore the literal and figurative connections between light and its obscuration among urban Mongols. In Mongolia, light and connected concepts are seen in opposition to darkness, dirt, corruption, stagnation, and pollution in its spiritual and environmental meanings. The dimming of light in the form of dirt, pollution, and dust opposes light, purity, and enlightenment, along with movement and wind. By exploring the use, understandings, and oppositions of light (*gerel*) and spiritual pollution / air pollution (*buzarlal, agaarin bokhirdol*), this book will illustrate how contemporary Mongols approach religiosity in a city enshrouded in an amorphous substance that is neither material nor immaterial. By focusing on light, its intersections and its oppositions, this ethnography will attempt to illuminate Buddhist practices and beliefs in a living urban context wherein worsening air pollution and growing social inequalities ubiquitously and viscerally demand consideration.

Light and Enlightenment

Before the socialist period Buddhist institutions were dotted throughout Mongolia in key positions for trade and communication with nomadic herders (Moses 1977). They were the custodians of enlightenment. Within the temple walls lived reincarnation lineages that were believed to have reached such high levels of attainment that they could choose their own rebirths. High lamas were thought to be Bodhisattvas—beings that indeterminately delay complete enlightenment to help others be free from suffering and the endless rebirths of *saṃsāra*[4] (*orchlon*). These lamas were called *Gegeen*, meaning daylight, splendor, and brightness (Sneath 2009). They, along with other monastic teachers, taught the knowledge and practices needed to follow the Vajrayāna lineage of Buddhism, sometimes known as "the thunderbolt school." This school is believed by its followers to contain highly volatile rituals and methods that blaze a quicker path to enlightenment.

In the pre-socialist period Buddhist institutions were the custodians of soteriological praxis and passed this knowledge on to the next generations within monastic communities through teachings and secret tantric rituals carried out within the temple walls. For those Mongolian pastoralists who visited monasteries—some of the only permanent dwellings in the country—to trade and to seek medicine or protection, the lights of the hundreds of butter lamps and the ornately represented mystical powers of the reincarnation lineages must have left a striking impression.

In the 1930s, as the socialist government began waging a campaign of brutal repression against Buddhism, the term enlightenment (*gegeerel*) was appropriated to mean secular education (Bawden 1997). It, along with power, influence, and property, was wrestled, in a campaign lasting almost twenty years, from the hands of the monastics and high lamas. The socialist state was now able to say *who could* and *who could not* become "enlightened" and, perhaps more importantly, *how.* As the term transitioned to refer to socialist education in the sense of the European Enlightenment, knowledge became democratized (Kaplonski 2014). Ordinary women and men could become "enlightened" and could teach others how to do so. Enlightenment under socialism became a pursuit not only available to all Mongols but also morally incumbent upon them.

Accompanying this transition, the socialist state began providing electricity for the first time in the countryside. This introduction of electricity, or "Lenin's Light" (*Ilyichiin Gerel*), as it was known, to the countryside in the 1930s and 1940s was used to metaphorically link the socialist regime with "light" (*gerel*) and with the western idea of enlightenment as both transcendent and illuminating (Sneath 2009). Just as the Buddhist missionaries before them had believed that they carried the light of Buddhism to the dark north (Kollmar-Paulenz 2014), the socialist state saw itself as bringing light to what they saw as the "backward" pastoralists of rural Mongolia (Bruun and Narangoa 2006). In the state's view, in order for progress to occur along Marxist economic lines, pastoralists had to be educated and urbanized. As such, increasing urbanization accompanied the electrification of the countryside, facilitating schooling for the children of herders and supporting the administrative functioning of the new regime (Bruun and Narangoa 2006).

If the idea of light during socialism was mobilized by the government to mean education and "enlightening" activities, there is another way in which this metaphor can be used to elucidate the period. As electrification "enlightened" the countryside, the state increasingly used surveillance to expose those who did not fit within the narratives of socialist progress. Light provided illumination, but it also generated exposure. During the purges of the

1930s, thousands of people were taken away at night, often never to be seen by loved ones again (Buyandelger 2013). The torchlight carried by state officials at once exposed its victims and obscured the perpetrators of violence (Kaplonski 2008). This is another way that the socialist period brought "light" to Mongolia. While this light was shone most intensely during the purges of the 1930s, the state never fully relaxed its agenda of the persecution of religious activities. It continued seeking out and persecuting those carrying out illicit religious activities right up until the 1980s (Buyandelger 2013).

Along with the birthing of the nascent democratic movement, the end of the socialist period saw the rapid demolition of state infrastructure and the socialist economic sphere more broadly (Rossabi 2005; Sneath 2002). Wages became infrequent or stopped altogether for public servants, and privatizing infrastructure struggled to keep up with regular demands. Electricity shortages became common across the country leaving many households with patchy and irregular light. As Pedersen (2011) notes, during the sharp economic crises of the 1990s, electricity shortages were interpreted cosmologically by some Mongols to indicate the coming "age of darkness" (*kharankhui üye*), a period of increasing difficulties.

During my fieldwork in Ulaanbaatar in 2009–2010, 2013, 2015, and 2016, the city still suffered from inconsistent electricity and blackouts. However, the far greater threat to "light" in the city is the physical dimming of the once abundant natural light as the seasonal winter pollution unfurls itself like a blanket over the city, transforming Ulaanbaatar into one of the five worst cities for air pollution in the world (Guttikunda et al. 2013). Coal, the very source of energy used to create electric light and heat in the city, is now the top source of winter air pollution. The smoke from Ulaanbaatar's coal-fired power stations creates light in the home while diminishing the visibility and clarity of the air outside. Hearth fires in the extensive ger areas, necessary for heat and cooking, further saturate the haze.

Following the economic fluctuations that accompanied the end of socialism, the population in the capital has risen from around 560,000 in 1990 to 1.35 million in 2016. Ulaanbaatar now is home to around half of the national population, and the infrastructure is creaking from the strain. This increase in population is partly due to a number of terrible *zud*s that occurred from 1999 to 2002 and during my fieldwork in the winter of 2009–2010. The *zud* of the winter of 2009–2010 affected almost three-quarters of Mongolia's land, decimating 8.5 million heads of livestock, nearly 20 percent of the national herd (Janes and Chuluundorj 2015). These winters have the greatest effect on the livelihoods of the poorer herders and female-headed households, whose livestock numbers are lower and who have very little money to buy feed for the cattle when conditions necessitate it (UNDP 2010). In the early 1990s collective farms were dismantled and state-run transportation and provisioning that used to buffer the blow of these extreme winters ceased to function (Sneath 1998). Partly due to the lack of transportation, the size of rangelands decreased, causing degradation in Mongolia's pasturelands (Lkhagvadorj et al. 2013). Herders living on degraded pastures without the same level of mobility are more susceptible to livestock deaths in harsh winters (Sneath 1998). The loss of a herd often means migration to the capital to borrow money from relatives and/or to look for work. Many, after being reliant on the hospitality of their kin, realize that they are unskilled in an urban environment and find it difficult to transition to urban life. It was estimated in 2010 that over 50 percent of the capital's population now lives in the ger areas that surround the city (UNDP 2010). These areas make up 83 percent of Ulaanbaatar's built urban area (World Bank 2015, 1).

As luxury shopping malls, expensive goods, and apartment complexes have cropped up to service the new urban elite in the center and south of the city, the ger areas have expanded—lacking basic infrastructure, such as running water and waste-management systems. Since the time that I began doing fieldwork in 2009 there has been a visible increase in segregation in the city. The distance between the wealthy sections of the inner city and the outer edges has increased in time, effort, and cost, due to the ever-worsening traffic jams that clog the city's arterial roads, increases in transport costs, and the privatization of services such as schools for the wealthy. The main developments expanding to the south of the city promise lower pollution levels and a lifestyle likened to Seoul and Tokyo. What connects the center and the surrounding neighborhoods is the suffocating winter smog, which effects, to varying extents, all city residents.

As the city's population has more than doubled, the long winters have become increasingly unhealthy for the city's residents due to pollution from traffic and burning rubbish and the smoke of coal burned for heating and cooking in the ger areas. Ger neighborhood residents need to burn around two bags of coal and half a bag of wood a day to survive the harsh winters (Hamilton 2011). If people cannot afford it, they burn tires, fences, or rubbish, whatever they can to prevent themselves from freezing in winter temperatures averaging below minus 25°C. In 2011 the Mongolian government admitted that the pollution problem had become so bad that it had reached "disaster" status (Hamilton 2011), with epidemiologists saying that hospitalization from respiratory-related complaints was causing a public health crisis (Jacob 2011). Conservative estimates state that one in ten people who die in Ulaanbaatar die from diseases related to air pollution in the city (Ryan et al. 2013). The air pollution has also been strongly correlated with an increase in spontaneous abortions in the winter months (Enkhmaa et al. 2014). Due to an increasing awareness of the effects that hazardous air quality can have on an unborn child, some doctors instruct women who have had a series of miscarriages to live in the countryside during their pregnancy (Fukuda 2017). For those living in ger areas, around one-quarter of Mongolia's entire population, the air quality is poorest. For the urban poor, health problems caused by continuous exposure to particulates are compounded by poor access to health care.

During winter the air quality index (AQI), used to measure pollution particulates on a scale from 0 to 500, is exceeded daily. On the fifteenth of September each year, additional coal-fired power stations used to heat the city's apartment blocks are turned on, and these power stations run until the fifteenth of May the following spring. As Ulaanbaatar is located between mountains the freezing temperatures create a thermal inversion, trapping the smoke from ger stoves, power stations, exhaust from cars, and burning rubbish. To give a sense of how bad the pollution is, Beijing, as of October 2013, issues a red alert if the air pollution reaches particulates of more than 500 in one day, above 300 over two days, or an AQI of over 200 for four days in a row (Tiezzi 2015). A red alert means that construction sites and schools are closed for the period. Ulaanbaatar's air during winter has high daily averages of 750 µg/m^3 (Guttikunda et al. 2013). In spite of this devastating seasonal problem, in 2015, due to the economic crisis, the government ended its funding to the Clean Energy Fund, a program that was created to deal with the pollution problem.

As smog infests the city in the long and cold winter, thermal inversion prevents the polluted air from escaping the valley it lies in, save through the exceptional achievement of unusually strong winds. When I asked people what they thought was the opposite of environmental pollution many replied that it was wind, as wind could rid the city of the air pollution. In winter the urban environment has become one of stagnation, but a kind of stagnation

Figure 1. Statue of a wind horse at a pilgrimage site near Sainshand in the Gobi Desert.

that contains within it unseen and potentially dangerous movement. Many believe that spirits capable of affecting people's fortunes are present in the city. Stagnation and immobility have powerful imaginative resonance in Mongolia. For Mongols immobility is associated with laziness (Benwell 2013). At the same time, stagnation is associated with the blockage of one's fortune (Humphrey and Ujeed 2012).

The symbol of the wind horse (*khiimori*) is common throughout the country, printed on Buddhist flags that are placed upon *ovoo*s and in high places where they can flutter in the wind. The connection of the horse to wind has a strong allegorical resonance in the imagination of Mongols who connect life-sustaining nomadic movement to horses. One's khiimori is one's internal energies. This energy is thought to be influenced from outside and can be adversely affected by external contamination (Humphrey and Ujeed 2012). Khiimori is associated with metaphors of air and movement. It is thought that in order to maintain one's khiimori a person should follow the movements of the sun. For instance, it is common for mothers to encourage their children to rise with the morning sun as aligning oneself with natural movements is thought to "raise their" khiimori (Humphrey and Ujeed 2012, 160). If one experiences a period of bad luck it could be thought that their khiimori is "lying down." A person's khiimori may be weakened due to normal fluctuations or because it has been polluted by outside forces. If outside forces are to blame, a lama or a shaman can carry out specific readings and rituals to cleanse one's khiimori (Humphrey and Ujeed 2012, 156).

In the context of the winter city, a lack of light is inextricably associated with a lack of wind. Pollution hangs in the air aided by a lack of sufficient air and movement. Movement and wind create clarity. These associations of purity with wind and clarity have a strong resonance in Buddhist teaching lineages both inside and outside Mongolia. Just as the clarity of mind is linked to a clear blue sky, one's breath is the primary place where one is clearly interdependent with one's surroundings. Breath animates and connects. The pollution of the air, with its actual limitations on light and breath, creates obscurations in both cosmological and tangible ways. Pollution blocks, suffocates, and delimits.

Urban Life in the Anthropocene

We are no longer poised on the edge of the abyss, contemplating its vastness . . . Instead . . . we have discovered that we are already falling inside the abyss, which is not pure empty space, but instead the fiery interior of a hyperobject . . . Flying through the universe in the space shuttle of modernity, we find out that we were driving with the breaks on, revving the engine while the fuselage lies rusting in a junkyard. (Morton 2013, 160)

In early 2009 the east coast of Australia, where I was traveling before I left for Mongolia, was experiencing a heat wave. The Department of Meteorology in Melbourne measured three consecutive days above 43°C (109°F) with the highest temperature reaching 45.1°C (113.2°F), the third hottest day in the city's history. The bushfires started when meteorologists registered the hottest temperatures since documentation began, including in Melbourne, where an all-time high of 46.4°C (115.5°F) was recorded. The wildfires that began on that day killed 147 people, and they were the worst recorded in Australia's history. These fires released an estimated 8.5 million tons of carbon dioxide into the atmosphere (Williams et al. 2011), adding to the problem of what many commentators are now calling "runaway climate change"—wherein rising temperatures cause the further release of carbon dioxide through events such as wildfires and the release of natural gas from the now melting Siberian permafrost. In Australia, the incredibly hot temperatures in the southeast, along with the dry conditions that enabled the fires to intensify, formed part of a complex of factors that are the preconditions for "megafires." These tremendous fires are fueled by drought and temperature extremes and are both the result of and further contribute to global warming (Williams et al. 2011). Megafires are so vast that they dwarf previously known natural disasters. They burn so ferociously that they irreversibly damage landscapes, even in Australia where ecosystems have evolved to regenerate through fire.

In early 2010, Mongolia was experiencing a natural disaster caused by an incredibly cold winter and the previous summer's drought. In the depths of the winter, Mongolia's government had declared a national emergency as the country's livestock began to be decimated by a terrible *zud*. The *zud* of 2010, like others of the twentieth century, was produced by a lack of rainfall in the summer months and was followed by inclement weather conditions, such as heavy snowfall, in the winter months (Janes and Chuluundorj 2015). Of the ten *zud*s that have been recorded since 1944, five have occurred since 1990, indicating that their increasing frequency is related to broader patterns of climate change produced by global warming (Janes and Chuluundorj 2015). The devastating effects of these disasters have been amplified by the dismantling of farming collectives (*negdel*) in the early 1990s as Mongolia switched to a capitalist economy. As a result, herders have now lost access to the state-run transportation that used to buffer the blow of these extreme winters (Sneath 1998). The dismantling of the *negdel*, along with growing inequalities in the countryside, has created conditions that aggravate problems with overgrazing, conflicts around grazing pastures and water, trespassing, and the theft of animals, all of which leave herders vulnerable to the extreme conditions caused by global warming (Janes and Chuluundorj 2015).

In both of these disasters other-than-human forces had a profound effect on human and nonhuman lives. A lack of rainfall was a precondition for both, along with temperature extremes. These climatic conditions are not part of the "normal" weather cycles in human history. Human activities since the Industrial Revolution have radically altered the global climate, which is now, in turn, dramatically influencing human lives. Since the eighteenth century, humans as a species have had such a measurable impact on the ecosystems and the geology of the planet that many geologists argue that it should be designated as a new era, departing from the Holocene, called the Anthropocene. Though still a subject of debate among geologists, this era's commencement has generally been linked to two key dates. The first being around 1784, the year that geologists have traced the residue of carbon from the coal-fired industries of the Industrial Revolution to the remotest regions of the world. And the second date 1945, when the atom bombs dropped on Hiroshima and Nagasaki caused radioactive material to be deposited all over the earth's crust (Morton 2013). From about 1950 onward, the impact of humans grew exponentially in intensity in a period some scholars refer to as the Great Acceleration. From the middle of the twentieth century, the net effect of human activity has, despite or due to intended motives, been the destruction of ecosystems, the release of greenhouse emissions into the atmosphere, the acidification and depopulation of the oceans, and rapid deforestation.

There have been several renamings of the Anthropocene by philosophers and social scientists, some of whom are concerned that the label merely reflects an amplification of human hubris regarding our control over the planet. These names include the Capitalocene, which foregrounds capitalism's impact on the planet (problematically obscuring the massive industrial impact of socialist countries during the twentieth century—Chernobyl and the drying up of the Aral Sea come quickly to mind); the Plasticene, which foregrounds the impact of human rubbish; and Haraway's Chthulucene (2016), among many others.

Latour (2014) argues that the label the Anthropocene can be seen as an opportunity for anthropologists as the term irreparably destroys the perceived dichotomies between "human society" and "nature." As he writes, in the

Anthropocene the idea of pristine nature untouched by humans has been ruptured: "there is no distant place anymore" (Latour 2014, 2). As the Anthropocene breaks apart the divide between nature and society, it contains within it a double movement. The first in the realization that humans now deeply and profoundly affect every part of the planet and the second in the awakening that we do not, and cannot, control the complex systems of the earth (Latour 2014).

During the natural disasters above, I was living in an urban environment where I felt the shocks of the temperature extremes and experienced the resultant devastation filtered through news media. I did not have my animals die or have my livelihood destroyed. Urban dwellers tend to be buffered from intimacy with the feedback loops of calamities that are increasingly affecting herders and farmers, informing them about the changes that are happening to the environment. Urban centers are examples of the ingenuity of human niche construction, whereby an organism, such as the iconic earthworm, actively alters its environment to make that environment more habitable for itself, reducing the immediate selection pressures of natural selection (Odling-Smee, Laland, and Feldman 2003). In large cities, most urbanites live largely disconnected from the processes that feed them and provide them with energy. For the wealthier inhabitants of cities temperature extremes are more of an inconvenience, to be alleviated with central heating or air conditioning, than the serious threat that they are for the urban poor. As Morton writes, the poor "perceive the ecological emergency not as degrading an aesthetic picture such as *world* but as an accumulation of violence that nibbles at them directly" (2013, 125). Yet it is wealthy urbanites who mostly decide which resources can be mined and logged, how industry should be regulated, how economic resources should be distributed, and how a nation should interact with their neighbors.

In spite of the many buffers that distance urban dwellers from broad environmental changes, the lives of even the wealthiest urban dwellers are profoundly affected by pollution. In 2016 the World Health Organization announced that air pollution is now affecting the lives of around 92 percent of the world's human population (BBC 2016). A recent study suggested that air pollution in Africa is responsible for more deaths than malaria, malnutrition, or dirty water (Vidal 2016). In the winter of 2016–2017 northern India was covered in a toxic blanket of smog (Safi 2016). At the same time even European cities, such as Paris, had to curb urban behaviors to limit serious air pollution problems (Willsher 2017). While the wealthy residents of Ulaanbaatar filter the air in ways not accessible to those living in ger areas, Ulaanbaatar's air pollution profoundly influences all of its inhabitants.

This ethnography will illustrate urban life in the Anthropocene. It will pay close attention to the ways that pollution, light, and purity are part of urban assemblages. As DeLanda (2016) describes them, assemblages are constituted from heterogeneous elements, which, through their interactions with one another, have emergent properties that are immanent rather than transcendent. By following the unfolding relationships that urban Mongols have with light and its obscuration this ethnography will explore urban religious assemblages, of which pollution is a part, in a bustling cosmopolitan capital city. Pollution intricately influences the fabric of urban lives, not only through the bodies that breathe the particulate saturated air but also in religious practices and understandings and the city's psychological underpinnings.

The Social Life of Difficult Things

> Still, on examining them with precision tools and exacting care, one may also find that some, many, or even all objects are blurry on the edges or fuzzy to the core. (Perl 2011, 444)

The "material turn" in anthropology has questioned anthropological tendencies to view nonhuman artifacts, agents, and things as symbols to be interpreted. This assumption was questioned when Appadurai (1988) argued that more attention should be paid to the "social life of things"—in particular, how objects have cultural biographies that change as they transition through different "regimes of value." Scholars, such as Miller, have suggested that a new materiality needs to investigate "how the things that people make, make people" (Miller 2005, 28). How, for instance, do materials craft religious life in religiously pluralistic Southeast Asia (Bautista 2012)? And what does a materialist anthropology look like when anthropologists take the worlds of their interlocutors more seriously by "thinking through things" (Henare, Holbraad, and Wastell 2007)?

These projects often look to human artifacts to explore how things influence social lives. Yet how does one conceptualize a "thing" as complex as air pollution or swelling oceans, which, while a part of human heritage, are "unruly" (Olsen and Pétursdóttir 2016)? How do we follow "objects" (or perhaps, rather, phenomena) so vast that they are difficult to conceptualize at all? The thick coal-soaked air of Ulaanbaatar is an element of global warming—a temporally vast and undeniably powerful object with its own agency and staggering force. Although it is the result of human activity, it is a difficult "object" to conceptualize, if it can be considered an object at all. Air pollution is a visible element of an enormously complex system, a part of what Morton (2013) calls a "hyperobject." It connects to global warming, a force that is so immense, both in time and space, that it is difficult to grasp and so colossal it is difficult to see (Morton 2013).

A hyperobject can only be viewed as though we were on a two-dimensional plane looking at a three-dimensional object passing through our world. Our narrow understandings of complex assemblages like air pollution are limited to partial identifiers, such as mortality rates and miscarriages. These statistics are highlighted by concerned policy makers and nongovernment organizations to demonstrate the urgency of Ulaanbaatar's plight. Yet somehow, even though these statistics speak directly about life and death, they seem to fall on deaf ears. Like the science that draws our attention to the terrifying consequences of global warming, it becomes a policy problem, to be filed like any other, that needs to be addressed at a later date with resources that seem to be hard to muster in the present.

This ethnography attempts to demonstrate some of the assemblages that are uniquely influenced by the persistence of the city's pollution. It will investigate the more troublesome or "ugly" human heritage of life in the Anthropocene (Dalby 2016). In doing so, it is a challenge to anthropologists working within the material turn to extend the kinds of "things" that are worthy of study in the Anthropocene. Air pollution marks the boundary between what is often considered to be the physical and the immaterial. One can't really hold onto it, but it is visible to the naked eye. Inhaled as breath, it intimately connects with every cell of a person's body. It insinuates itself into all parts of the city, yet it ultimately eludes capture and control.

It is precisely this lack of clarity, this ambiguity or fuzziness, that makes pollution resonate powerfully within the minds of Ulaanbaatar's residents. It is a metonym for the persistent unpredictability of the urban environment, from the day-to-day issues of whether a debt will be repaid or a permit approved to the more complex issues of an unstable economy. As these radical economic uncertainties have replaced the sense of continuity that the socialist system (though often oppressively cast) had provided in the decades preceding 1990,[5] public religious institutions and practices have revived. Yet these institutions, along with an array of independent religious specialists, are not detached from the broader uncertainties that characterize the city. They too, as this ethnography will explore, are plagued by vagueness, uncertainty, and feelings of ignorance.

A condition of fuzziness or blur is not necessarily a problematic state. Indeed, as I will argue in chapter 4, feelings of ignorance and uncertainty in Mongolia are in fact generative of religious practices of all kinds. Uncertainty, in Buddhist texts, is a state of being for all living things. Acknowledging one's ignorance is a necessary precondition for entering the path toward enlightenment (Cassaniti 2006; Mair 2007). Since Buddhist soteriology is ultimately about awakening to some state of non-delusion, a Buddhist who is no longer ignorant as to the true nature of reality is enlightened, a difficult state to achieve indeed. However, as very few people engage with this level of Buddhist philosophy in the capital, a condition of ignorance, while generative of a variety of religious practices, interacts with other urban anxieties and is viewed predominantly from outside of Buddhist philosophy rather than from within its frame (see chapter 4).

Most of Ulaanbaatar's urban population by necessity navigates through "fuzzy thinking." As the urban economy rises and falls in unpredictable ways, sustaining life in the capital for much of Ulaanbaatar's inhabitants is characterized by instability (Højer and Pedersen 2008). Chapter 1 describes how dust, dirt, pollution, and attending metaphors instantiate and exacerbate the reduced visibility within Mongolia's vacillating capitalist economy. It discusses how the post-socialist economy, which is reliant upon mining activities, creates dust, pollution, and dirty money, along with increasing debt. It demonstrates the links between Mongolia's mining economy, corruption, global warming, dust, and dirt.

Chapter 2 explores the history of light and enlightenment in Mongolia. It looks at how light and its obscuration were mobilized during the pre-socialist and socialist periods, specifically from the Mongolian Empire to the end of the socialist period. It examines how the revisionist histories and ideas of purification encouraged by the Qing Empire resonate in contemporary religious practice in Mongolia today. Following the end of the Qing Empire and the brief period of independence, the mastery of light, enlightenment, and purification were taken from the control of Buddhist institutions and placed under the responsibility of the socialist government. It examines each period and its specific relationship to light, purification, and enlightenment.

Chapter 3 looks at the role of Buddhism within nationalist narratives since the beginning of the Democratic Revolution. It explores how ideas of purity and purification are common within post-socialist nationalist narratives that contain anti-syncretic impulses. It will also show that while there are loud anti-syncretic nationalist elements present, many of which have an overt Sinophobic orientation, cosmopolitanism still dominates religious practice in the capital city.

Chapter 4 explores contemporary anxieties about religious ignorance in Ulaanbaatar. It discusses how instead of distancing laypeople from religious practice, concerns about religious ignorance are generative of religious practice. Through frequently describing their own or others' ignorance about Buddhism, lay Buddhists indicate that Buddhism and the renewed possibilities of knowledge or ignorance about Buddhism are a matter of considerable importance. Concerns about religious ignorance also indicate a change in Buddhist epistemologies from the pre-socialist era. Religious knowledge and enlightenment, rather than being something that only a small number of high lamas have access to, has become to a certain extent democratized. This chapter discusses how talk about religious ignorance in Ulaanbaatar presents itself in a variety of complementary and conflicting ways: as a reflection of anxiety over lost traditions, as a source of power and deference, and as a blossoming space for hope and religious enthusiasm.

Chapter 5 describes how the changing architecture of the city blurs the once prominent Buddhist institutions from view. It discusses the presence, or lack, of Buddhist practices in the daily lives of urbanites and the visible and invisible connections that support and undermine Mongolian Buddhist religious institutions in the capital. It discusses several Buddhist figures associated with bringing light and enlightenment to the capital and their geopolitical importance for the country.

Chapters 6 and 7 investigate the ways that environmental pollution is connected to the unseen causal systems that are believed to influence unfolding fortunes. Chapter 6 examines karma as a moral mode of causality that creates recompense for immoral activities, including corruption and polluting. It explores karma as a model of causality wherein immoral actions create negative ramifications for individuals and collectives. Chapter 7 describes ritual activities to purify obstacles that are thought to inadvertently cause blockages or affect the energetic systems of individuals, families, and businesses. These operate in a nonmoral or minimally moral causal mode, involving disruptions and reorientations of one's fortunes. It discusses rituals carried out at Buddhist temples and their interpretation as unblocking, purifying, and encouraging free-flowing energy and movement. While chapter 7 explores accidental blockages and restrictions, and chapter 6 investigates religious interventions into the negative consequences of actions carried out with bad intentions, these are not posited as ideal and distinct operations, and both require ritual purification.

Chapter 8 looks at how anxieties regarding moral decline in the postsocialist period influence the economic stability of newly revitalized Buddhist institutions and attitudes toward religious specialists. It explores how narratives of pollution and purity interweave with concerns about corruption, fiscal imperatives, and ignorance within Buddhist institutions in the capital.

Chapter 9 discusses the influence of vegetarian New Religious Movements on ideas of enlightenment, light, and purification in the capital. Given their popularity among my interlocutors, these groups have a profound effect on religious ideas. How Mongols approach the possibility of enlightenment is frequently related to ideas of purification, and, with the popularity of vegetarian New Religious Movements encouraging purification through radical lifestyle changes, this is no longer simply the domain of high lamas within Buddhist institutions. This chapter will explore how vegetarian New Religious Movements offer purification through meditation and the eating of vegetarian or "white" foods, which have a long association with purity and purification.

Fieldwork

This monograph is based on around twenty-two months of fieldwork that I carried out in Ulaanbaatar from 2009 to 2010 and on subsequent trips in 2013, 2015, and 2016. During this ethnographic research, I spent time with lay Buddhists that coalesce around two discernible but connected paradigms of Buddhist practice and community encountered in Dharma Centers, at local temples, and among the urban community more generally. The first loose "group" of lay Buddhists that I spent time with were those that frequently attended educational classes at Ulaanbaatar's Dharma Centers. These were from diverse socioeconomic backgrounds and most spoke only Mongolian. With the students of these centers I participated in ritual services, educational classes, and social activities, and conducted formal interviews. The second group of lay Buddhists (and some non-Buddhists) was composed of those I met when visiting Buddhist temples and rituals and in my daily life. These were friends, acquaintances, chatty middle-aged or older ladies at rituals, friends' family members, friends' friends, and friends' colleagues. As I lived in the center of the city in an apartment this second collection of urbanites tended to live centrally in apartments. They were mostly highly educated, and, although many had been born in the countryside, most were relatively well off. The lamas that I met during my fieldwork worked (or had previously worked) at temples or Dharma Centers. Many had studied in southern India with Tibetans in diaspora, while others were locally trained.

The Dharma Centers where I carried out research were positioned at two key locations in the city. The first of these was a charity and Dharma Center in the Third and Fourth District called Jampa Ling. The second was the Foundation for the Preservation of the Mahāyāna Tradition's (FPMT) centrally located Shredrup Ling. At Jampa Ling, my husband and I taught English classes to young children and to university-age students who attended Buddhist teachings at the center. We traded English lessons for lessons on the *Lam Rim Chen Mo*, a key Gelug text, from Lama Zorigt Ganbold, a twenty-four-year-old Mongolian lama who had trained in southern India at the Drepung Gomang Monastery and was teaching the weekend classes at Jampa Ling during our stay. As a result of the charitable work that Jampa Ling does, students attracted to the center come from a wide range of socioeconomic groups. While some of the students traveled from the wealthier sections of the inner city to learn about Buddhism, others came from nearby apartments or ger areas or attended classes because they had connections to the center as a result of receiving charity.

The organization, like most in Mongolia, is part of the Gelug lineage, or "yellow religion" (*sharin shashin*). It is headed by Panchen Ötrul Rinpoche, a Tibetan-born lama who was born in 1939 and was chosen as a candidate for the reincarnation of the Panchen Lama at the age of seven. In 1960 he escaped to India as a refugee and has lived in Ireland since 1990. In 1995, he made his first visit to Mongolia with His Holiness the Fourteenth Dalai Lama. During the trip the Dalai Lama asked if he could stay to teach Buddhism in Mongolia. As a result, Panchen Ötrul Rinpoche now returns annually to give teachings in Mongolia during the summer (Jampa Ling Tibetan Buddhist Center n.d.).

The light-yellow two-story building that houses Jampa Ling was built in 2003, on the very edge of the spreading western ger areas. From 2009 to 2010, it housed two residential lamas, along with visiting teachers and volunteers. One of my main interlocutors was Lama Zorigt Ganbold, an affable Mongolian lama who taught most of the weekend classes at Jampa Ling during my fieldwork in 2009 and 2010. His opinions about Buddhist practice were heavily influential on the perspectives of the young and old students that he taught weekly on Saturdays and Sundays. Born in Ulaanbaatar to a middle-class family, when he was eleven years old his grandmother was approached by a number of lamas looking for new disciples in 1997. These Mongolian lamas from Gandan and the nearby Lam Rim Temple (a temple just south of the main temple complex) were looking specifically for children born in the Year of the Tiger. Men born in the Tiger year, according to Mongolian astrological systems, are believed to become good lamas or good politicians. After some initial resistance Zorigt became interested in the idea of becoming a lama and, as he told me, wearing a lama's clothes and being able to speak in an educated way. At age eleven he began studying Buddhism with Tibetan-born Geshe Lhawang Gyaltsen.

At fourteen Zorigt was granted permission by Panchen Ötrul Rinpoche to become a monk, and traveled to southern India to be educated at the Drepung Gomang Monastery. There he studied for seven and a half years and lived a strict life of study and renunciation. Lama Zorigt rarely left the monastery compound, as novices had to get several high-ranking lamas to approve their leave. He returned to Mongolia because he had problems with his back and was encouraged to stay in Mongolia by Geshe Lhawang and Panchen Ötrul Rinpoche. In Ulaanbaatar he taught dharma classes and helped with translations. Although he was given a Tibetan name when he was in India, upon returning his friends and students preferred to call him by his Mongolian name. The other residential monk, a quizzical young lama named Pürevsükh Urtnasan, studied with Lama Zorigt at the Drepung Gomang Monastery and was working as a translator, translating untranslated and modern Tibetan texts into modern Mongolian, as well as undertaking research on the Indian Sanskrit poet Kalidasa. Jampa Ling received funding from one of the Dalai Lama's charities to build a printing press, and this was used to print translations of important Buddhist texts into Mongolian.

Figure 2. Lama Zorigt sitting in front of the main shrine at Jampa Ling.

Jampa Ling is connected to a charity called Asral that provides funding and employment for women who head or are part of impoverished families. During 2009 and 2010, they had a felting company called Made in Mongolia that employed local economically disadvantaged women. The center provides English-language classes, additional tutoring, and hot meals for their children before they go to school. In winter they provide coal, warm clothes, and other essential services for poor families. They run three rural charities, one in the nearby town of Gachuurt, another to the southeast of Ulaanbaatar in Shankh, and one at Öndörshil in Dundgov Aimag.[6] In Shankh they have a temple that provides education for novice lamas from Ulaanbaatar during the summer months. On the weekends, during my initial fieldwork, Jampa Ling taught Buddhist philosophy and transformative practices (such as meditation and prostrations) to old and young students. It also conducted bimonthly *pūjā*s (*takhil*),[7] held public rituals, and gave public teachings by foreign and local teachers. The ages of the participants I formally interviewed there varied from sixteen to seventy-five, were mainly women (reflecting the broader tendencies for women to be more involved in Buddhist educational activities), and came from a variety of socioeconomic backgrounds.

When I returned to Mongolia in 2013 Jampa Ling had radically changed.

Geshe Lhawang, the main Tibetan lama who had been living at the center, had left, and many of his students had followed him to build a new center called Arvidin Oron Töv. His followers, equipped with the skills they had acquired working at Jampa Ling, raised funds and built a new Dharma Center and temple to the east of Narantuul market. It, like Jampa Ling, has a charitable outreach, houses live-in Tibetan lamas and lay Buddhist staff, and maintains regular educational activities. They also have a center outside of the city limits in the nearby town of Nalaikh, which is used for meditation retreats and, no doubt, as a refuge for urbanites from the city's air pollution. The two residential lamas at Jampa Ling, Lama Zorigt Ganbold and Lama Pürevsükh Urtnasan, are no longer at Jampa Ling and have both disrobed due to personal reasons. They continue to actively participate in Buddhist centers and in educational activities and have traveled extensively since my initial research.

The other main field site where I met people attending regular Buddhist classes was Shredrup Ling, an inner-city Buddhist center run by the FPMT. The FPMT is a global Buddhist organization headed by Lama Zopa Rinpoche. Like Jampa Ling it is part of the Gelug lineage. The FPMT supports a number of charitable projects, predominantly, at the time of my initial fieldwork, through their nunnery, the Dara Ekh Khiid (or Dolma Ling Nunnery). In 2009 they had a soup kitchen there that fed over seventy people every day and a small medical center that provided basic medical services. They also ran a sewing center for unemployed women. The Dara Ekh Khiid is the only residential nunnery in Mongolia. Initially it had fourteen Mongolian nuns and two that were studying in India.

Before arriving in Mongolia I had intended to make the nunnery Dara Ekh Khiid my primary field site. However, due to some difficulties management was having with the operation of the nunnery, it was impossible for me to participate in regular activities there. The inaccessibility of the nunnery culminated in an electrical fire that burned down a substantial part of it at the beginning of December 2009. Luckily no one was hurt, although the oldest nun, who was ninety-five at the time, was almost killed because she was sleeping in the building adjacent to the kitchen, which was the first to catch fire. I was told that in spite of her advanced years she managed to escape through a window and was unharmed. Because of her age and a desire to not be a burden on the organization, she had hidden money for her funeral in between the pages of a *sūtra*. After the fire had been put out, even though most of the other things in the room had been thoroughly burned, providence preserved the *sūtra* and the money that it contained, as well as a portrait of Lama Zopa Rinpoche.

Shredrup Ling itself has maintained its presence as a central Dharma Center with ongoing classes, international volunteers, and the hosting of a vegetarian restaurant. It has weekly meditation classes, beginner's courses on Buddhism, yoga lessons, and Tibetan-language classes and regularly holds *pūjā*s and other rituals. It is a popular place for people to learn about meditation and Buddhism, and most of the people I spoke to at Jampa Ling had at some time attended or were currently attending classes there too. The teaching room, which is located on the second floor, is frequently filled with more than a hundred people, especially when a new teacher arrives to give teachings. During all of my visits, an Australian nun, Ani Gyalmo, was the main spiritual teacher at the center. She taught Buddhist courses, meditation, and yoga classes at Shredrup Ling and volunteered weekly to teach prisoners meditation in Mongolia's high-security prison.

In addition to my fieldwork at these Dharma Centers, I spent time attending rituals, chatting with laypeople, and visiting lamas at Ulaanbaatar's Gandantegchenlin Khiid (locally known as Gandan), the largest temple in Mongolia; Dashchoilin Khiid, which once dominated the cityscape; and some other smaller temples, such as the single Sakya temple, the Sakya Pandita Dharma Chakra Monastery in Bayanzürkh District. At these temples, I circumambulated and prayed to sacred objects, sat in public services, and bought prayers just as other laypeople did (see chapter 6). I interviewed lamas, attended conferences, and viewed sacred objects. Gandan Khiid is the largest of the temples in Mongolia and was the only temple that remained open during the socialist period. While linked administratively through a central governing body and proximate in space, it is split into a number of smaller temples, which finance and govern themselves somewhat independently. Gandan's head lama, Khamba Lam Choijamts, is considered by some Mongols to be the head of Buddhism in Mongolia, though this is contentious (see chapters 3 and 5). It is undoubtedly the most visible temple in the urban landscape. In spite of this, even the imposing white temple that houses Mongolia's most popular icon of the Bodhisattva of compassion, Avalokiteśvara (Mong., Janraisig), is increasingly overshadowed by new high-rise apartment blocks that are being erected on what remains of the city's former parks (see chapter 5).

Chapter 1

Dust and Obscuration in a
New Economy

It's July 2015 and some friends and I have piled into a van to drive out to see the horse racing at the yearly Naadam celebrations. Naadam is one of the biggest festivals in the Mongolian calendar, along with the Lunar New Year (*Tsagaan Sar*), and celebrates the "three manly sports" of wrestling, archery, and horse racing. It, like many other "traditional" activities, was reinvigorated as a national celebration after the end of the socialist period. The month preceding Naadam has been abuzz with complaints about wild government spending on the various events. One rumor concerns the possibility of a famous international headlining act for the opening ceremony, with people debating the likelihood and desirability of Beyoncé, J. Lo, or the Backstreet Boys. Most people, though simultaneously enthusiastic about a possible visit from Beyoncé, complain to me about the obscenity of spending $1 million on a pop star when the Mongolian economy is in such dire straits. The government has recently stopped paying public servants for one month out of every three, and my middle-class friends that were previously employed in the mining industry are struggling to find work. A third of the newly built apartment blocks financed during the mining boom now stand empty. Many Mongols who had taken out housing loans in US dollars when the Mongolian *tögrög*[1] was strong are now crippled with almost twice the debt. The value of the tögrög, reasonably high against the US dollar in 2011, precipitously lost value to nearly half its relative worth in 2015. In August 2016 the value of the tögrög dropped again, making it one of the worst performing currencies in the world (Reynolds 2016). In spite of these economic troubles, parliament spends a full day's session arguing about whether the cost to fly in J. Lo is worth the "prestige" that she could offer Mongolia.

As Naadam arrives it is clear that no pop star is coming and that, due to the severe drought in the surrounding Töv region, it is to be a hot and dry celebration. On the first day of the wrestling it is 33°C and, even with their open-breasted red midriff shirts and blue short shorts, the wrestlers are clearly suffering through the heat. The following day, as I find myself in a traffic jam driving out of the city to see the horse racing, the steppe is drought-ridden, a sullen uniform brown—in sharp contrast to its usually luscious green in the month of July. The city itself is shrouded in dust, a perturbing hint of what we can expect at the notoriously disturbed site of the racetrack. Arriving at the horse race and reluctantly exiting the van, the wind blows fiercely, unsettling the dust into a swirling suffocating storm. Undeterred, the festival that has sprung up around the occasion continues, albeit with some difficulty.

As the horses and their child riders approach the finish line the ferocity of the dust storm redoubles. Even my husband and I, having taken refuge in a three-sided refreshment tent, can hardly breathe. As the wind is surely peaking in intensity (the tent won't take much more, we're certain), we peer out of the tent, and there in the midst of it all stands a small, bespectacled middle-aged woman dressed in a smart *deel*[2] and hat serenely making offerings of milk in all directions into the dust storm. She calmly carries out this ritual, associated with purity and thought to placate local spirits (see chapter 9), in the lashing storm. Who knows if her efforts yield a result, but as the storm continues, and we struggle blindly through it to the sheltering van and homeward, the horses and their child riders somehow manage to finish the race.

While these aspects of the festival, economic uncertainties and scattering dust, may seem unrelated, in the minds of many Mongols—and as I will argue, in reality—they are intimately connected. Sitting at a Taiwanese restau-

Figure 3. A dust storm envelops the festivities at Naadam.

rant eating vegetarian dumplings in 2015 with an academic friend and former lama, I inquire about the slumping economy. The economic situation, he says, seems to be "dusty" (*toostoi*). When I asked him what he means by this comment, he elaborates that people in Mongolia are unable to see clearly, to see themselves out of the situation, and in effect to navigate capitalism. Dust (*toos*) and other air pollution, or "dirty air" (*agaariin bokhirdol*), have come to be associated with contemporary times and the social, economic, and environmental realities of life in Mongolia. Dust not only literally and metaphorically relates to climatic and economic uncertainties, it also relates to blockages, boundaries and restrictions. In the southern Gobi, as Jackson (2015) writes, the dusty present contrasts with herders' memories of a boundless and clear past. Dust produced by mining creates an unwanted fuzziness through which one cannot see, and undesirable blockages that were not previously present (see chapter 7).

Although Mongolia has been a market economy (*zakh zeel*) for over twenty years, many Mongols, even those who were born near to or after the end of socialism, discuss capitalism as though the country does not yet understand it. Most Mongols discuss money, as is common in other modern economies, as though they consider "stability to be its nature and wide fluctuation to be a treatable pathology" (Guyer 1995, 7). Though the value of the local currency has fluctuated considerably since 1990, many of my friends optimistically tell me that in order to lift the country out of its difficulties Mongols need to come to understand capitalist economics and the market economy. In 2015 and 2016, when the economy is not going well, most people I speak to blame, quite reasonably, corruption and mismanagement. Corruption and misunderstanding are mobilized as oppositional concepts to light and clarity. Just as ignorance surrounding religion has led to the artifacts of Buddhism being enshrouded in mystery and secret power (see chapter 4), the artifacts of capitalism—reified as money—are thought to contain power. Money can be collected by nonfiscal means and can become polluted and polluting, depending on how it is obtained.

The "Transition Period" after the Democratic Revolution

In Ulaanbaatar the period following Mongolia's rapid entry into global market capitalism was characterized by redundancies, failing infrastructure, and a lack of food. When reflecting on the decade after the Democratic Revolution most people describe inflation, rising prices, ration lines, and instability. One acquaintance told me that there were rumors circulating that the centrally powered heating system was going to stop because the power factory workers were unable to find replacements for the moving parts. If this had happened urbanites would have had to abandon their freezing apartments to live with their family members in gers, which are internally heated by stoves. While a major continuous power failure never happened, navigating the new economy without the certainties of employment and stability that socialism provided ushered in a difficult period for many Mongols.

In spite of economic uncertainties, most Mongols I meet during my fieldwork describe the beginning of the 1990s as an optimistic time. Following a peaceful revolution, new freedoms impossible during the socialist era were enabled by the new system. Laws ensuring freedom of speech, religion, and movement brought in a new era of possibility, especially for Mongolia's disproportionately young population. During this time many temples reopened and some were rebuilt, along with the colossal Avalokiteśvara statue at Gandantegchenlin (Gandan) Temple. Those who were able to mobilize resources could potentially travel and study abroad. Many others lost their livelihoods and were not able to successfully navigate the new economic landscape. In many ways, the switch in system, economically and politically, traded in "freedoms from" poverty and precarity for "freedoms to" practice religion, move, and choose one's livelihood (albeit contingent upon possessing the means and connections).

In the early 1990s the government had high hopes that it would become the fifth Asian Tiger economy (Sneath 2002, 191). Davaadorjiin Ganbold, an economist and deputy Prime Minister (1990–1992), was enthusiastic about Mongolia's potential for economic transition and keen to involve the International Monetary Fund (IMF), the Asian Development Bank (ADB), and the World Bank. In 1990 and 1991 the IMF and ADB sent teams to talk to and advise the Mongolian government's economists about how they could shift to a free-market economy (Rossabi 2005, 43). Previously, socialist paradigms of progress through social evolutionism had legitimated power and assisted in the interpretation of everyday life. As Buyandelger writes:

> Ironically, the end of Marxist-Leninist evolutionism was also the beginning of the transition theories, another version of evolutionism that operates on the assumption that all societies are parts of a global developmental continuum based on a free-enterprise-driven global economy. The practitioners of the transition theory—the neoliberal economists—hold that the road from totalitarianism to capitalism runs through a rupture known as "shock therapy"—a rapid demolition of state enterprises and support systems. (2008, 236)

Just as the USSR had advised the Mongolian government in accordance with their own principles of progress, so did neoliberal organizations. As a reflection of neoliberal paradigms, the IMF and ADB advised the government to privatize state-owned enterprise and start the transition to a market economy. State enterprises were seen as inefficient, and it was assumed that their privatization would increase their efficiency and hence, profitability. In accordance with neoliberal economic imperatives, taxes and barriers to trade were reduced (Rossabi 2005).

After 1989, as the Soviet Union withdrew its economic advice, two other external factors affected Mongolia's transition. First, Soviet aid, which previously accounted for around a third of Mongolia's GDP, began to decrease in 1989 and was completely withdrawn by 1991. Some of this money was replaced by aid from western nations, Japan, and international organizations, and already in 1991, alternate foreign aid accounted for 15 percent of the GDP (Sneath 2002, 194). Second, there was a sharp drop in exports and imports as the former Soviet trading blocs collapsed. The old Soviet nations started to demand hard currency for goods, and the transportation of products became unreliable. This meant that in the early 1990s shortages of fuel, materials, and spare parts were common. Due to these shortages, factories closed, leading to unemployment, and some crops were not planted and harvested. In the cities, sugar, butter, milk, meat, and matches had to be rationed, and rural areas had shortages of flour and sugar (Rossabi 2005, 35).

Sneath (2002) argues that these external factors can only partially account for the dramatic decline in Mongolian living standards during the 1990s. Following western economic advice, at the same time as these external forces were placing pressure on the Mongolian economy, the prices of milk were liberalized on the assumption that by liberalizing prices incentives to produce milk would increase. Following this would be an increase in supply that, in turn, would drive the price of milk down. Within six months of the reform the price of milk had increased by nine times, and the actual amount of milk available in the city had halved (Sneath 2002, 194–195). The economic policies that the government had started to follow meant that liberalized prices for meat and dairy were being introduced at the same time as the state-run procurement systems were being destroyed:

> Without the transportation arrangements of the official procurement system, selling meat and milk represents a good deal of effort for hard-pressed pastoral families, and there was no longer any official obligation for them to do so. In rural Mongolia the reality of institutional settings and their associated methods of operation and transportation had a greater influence on pastoralists than the prices for commodities paid in distant urban markets. (Sneath 2002, 195)

The World Bank estimates that between 1990 and 1992 wages halved and by 1993 again decreased by a third (Sneath 2002, 193). By the time that products came back on the shelves in the mid-1990s, few people had enough money to buy them (Rossabi 2005, 53). Along with cutbacks to state economic institutions came cuts to education, welfare, health, and culture. After visiting Mongolia in 1991, the Asian Development Bank spoke highly of the health system, saying that overall the population had good access to health care. In the same report it advocated the introduction of fees to make the health care system more "efficient" and advised for the reduction of the doctor-to-patient ratio (Rossabi 2005, 169). This advice did not take into account the demographics of Mongolia, where the population density in rural areas is very low and therefore the doctor-to-patient ratio needs to be high in order for herders to be able to access doctors. From 1990 to 1992 government spending on health decreased by 43 percent, and spending on education fell by 56 percent (Sneath 2002, 193).

In many ways, in spite of radical economic changes, the attitudes and practices of people during socialism have been carried through into the present economy. The Mongolian economy before and after the end of socialism has been partly shaped by strong kinship networks, the valuing of gifts and hospitality as social lubricants, and mixed attitudes toward the acquisition of wealth and its distribution (Empson 2012). While the imagery of wealth-producing capitalism with its success stories and big men are certainly attractive in the post-socialist context, Mongols have a relatively recent memory of an alternative economy and, for urbanities, the possibility of romanticizing the idealized, low-spending self-sufficiency of nomadic herders.

During the early 1990s many fell back on kinship and friendship networks to support themselves, and this reliance still continues today. This was not however always a possibility or necessarily the most appropriate response. In 2015, Turuu, a friend who was born in 1980 in Ulaanbaatar, described his experiences while we holidayed in a ger camp[3] in Terelj, a national park two hours' drive from Ulaanbaatar. In the early 1990s his mother rang him unexpectedly from her work at a local television station to tell him to find all the money in the house and to go and buy as much rice as he could. Because of her job she had received information about the immediate, looming economic crash. He told me that he went out and bought twenty kilos of rice, and the next day the economy collapsed, precipitously raising food prices and reducing the value of the tögrög.

During the economic changes some people tried to set up new businesses to make the most of the new market economy. Turuu's father (a successful artist) went to a bank in the early 1990s to help a family friend get a loan to start a business. The friend was trading goods in Russia, and after some initial success, he was able to pay back the loan. Having proved himself as independent to the bank he was now able to secure a loan on his own without support from Turuu's father. This second time, however, he did not return; nor was he ever seen again by the family, a common way of dealing with debt in Mongolia (see Pedersen 2016). Because of a feeling of indebtedness to the bank, though no real debt was actually acquired, Turuu's father felt that he was responsible for the debt and slowly paid it back to the bank. It took five years to pay back the loan, causing considerable hardship for his family. Not having internalized an understanding of the new depersonalization of the market economy, his father had relied on former values of honor and social obligation in a new system marked predominantly by disinterest and calculation.

There are countless other families that were not able to successfully navigate the rapid changes after 1990, with terrible consequences. Single-parent families in particular suffered greatly as there were no longer support systems for single mothers. For those unable to access alternative support, this was and still is a devastating change. One of my friends was found by a Buddhist charity when she was ten, living in squalor in a half-built, abandoned apartment building with her mother. Another family that I have been friends with for many years were left by their father in the early 2000s, during the mother's fourth pregnancy. They were so destitute that they were unable to find enough food to eat. Because of a lack of food, the family's fourth child was not able to develop fully in the womb and suffers ongoing effects.

While the Mongolian currency and economy have fluctuated considerably since 1990, the early 2010s saw some reductions in poverty. It is estimated that in 1989, the year before the end of the socialist period, income poverty was at 0 percent (Sneath 2002, 193). In 1994 it had risen to 24 percent of the population (Sneath 2002, 193). In 2007–2008, the United Nations Development Program (UNDP) wrote that 35.2 percent of the Mongolian population were living below the poverty line (UNDP 2009, 7). This poverty was worse in rural areas, where 46.6 percent of the population were reported to be living below the poverty line (UNDP Mongolia 2009, 7). Due to growth in the economy around 2011 and the successes of some poverty-reduction programs, overall poverty reduced from around 39 percent in 2010 to around 27 percent in 2012 (UNDP 2016). Though poverty rates fell as Mongolia's economy expanded rapidly during the mining boom of the early 2010s, around one in five Mongols still lived below the poverty line in 2014 (UNDP 2016).

Dust and the Mining Boom

> In South Gobi, dust rising behind herds of livestock and wildlife, soot from
> stoves, fluff from sheared sheep and camels, and snuff are natural dusts.
> These dusts symbolize livelihoods in the desert associated with nomadic
> herding, whereas fine dust from roads symbolizes development and enclosure.
> (Jackson 2015, 96)

Ömnögovi, a province in the south of Mongolia, is home to Tavan Tolgoi, the world's largest unmined coal deposit, and Oyu Tolgoi, a gigantic
copper and gold mine. As most of Mongolia's roads are unpaved, many of
the heavy vehicles used for transporting minerals to China and those that
service the mines travel on unsealed roads, spreading dust to the surrounding regions (Jackson 2015). As Jackson (2015, 99) has written, for nearby
herders, the dust plumes act as enclosures around herding pastures, limiting herding activities within the boundaries drawn by transportation networks. Nomadic pasture and water resources are degraded by mining activities along with the health of both the herders and their animals as they
breathe in the dust-soaked air. These herders speak with nostalgia for the
dust-free past, describing previously unbounded pastures and visual clarity
(Jackson 2015). For these herders the roads and dust act as blockages in the
present era, literally and metaphorically. Mining roads, both paved and unpaved, dissect and create distance rather than building connections (Jackson
2015; Pedersen and Bunkenborg 2012).

Although the Gobi dust dissects the landscape creating obstructions for
herders, it does connect mining activities in the Gobi to Mongolia's neighbors. Gobi dust now regularly inundates vast regions of Russia, China, Korea,
and Japan, in plumes that are so large that they can be seen from space. As
the processes of mineral extraction disturb the ground and add directly to
the dust, they also contribute to global warming, of which increased deserti-
fication and intensifying sandstorms are predicted consequences in the region (MARCC 2009, 149). It is estimated that Mongolia's coal deposits
represent 10 percent of the world's untapped coal resources. As such, the
relationship between global warming, dust, and the mines in the Gobi
become ever more enmeshed. Tavan Tolgoi, having been stalled significantly for a number of years, plans to export this vast deposit of coal internationally, on industrial scales.

While many Mongols are ambivalent about mining due to its effects on the environment, as a low-income country now shackled with a large amount of debt, the Mongolian government sees the mines and their increased operations as an economic and political necessity. The global and local effects of exporting and burning mineral resources from Mongolia's domestic coal mines are critical. Scientists estimate that 80 percent of known coal deposits must not be burned in order to have at least a 50 percent chance of limiting global temperature rises to 2°C (McGlade and Ekins 2015). Since the beginning of the twentieth century, there has been an existing global temperature rise of 0.8°C, which has resulted in a disproportionate temperature increase in Mongolia of 2.14°C due to its inland northern location (MARCC 2009, 8).

An increase of 2°C can now only be met by reducing current fossil-fuel consumption. As estimated by the UN's climate report (IPCC 2014), the results of this temperature rise are as follows. Temperature increases will mean an escalation of extreme weather events, such as floods and hurricanes. Low-income countries are likely to be disproportionately affected by global warming as they are less adaptable both in their reaction to extreme weather events and relating to long-term changes to deteriorating ecosystems, crop yields, and sea-level rises. The predicted loss in biodiversity brought about by changing weather patterns will render both crops and communities more susceptible to global warming, as impacts on one crop species could have devastating effects on agricultural yields, forcing communities to search for other food options and further taxing overstressed ecosystems and wildlife populations. Rising global temperatures will decrease food and water security along with the overall habitability of some countries. These in turn will increase the chances of global destabilization (including an increase in conflicts), significant economic losses, and the large-scale displacement of peoples. These are the effects of a 2°C warming (IPCC 2014). If we continue to burn coal and other fossil fuels at the present rate, the world is set to warm globally by 4°C by the end of the century, for which the projections are simply catastrophic.

Mongolia's ecosystems and pasturelands are highly sensitive to the temperature changes and altered precipitation attendant to climate change. Because of its location, it is predicted that surface temperatures will rise by at least 5°C by the end of the century (that is, if the global climate rises by only 2°C). As a low-income country Mongolia possesses limited capacity for large-scale adaptation in the face of environmental disasters. It is estimated that although there will be some increase in precipitation in the northern regions that the desert areas in the south are likely to increase in territory, spreading northward (MARCC 2009, 63). The country will also suffer from decreased surface water and droughts in river basins (MARCC 2009, 62). Ninety percent of its landmass will become vulnerable to natural disasters in the form of droughts and heavy snowfalls (MARCC 2009, 71). Mongolia will see more natural disasters, such as extreme hot and cold weather events, flooding, *zuds*, sandstorms, the melting of snow, and the degrading of land surfaces due to the melting of permafrost (MARCC 2009, 149). "In the case of Mongolia, its fragile ecosystems, pastoral husbandry and very limited irrigated agriculture are extremely sensitive to climate change. As such, Mongolia's traditional economic sectors and its people's nomadic way of life are highly vulnerable to climate change" (MARCC 2009, 70).

Natural disasters disproportionately affect poorer herders with herds under one hundred head of livestock (UNDP 2010). Climate-related catastrophes have already affected the movement of people within Mongolia, including the mass migrations that increased Ulaanbaatar's population following the *zud*s of 1999–2002. Future calamities, if they occur without disaster preparedness, will likely cause those that lose their herds to migrate to the city. With current trends in urban planning, this movement of people will add to the strain on Ulaanbaatar's infrastructure and will likely increase the city's air pollution problems. As Mongolia's governance is highly centralized, the national government makes decisions about mining projects and collects revenues from these enterprises. The taxes that the government collects from the mines flow directly to Ulaanbaatar, with very little making its way back to the local communities directly affected by mining activities (Janes and Chuluundorj 2015, 142).

Dirty Money

At a dinner party in an apartment in the Third and Fourth District of Ulaanbaatar one night I was part of a conversation about the global and local political upheavals of 2016. This was characterized by a small amount of hope and a large amount of disappointment in the upcoming global and local elections. During the conversation our sharply dressed middle-aged Buddhist host piped in, saying:

> People are always complaining about politicians. They are stealing from us. They are always taking, taking. But my mother used to say that they are always taking because they are the reincarnations of Chinese merchants and Sheiks that the Mongols robbed in the past. Now they have been reborn to take from us. They take our wealth and our minerals and they give us nothing back. It is our karma.

There was a general agreement at the table that it was possible for a nation to have collective karma and that the actions of a country's past could influence the unfolding fortunes of an entire nation (see chapter 6). In this way, the global distribution of wealth is not only defined by the ambiguities of fluctuating fortunes in a global economy, it is influenced by karmic reverberations from previous activities. Later at the dinner party our friend described to the table how she had heard that the Mongolian director of a mining company had become very ill with a host of rare diseases. These diseases, she said, were the result of the disturbance of local spirits through mining activities. Though mining profits are significant, they are considered by many Mongols to be a perilous way to make money due to spiritual pollution and acquiring bad karma.

The mining boom began in the early 2010s, and with it, the economy started to grow. In 2008, 80 percent of Mongolian exports were mineral (Chuluundorj and Danzanbaljir 2014, 282), and by 2011, Mongolia's economy, boosted by the mining sector, had expanded by 17.5 percent (Chuluundorj and Danzanbaljir 2014, 276). In 2014 it was estimated that around one hundred thousand people were employed in the mining industry with an extra forty thousand working as artisanal miners, or, as they are colloquially known in Mongolia, "ninja" miners[4] (Damba 2014, 305). The two giant, largely unexploited mineral reserves at Oyu Tolgoi and Tavan Tolgoi have been the subjects of economic speculation, and contracts have been negotiated and renegotiated by successive democratically elected governments.

The mineral resource boom, while bringing money and economic growth, has made the Mongolian economy reliant on external economic conditions for its continued expansion and viability. Mongolia now depends largely on external trading partners, in particular China, for trade and the use of its rail and ports (Chuluundorj and Danzanbaljir 2014; Reeves 2011). As Reeves (2011, 170) points out, it has been the exception rather than the norm that resource-wealthy countries don't fall victim to the "resource curse," a condition where the export of raw materials and the injection of the money that it brings does not improve the living standards of its citizens. Because of the emphasis on mineral exports and the incoming revenue that they attract, Mongolia, as is common of other resource-rich countries, has neglected its other domestic products (Reeves 2011). The crop sector that serves domestic needs had declined by 2009 from around 550,000 hectares in 1990 to 250,000 (Reeves 2011, 180). Without ensuring the continuation and provisioning of domestic production and industry, Mongolia is highly vulnerable to fluctuations in the global market and its reliance on ever higher volumes of mineral exploitation.

Like the attitudes during the mining boom in my hometown, Perth, Western Australia, many Mongols in the early 2010s normalized the influx of money, assuming the mining boom would last forever. According to Bonilla (2016), when she was first carrying out research on the mining boom in 2011 and 2012, her interlocutors seemed unaware of the potential burden of debt created by borrowing, both personally and as a nation. In 2012 the government acquired $1.5 billion of debt in the form of Chinggis bonds, and in 2013 it acquired another debt in the form of a ten-year "samurai bond" of ¥30 billion (Bonilla 2016). Just as many young Australians in Western Australia and Queensland took out loans to buy luxury goods that they were soon unable to repay, many Mongols acquired large debts during the mining boom. As Bonilla writes: "The word '*bond*' has since become normalized in colloquial Mongolian, referring specifically to a loan financed by investors on international markets. More generally, and perhaps significantly, bond is also used to refer to debt that Mongolia, as a nation, owes to foreigners" (Bonilla 2016).

As China's hunger for raw minerals began to wane and economic downturns continued to depress the global market, Mongolia's economy began to slow. Late in 2014, the government signaled that Mongolia was now in a national economic crisis (*ediin zasgiin khyamral*). Many Mongols feel personally implicated in the national debt, relating to this national debt through their understanding of personal indebtedness (Bonilla 2016).

While I heard many urban Mongols praise the benefits of the mining industry, many also talked about the negative effects that the industry was having on the environment and that, due to corruption, money was not able to flow from the pockets of the elites to the broader population. During the Qing era, mining was a taboo due to notions about sullying the purity of the pristine Mongolian landscape (High and Schlesinger 2010). As High (2013) writes, following on from this historical precedent, today money made from mining can be considered by miners to be polluted. She noticed that individual notes that are physically dirty after being at mine sites are considered to be of less worth than other clean notes of corresponding value (High 2013). Because of the dirtiness of the money many miners believe that they should spend money they make from mining on consumables (such as entertainment and alcohol) rather than durable objects, which would instantiate the pollution and bring ill luck (High 2013).

While High's (2013) interlocutors, who worked at or near mining sites, identified specific notes as being dirty and corrupted, and having different "regimes of value" (Appadurai 1988), for urbanites this sense of defilement is more abstracted. The economic benefits attendant to the resource boom in Mongolia has meant that some urban Mongols have benefited financially from an industry that for them is largely invisible. Though rumors of environmental pollution in the countryside disturb many urbanites, it remains an abstract idea for many city residents. In spite of this detachment, coincident with the growing mining economy and increases in wealth disparities, the urban problem of air pollution has grown. This, for many people, is metaphorically and literally linked to broader problems of greed and corruption in the city and the country as a whole.

Many of my interlocutors told me stories of karmic and non-karmic forms of retribution that follow from the acquisition of money made through corruption or from accidentally disturbing sensitive landscapes. Some urbanites told me that money made from corrupt activities would create bad karma and that this would create ill effects in their next life. Others told me of the karmic repercussions in this lifetime, while others still described tales of karmic retribution that had flowed on to the children of corrupt officials and businesspeople. Along with karma, spiritual contamination from disturbing landscapes was mentioned as a reason for illness or blocked fortune, and many people visit temples to remove blockages and in an attempt to purify bad karma (see chapters 6 and 7).

In a 2006 survey documenting Mongolia's attitudes toward corruption, two-thirds of Mongols believed that it was unacceptable, yet two-thirds also thought it was common and was getting worse (Reeves 2011, 178). Most Mongols seem to agree that there are clear-cut cases of corruption and the embezzlement of public money. Along with high government officials and businesspeople doing deals with foreigners, I heard of corruption at universities and among the medical profession. One female friend in her early thirties told me that her friend's baby died during childbirth because her husband refused to pay the attending doctors and nurses extra money so that she would be properly attended to. Others told me of a woman from the ger areas who was forced to give birth outside a hospital because she did not have enough money to pay the hospital. In 2015, two female friends independently described how they had tried to bribe police officers because they were caught speeding. While one was successful, the other was not. Because he would not take her money and made her pay the fine, she said, "I was surprised—that's good. But . . . [they still have to] change the bad people who try to corrupt the others."

It should be noted that not all gifts in Mongolia are thought to be instances of corruption. As Sneath (2006) has pointed out, during the socialist period it was common to give gifts, such as vodka (*arkhi*), as part of patterns of exchange. However, as the distinctions between the incomes of the wealthy and the poor have increased, gifts that were once accepted patterns of reciprocity have become dubious (Sneath 2006). As some Mongols have become very wealthy, gifts given in exchange for instrumental results have become larger and their associations more problematic (Sneath 2006).

As well as overt examples of corruption and concerns that mining can cause health or other problems, other ways of making money can be thought to carry pollution or bad energy (*muu energi*). Money made from other people's suffering, even inadvertently, can be thought to cause problems in the future. Asking for specific amounts of money when carrying out religious activities can be seen as problematic, as a religious practitioner is meant to help alleviate the difficulties put on people (Buyandelger 2013). Likewise, trading on interest loans or debt could present potential spiritual danger. Pawnshops (*lombard*), an increasingly common form of high-interest lending in Ulaanbaatar (Empson 2016a), trade on indebtedness and an individual's financial difficulties. Because they contain objects unwillingly parted from owners, they are believed to be places of spiritual danger that can affect the lombard's employees (Højer 2012).

It would be misleading to suggest that due to these problems Mongols try to avoid the accumulation of money. Most people in the capital actively try to make and accumulate money. Many people carry out religious rituals aimed at removing obstacles in the home or in temples when suffering from money problems. There are now a number of high-profile new religious teachers who sell ritual services as a way of navigating the unstable economy. Sarandavaa, a former aura reader, now instructs large audiences about how to attract and multiply wealth. She carries out public talks during which she encourages followers to lift up their wallets and circle them in a clockwise direction three times. This ritual element is used in Buddhist ceremonies, often using a blue *khadag* (prayer scarf), and is meant to generate blessings and multiplication. After carrying out these public blessings, she instructs her followers to keep a certain colored wallet so that money will be attracted to it. I participated in other rituals, such as the enduringly popular prosperity ceremonies (*dallaga avakh*) that are now carried out at Gandan Khiid and elsewhere, which are believed to help generate prosperity and wealth for the home.

A Fuzzy Economy

Coincident with worsening air pollution in the capital, Mongolia's economy has become "fuzzy," unclear, and difficult to predict. As uncertainty and ambiguity characterize the economic landscape, individuals, families, and the Mongolian nation all attempt to navigate the global economy with increasing debts and without a clear sense of how to proceed. Mongolia's mineral wealth is looked to as the major future source of income for the country and as a way out of the nation's rising international debts. Yet, money made from mining carries with it problems of corruption and spiritual contamination. As mine sites encroach upon herders' pastures they degrade the environment, create dust, and compromise clean water supplies. For herders in the Gobi, dust from the mines is associated with contamination, containment, and restriction.

The extraction economy literally creates dust both in the short and long term. Mining adds to global warming, the consequences of which will be devastating for Mongolia economically and environmentally. At the same time, the money made from mining is considered to be dirty (*bokhir*) by many Mongols, carrying with it potential misfortune to those who earn it. As vast sums of money are injected into the economy, this encourages corruption, which is believed to bring ill health and other problems to its beneficiaries and their families.

Urban air pollution followed Mongolia's shift to a capitalist economy. For many Mongols, dust and air pollution have become associated with corruption and a lack of clarity about how to navigate capitalism. Within Buddhist ideas of karma, corruption brought about by the motivation of greed is seen in opposition to the pure intentions of enlightened beings. Many Mongols believe that the karmic effects of making money in negative ways will be experienced in this life, the next life, and/or by one's children (chapter 6). Likewise, ignorance, along with a lack of knowledge and education, is seen in opposition to enlightenment (*gegeerel*) in both its socialist and religious meanings (chapter 4).

The next chapter will detail the history of light and enlightenment before 1990, providing context to the materiality of light and its dimming in contemporary Ulaanbaatar. By looking at the history of Buddhism in Mongolia this chapter will illustrate the importance of light and purification, both religiously and politically, and provide background for their continuing relevance today. In the pre-socialist period, as the increasingly politically charged Buddhist monastic institutions attempted to purify the Mongolian religious landscape, hybrid forms arose, creating a unique northern tradition of Vajrayāna Buddhism. In the tumultuous beginnings of the twentieth century, another form of purification began, this time manifesting itself in the brutal purges of the 1930s. Buddhism was seen to be too powerful for the new socialist government to tolerate and was all but erased from the public sphere. In place of Buddhist institutions, new ideas of enlightenment and light were encouraged by the socialist government, creating their own long shadows and blind eyes.

Chapter 2

A History of Enlightenment in Mongolia

At the turn of the twentieth century Buddhist institutions were established in strategic positions for trade and religious practice all across Mongolia. Over centuries Buddhist missionaries had shrewdly chosen the sites for new temples based on old trading routes and the position of shamanic sacred sites. They were located at key positions for ritual prestige and to ensure that nomadic families, who came to these places for social gatherings, would frequent the monasteries (Moses 1977, 114). Lit by throngs of butter lamps, the seats of Mongolia's most respected lamas, and housing the country's most prized art works, the temples were places of light and enlightenment. Here people came to trade and to seek out religious rituals, medicine, and advice. For some lamas the temples provided literacy and education. For the nobles, serfs, and laypeople that paid tribute to these temples they must have appeared as impressive structures in an otherwise predominantly transient landscape.

The history of Buddhism in Mongolia has been a turbulent one since its arrival in the region in the fourth century AD (Heissig 1980, 4). The passing centuries have seen Buddhist institutions mobilizing and being mobilized by a variety of political interests, until their very existence became politically untenable for the socialist government in the early twentieth century. Following the diversity of religions in the courts of the Mongolian Empire, the region experienced a shift in the centralization of Buddhist power to Tibet during the Qing Empire. During the lifetime of the Fifth Dalai Lama (1617–1682), the clergy of the Gelugpa lineage of Vajrayāna Buddhism encouraged Tibetan-centric hierarchies and anti-syncretic policies that were designed to "purify" Buddhism in the peripheries of the Qing Empire. As Manchu leaders sought to bring stability to the Empire by affirming Tibetan Buddhism as the source of spiritual power,[1] the desire to bring light and purification to the edges of the Empire's imagined mandala grew. Tibetan Buddhist missionaries who transmitted Buddhism to Mongolia commonly employed the narrative that they were bringing purifying light to the dark and backward northern lands (Kollmar-Paulenz 2014).

As the Manchu nobility and Tibetan Buddhist hierarchs sought to "purify" the religious landscape of perceived syncretic elements, a number of trends that are now contested elements of Mongolian Buddhism developed. First, they posthumously linked Chinggis Khan to the introduction of Buddhism in Mongolia, identifying "the Khan of Khans" as a *Cakravartin*[2] and as an emanation of Vajrapāṇi[3] (Ochirvaani). Second, the Gelug lineage became dominant in Inner Asia and positioned itself as the "traditional" lineage of Buddhism in the region. Third, Tibetan became the main liturgical language for Buddhism, and the translation of texts into Mongolian was discouraged. Fourth, Tibet became centralized in Buddhist topographies, both symbolically and literally as the seat of Buddhist learning, the birthplace of reincarnation lineages, and the landscape in which hagiographies and stories of spirit conversions were set.

In spite of the Qing Empire's policies aimed at purifying religion, hybridized religious practices emerged in the Mongolian cultural region. In Inner Mongolia key Tibetan missionaries, such as Neichi Toin, attempted to translate Tibetan Buddhist ideas into localized practices. Further from the center of the Qing's imagined mandala, charismatic Buddhist figures became exemplars for unique and unorthodox forms of Buddhist practice. Though the Qing Empire attempted to purify religious practice to support their political agenda, localization, interpretation, and negotiation characterized Mongolian interactions with Buddhism in this period.

In the unstable beginning of the twentieth century, Buddhist institutions saw a brief intensification of their power as the Tibetan-born eighth reincarnation of the Javzandamba lineage, the Bogd Gegeen, was enthroned as king in the newly independent Mongolia in 1911. This power was short lived. As revolutions swept across the steppe, the very existence of Buddhism soon became politically intolerable for the socialist government, who ruled from 1921. The new government set out to erode the power and wealth that Buddhist hierarchies had accrued. Their attack on Buddhism culminated in the late 1930s with the assassinations and imprisonment of thousands of Buddhist lamas, as well as nobles, shamans, intellectuals, ethnic Buryats, and politicians.

Concurrent with the socialist government's destruction and repression of religion, the state appropriated the term "enlightenment" to mean education. Like the Tibetan Buddhist missionaries who preceded them (Kollmar-Paulenz 2014), the socialists saw themselves as bringing light to the "backward" and "superstitious" Mongols (Bruun and Narangoa 2006). They attempted to sever enlightenment's association with secret tantric practices and miraculous rebirths. Men, women, and children could now "find" enlightenment (*gegeerel olokh*), with its new meaning of "to become educated" (*gegeerekh*), and they could educate others (*gegeerüülekh*).

Along with policies encouraging the education of laypeople and poorer lamas concerning the feudal nature of Buddhism, the government desacralized enlightenment and the secret knowledge that was believed to facilitate it. Socialist authorities opened and exhibited previously hidden sacred objects and spaces, such as those housed in the Choijin Lama Temple that contained the shrines of Mongolia's short-lived state oracle. The temple was opened as a museum in 1938, having the dual effect of desacralizing sacred objects and demonstrating the "ferocious" and "dark" tantric iconography that the temple contains (see Højbjerg 2002 for a discussion of processes of desacralization in Guinea).

While the socialist government decoupled the association of temples and light, they themselves brought electricity to the countryside, signaling the power of their own light of modernization. Naming electricity "Lenin's Light" (*Ilyichiin Gerel*), the socialist government did all that it could to link itself to enlightenment, in the sense of education, and light in its literal and metonymic associations (Sneath 2009). The state successfully stripped the monastic establishments of their capacity to generate light, enlightenment, and purification.

If light was used by the new government as a metaphor for modernity and socialist programs of education and electrification, there was another way in which the socialist government brought light to Mongolia. By the end of the 1930s as the purges intensified, the socialist government used light to interrogate and expose those they labeled to be enemies of the state. For those who were arrested during the night (Buyandelger 2013, 72), torchlight obscured the perpetrators, hiding the identities of those who persecuted and murdered lamas and laypeople. Around half of the people killed during the purges were lamas. Toward them, the exposure that the socialist government encouraged was a selective one that exposed real or imagined plots to overthrow the government and sought to cast religion in the light of corruption, superstition, and archaic hierarchies. Those Mongols who opposed the new government through religion (including shamans), wealth, ethnicity, or differing ideologies were taken from their homes, monasteries, or pastures and often never seen again. The light once associated with the reincarnation lineages was extinguished, and the socialist government outlawed the finding of any new reincarnations.

Chinggis Khan as the Wheel-Turning King

Although Buddhism was present in Inner Asia long before Chinggis Khan's birth, many Mongols believe that it was Chinggis Khan who first brought Buddhism to the country, after he united the Mongolian and Turkic tribes in 1206.[4] While Chinggis Khan certainly had contact with Buddhism as he waged war against the Jin State (Sagaster 2007), the stories that link Chinggis to the introduction of Buddhism in Mongolia likely originated in apocryphal stories told by the missionary lamas of the sixteenth century. They proposed Chinggis Khan to be an emanation of the wrathful figure of Vajrapāṇi, one of the three main protectors of the Buddha. As the missionaries attempted to incorporate the influential cult of Chinggis Khan, which had existed since the thirteenth century, into the Buddhist cannon, the idea of the Khan as a Buddhist deity grew (Hurcha 1999).

During the rule of the Qing Dynasty, histories linking Chinggis Khan to the introduction of Buddhism were incorporated into the Qing's revisionist histories as an expedient way of cementing their alliances with the Mongolian rulers and the politically astute Tibetans (Elverskog 2008). It was in the interests of the Qing to forge strong alliances to stop the notoriously fractious Mongols from fragmenting into opposing groups. The Qing, along with inserting themselves into the mythologies of divine kingship surrounding the worshipped ruler Chinggis Khan, linked their right to rule to the Buddhist idea of divine kingship (Elverskog 2008, 48). By reimagining Chinggis Khan as an emanation of Vajrapāṇi, they absolved him of any troubling narratives that may have undermined their associations. In doing so, they strengthened the image of Buddhism as the natural religion in the northern parts of the Empire.

The idea of the Buddhist Cakravartin is of a noble ruler who protects and supports Buddhist institutions by limiting civil unrest. Such a ruler is said to be noble and virtuous so long as they do not undermine Buddhist institutions' abilities to carry out their religious practices. The Cakravartin concept is an acknowledgment that rulers must make difficult decisions, including punishing those who commit crimes within their kingdom and protecting the kingdom from external threats through war when necessary. These actions, frequently involving enacting physical harm on wrongdoers, would be seen as sowing the seeds of bad karma for ordinary Buddhists. However, because of the greater good that these leaders are said to enable by protecting the dharma,[5] the Cakravartin's role as virtuous ruler remains untainted by the creation of negative karma.

In Tibet this idea has often been accompanied by the naming of leaders as emanations of important deities. As Mills writes, the idea of emanation is used "as a narrative means to resolve the contradictions of a virtuous king acting in his capacity of lawgiver, and therefore, a violent punisher of wrongdoing" (2012, 236). Reflecting tantric ideas, this proclamation of leaders as emanations of deities indicates that they have special knowledge that enables them to act with "pure" intentions even if what they are doing appears to be negative (Mills 2012). This practice of declaring leaders to be emanations of deities has had a recent revival in the Mongolian cultural region when, as Bernstein (2013) reports, in 2009 the leader of Buryat Buddhism, the Khambo Lama, named then Russian president Dmitry Medvedev to be an emanation of White Tārā[6] (Mong., Tsagaan Dara Ekh).

Today the idea that Chinggis Khan was an emanation of Vajrapāṇi remains an important part of Mongolian Buddhist narratives. During my

Figure 4. Young lamas participating in the revitalized Danshig Naadam festivities
(in the background is a large thang ka depicting Vajrapāṇi).

initial fieldwork in 2009 and 2010 his image was prominently displayed in
the largest temple in Ulaanbaatar behind the towering Avalokiteśvara
statue in the central shrine of Gandan Khiid,[7] pictorially represented
beneath the wild blue figure of Vajrapāṇi in an impressively large *thang
ka*.[8] This image, painted by the famous Mongolian artist Lama Pürevbat, has been reproduced in postcards and was, during my initial field-

work, commonly seen enshrined in shops, houses, businesses, and Buddhist centers all across the country.

Like other post-socialist nations[9] Mongolian national identities have been reconstructed from ideas of the pre-socialist past (see chapter 3). By placing Chinggis Khan's image next to the newly rebuilt statue of Avalokiteśvara, contemporary Buddhist institutions underline the idea that Buddhism and Chinggis Khan are "traditional" parts of Mongolian heritage. Just as Buddhism is anchored by the image of Chinggis Khan, so too is the image of Chinggis Khan, as peaceful ruler and lawgiver, strengthened by its placement in this holy site. This monumental Avalokiteśvara statue has particular significance in the historical narratives around rebuilding Buddhism after the socialist period. The original statue of Avalokiteśvara was erected between 1911 and 1913 following the establishment of a newly independent Mongolia under the leadership of the highest Mongolian lama, the Bogd Gegeen (see below). It was destroyed between 1937 and 1938 during the socialist purges and was restored with great enthusiasm in the mid-1990s during the economic meltdown that began in the early 1990s (Vanchikova 2014). As this statue was originally built during a brief period of Mongolian independence, it has come to represent the importance of Buddhism during the pre-socialist past and symbolically links Buddhism with freedom from both the Manchu Dynasty and the Soviet Union. The shrine therefore enables the symbolic associations of Chinggis Khan as the protector of Buddhism and of Buddhism as associated with a free and independent Mongolian nation (Mongol *uls*).

Buddhism in the Mongolian Empire

The Mongolian Empire had contact with various forms of Buddhism, but it was the Tibetan schools that were to have the greatest continuous impact on Buddhism in Mongolia, and the later "reform" Gelug school that would come to dominate under Manchu rule. The Empire first had sustained contact with the Tibetans in 1240, when Ögedei Khan's son, Prince Köden, sent an army to Central Tibet (Sagaster 2007). The army's military leader, Doorda Darkhan, was apparently so impressed by the Tibetans that he encouraged Prince Köden to invite an important Tibetan lama to the Mongolian court. Whether a purely tactical move designed to bring a respected representative to surrender the Tibetan plateau (Wylie 2003, 321–322) or partly due to the prince's desire to encourage extra-worldly forces to work in his favor (Sagaster 2007, 385), in 1244 an invitation was sent to the Sakya Pandita,[10] the head of the Sakya lineage, to visit Liangzhou. At age sixty-three, and in the company of his two nephews, the Sakya Pandita set out for Liangzhou. In 1246, when he met with Prince Köden, the lama is said to have healed the prince from an intractable illness. The prince became a patron of the Sakya lineage in 1249 (Sagaster 2007, 386).

During Möngke Khan's rule (r. 1251–1259), religious groups were so plentiful in the courts of the Empire that he held religious debates in an attempt to dissuade religious groups from ongoing power struggles, some of which were adjudicated by his younger brother Khubilai Khan. Initially interested in the Chan style of Buddhism, after Möngke Khan's death, Khubilai Khan (r. 1260–1294) began to treat the Tibetan style of Buddhism preferentially (Rossabi 1988). Khubilai first met with the Tibetan form when he was leading a military expedition to Dali (in modern-day Yunnan province). He passed through Liangzhou and met with the Sakya Pandita's nephew 'Phags pa.[11] On his second encounter with 'Phags pa, who by then was the head of the Sakya lineage, it is said that Khubilai "received the consecration of the tantric deity Hevajra from 'Phags-pa and chose him as his spiritual guide" (Sagaster 2007, 387). As Rossabi writes, in addition to the "purported magical powers of the Tibetan Buddhists," Khubilai was aware that "the politically experienced lamas could be useful political allies" (1988, 40). After Khubilai's conversion, and in the same year as his ascendancy to Great Khan in 1260, he appointed 'Phags pa as State Preceptor.[12] An alliance with the Sakya lineage was forged, and the school gained a position of leadership over the other Tibetan lineages and the Chinese Chan Buddhists who had held power during Möngke Khan's administration (Sagaster 2007, 391–392).

Following the fragmentation of the Mongolian Empire Buddhism's influence in the region was significantly weakened. However, many monasteries survived, and a number of important translations of Buddhist texts were made during this period (Sagaster 2007). At the end of the thirteenth century and throughout the first half of the fourteenth century, the first translations of popular *sūtra*s into Mongolian, such as *Altan Gerel*, the *Sūtra of Golden Light*, were commissioned (Sagaster 2007, 394). Buddhism, though its strength had diminished, survived during the centuries after the

Mongolian Empire, but it did not again become a powerful force until the late sixteenth century (Sagaster 2007).

Revisionist Histories

By the sixteenth century the region now known as Mongolia was split into semiautonomous communities ruled by sometimes-warring nobilities (Elverskog 2008). It was during this time that Altan Khan (1507–1582), the leader of the Mongolian Tümed people, met with the Gelugpa lama Sonam Gyatso[13] (1543–1588) at the Chabchiyal Monastery, near Lake Kökenuur, now in the Qinghai Province of China (Sagaster 2007, 396). During their meeting, Altan Khan bestowed the Gelugpa lama with the title of Dalai Lama (literally meaning "ocean-like teacher") and posthumously recognized his two previous incarnations, the First and Second Dalai Lamas. Sonam Gyatso became the Third Dalai Lama, and, in return, he bestowed upon Altan Khan the title of Cakravartin Sechen Khan, "the real ruler of the world . . . whose epithet was Sečen, 'the wise one'" (Sagaster 2007, 397). Ritualizing this relationship reinforced the power of both Altan Khan and Sonam Gyatso, raising the profile of the newly established Gelug sect.

Although a bond was established with the Gelug school and Altan Khan himself had become a Buddhist in 1573 (Bawden 1968, 28), Altan Khan's court maintained its religious diversity (Elverskog 2008, 102). This heterogeneity was ignored in the revisionist histories written sixty-five years later that wanted to establish the idea that, following this ritualized transferal of names, Gelugpa Buddhism dominated the region (Elverskog 2008, 104). These histories have Altan Khan and Sonam Gyatso proclaim themselves to be incarnations of Khubilai Khan and 'Phags pa respectively and record that after their meeting a rapid transformation of the religious environment throughout the Mongolian region ensued (Elverskog 2000).

Some historians have used these texts to argue that the Buddhist missionaries of the sixteenth century brutally repressed local religions (Atwood 1996; Bawden 1968; Heissig 1980). However, texts contemporary to Altan Khan indicate that it is unlikely that the relationship between Altan Khan and the Gelug sect ushered in a period of religious intolerance. Although the Khan's power was symbolically strengthened through the unification of the two spheres of religion and state, after his meeting with Sonam Gyatso,

Altan Khan continued local religious practices that incorporated both Buddhist and non-Buddhist elements. As Elverskog writes:

> During the reign of Altan Khan there was an amalgamation within the rit-ualisation of emperorship which included both the indigenous Mongolian religion and the newly adopted Dgel–ugs–pa [Gelugpa] lineage form of Tibetan Buddhism. The notion that it was some form of Caesaropapism, emu-lating an idealised Buddhist conversion that inherently dissociated the Mongols from their own cultural traditions, privileges later narratives that are intrinsically tied to the narrativisation and ritualisation of colonised Mongolia. (2000, 403)

The symbolic exchange of titles did however have important ramifications for Buddhism in the region. Following the conferral of titles, Altan Khan built new monasteries and commissioned translations of important Buddhist texts from Tibetan into Mongolian. The Dalai Lama encouraged him to implement a number of edicts. He outlawed the killing of women, slaves, and animals during funerals and the killing of animals and human beings for monthly offerings. He also made the possession of the *ongod*, the sacred ritual objects of the shamans, unlawful (Heissig 1980, 26–27) and repressed, often brutally, the shamans themselves (Elverskog 2008, 119).

Such was the importance of Mongolia for the Gelug sect that before the Third Dalai Lama died he declared that his next incarnation would reappear in Mongolia. Seven years after Altan Khan's death, Altan Khan's great grandson was recognized by Gelugpa lamas as the Fourth Dalai Lama and was sent to Lhasa at the age of twelve to gain a Buddhist education (Sagaster 2007, 401). A contemporary of Altan Khan's, Abadai Khan (a Khalkha Mongol),[14] met with the Dalai Lama at Altan Khan's city Hohhot in Inner Mongolia and, after this meeting, built the Erdene Zuu Monastery at the old site of Kharakhorum. This monastery is now thought to be the oldest surviving monastery in Mongolia (Jerryson 2007, 21).

The Qing Empire and Anti-syncretism

During the rule of the Fifth Dalai Lama the relationship between the Gelug lineage and the Manchu Dynasty was strengthened. The idea of the one priest, one patron relationship was established, and Buddhism in Mongolia became more tightly administrated. As the Kagyupa and other Buddhist lineages were relentlessly repressed in other parts of the Empire, the Gelug lineage became the dominant form of Buddhism within Mongolia.

The revisionist histories commissioned by the Fifth Dalai Lama linked the project of purifying Buddhism with the idea that Tibetan missionaries were bringing light to the dark lands in the north. In his histories, the Sečen Qung Tayiji, upon witnessing the meeting of Altan Khan and the Third Dalai Lama, says: "Our country was like an island in the ocean of darkness and blood, because nothing but evil as deeds and flesh and blood as food were enjoyed. Out of the grace of the union of priest and donor, like the sun and the moon, the way of the pure Dharma was shown. The sea of blood has been turned into milk" (Ngag Dbang Blo Bzang Rgya Mtsho 1984, 147; quoted in Kollmar-Paulenz 2014, 52).

The powerful image of Buddhism transforming blood to milk (see chapter 9 for the relationship between milk and purity) indicates the tendency of Tibetan missionaries to see themselves as bringing purification and light to the outer reaches of the Empire.

As the pre-Qing history of religious diversity was "purified" during the Fifth Dalai Lama's rule, the Gelugpa naturalized itself as the traditional form of Buddhism. Tibetan became the official "church" language for rituals and sacred texts. Rather than incorporating local Mongolian deities into the Buddhist canon, local spirits remained peripheral to earlier incorporated Tibetan deities (Elverskog 2008, 121). Lhasa was imagined as the spiritual center of Mongolian Buddhism, and those who deviated from this impression were disciplined. As the relationship between the Qing Emperors and the Gelugpa strengthened, the Manchu Dynasty became increasingly involved with some of the more important aspects of Buddhism, including finding the rebirths of reincarnation lineages.

This policy of religious purification reflected the Qing Empire's anti-syncretic policies toward land and ethnicity. Manchu bureaucrats worked to ensure that the local populations who were ruled under local "banners" (*khoshuu*) were distinct from one another. By the mid-nineteenth century, as High and Schlesinger write, "aspects of a Mongol 'way of life' specifically included the pursuit of steppe pastoralism, respect for the Dge-lugs-pa school of Buddhism, and the subjugation to banner and imperial authorities. In order to ensure this protection, the Qing Emperors sought to rule their

Mongol constituency in an acceptably Mongol fashion, as *khan* and patron of Buddhism" (2010, 293).

The dilution of ethnic identities through intermarriage or the adoption of non-Mongolian cultural and environmental practices was discouraged. In order to keep ethnicities separate, marriages between Khalkha Mongols and others were forbidden. Different ethnicities lived within their own banners and if they committed crimes they were punished by their own set of laws specific to their banner (Elverskog 2008).

Hybridization

As the Qing Empire tried to spread a purified form of Tibetan religious orthodoxy, hybrid forms emerged. Though the Qing attempted to spread projects of anti-syncretism (often by force), a number of Tibetan missionaries and Mongolian-born Buddhist figures encouraged processes of localization and hybridity. When Mongols look back to their history to reimagine their Buddhist past, a number of figures stand out as exemplary as they advocated a uniquely Mongolian form of Buddhism.

One of these early figures was the unorthodox missionary Neichi Toin, who traveled throughout Inner Mongolia. He was known for his abilities to "cure" shamans of spirit possession and to liberate ancestral spirits possessing their descendants (Ujeed 2011, 270). Neichi Toin was exiled by the Fifth Dalai Lama and sent to live in Hohhot for his unorthodox methods of proselytizing. He was particularly disliked by the Buddhist establishment and the Manchu nobility for translating religious texts into Mongolian, wearing unconventional green and blue robes, donating monastic money to the poor, and bestowing tantric empowerments on the uninitiated (Elverskog 2008, 105).

Zanabazar (1635–1723), the great grandson of Abadai Khan, was the first of the Javzandamba lineage and was born before "Outer" Mongolia[15] became part of the Qing Empire. According to legend young Zanabazar did not speak until he was three, and when he did his first words were a Tibetan Buddhist prayer (Pozdneyev 1892, 325). During the same year he took his monastic vows from a Sakya lama and was given the Sanskrit name of Jnanavajra (meaning "thunderbolt of wisdom"). This, in Mongolian, became Zanabazar. The child was later to be known as the Öndör Gegeen, *öndör* meaning "tall or high" and *gegeen* meaning "brilliant and bright" (Bawden 1997, 275).

Zanabazar's depictions of Tārā, based on his wife or consort, Dorjiinnal-jirmaa, survived destruction during the socialist period and are still on display in Ulaanbaatar today. Zanabazar and his students left behind many highly regarded sculptures and depictions of Buddhist iconography. His moving ger temple called Örgöö, literally meaning "palace," eventually became the basis for Ulaanbaatar. An influential political figure, he is also remembered for his role in the Mongolian submission to the Qing at Dolonnuur in 1691 (Pozdneyev 1892), a fact that was later emphasized by socialist historians (see below).

Over the course of his life the Mongolian region was politically unstable and Zanabazar had to flee on several occasions to escape the encroaching armies of the Oriat leader Galdan Boshogtu Khan (1644–1697). Pozdneyev writes that it was as a result of this instability that Zanabazar encouraged the Khalkha Mongolian princes, with whom he had considerable influence, to join the Qing Empire to avert their own destruction (1892). As Pozdneyev recounts:

"To the north of us," said the Gegeen, "there lies the great state and peaceful government of the Russian tsar . . . Buddha's faith has not yet spread there, and, besides, these people button up the skirts of their dress on the left side— to go there would be impossible; to the south of us lies another great and peaceful government, that of the Chinese . . . peace and tranquility, the faith of the Buddha is found there, and, as far as the Manchu dress is concerned, it is in truth just like the clothing of the inhabitants of heaven; their property and riches are equal to the precious stones of the sovereign of the dragons, and they have delicate silk fabrics, khadaks, and damask materials beyond counting; if we should go to this land we would live in quiet and contentment." (Pozdneyev 1892, 332)

In 1691, encouraged by the Öndör Gegeen and other political interests, Mongolia became part of the Manchu Empire. Zanabazar died in the Yellow Temple in Beijing on a visit to the heart of the Manchu Empire in 1723. Following his death the Kiangxi emperor thought it proper that a monastery should be built to house Zanabazar's remains. His successor, the Youngzhen emperor, commissioned the building of Amarbayasgalant Khiid in 1728, and Zanabazar's remains were moved there in 1779 (Pozdneyev 1892, 338).

Since Zanabazar there have been nine more incarnations in the Javzand-amba lineage. Only two of these, the Second Javzandamba and the recently born Tenth Javzandamba, have been born in Mongolia. Following a rebellion against the Manchu led by Khalkha nobles in 1756 that was initially supported by the Second Javzandamba, the Qing Dynasty, worried about the powerful political influence that the Javzandamba held, decreed that all subsequent incarnations within the lineage were not to be found among the Mongolian nobility (Bawden 1968, 33; Even 2011, 629). The Eighth Javzandamba was, like Zanabazar, both an enigmatic and controversial figure. He was renowned for his exceptional character and because he had the unfortunate task of steering Mongolia through the revolutions of the early twentieth century. The Ninth Javzandamba died in 2012 and his rebirth has been identified by the Fourteenth Dalai Lama to be a yet unnamed young child born in Mongolia (see chapter 5).

Pre-revolution

From the seventeenth to the early twentieth century, under the suzerainty of the Manchus, the power and wealth of the Mongolian monastic institutions grew. As part of the Qing Empire the territory of what is now known as Mongolia (or Outer Mongolia) was divided into different banners. *Chinggisid* families, Mongolian nobility who claimed their legitimacy through their ancestral connections to Chinggis Khan, headed each banner (Even 2011). These nobles coexisted with and were connected to religious establishments that were led by important reincarnations. The system was essentially feudal in its configuration; hierarchies were organized beneath secular nobles and decentralized monastic institutions (Kaplonski 2014, 47).

The power of the monastic establishments was decentralized in the sense that no one figure or monastery controlled the activities of the others. Yet their access to resources and wealth varied considerably, with some key Buddhist institutions amassing vast amounts of wealth and influence while others remained relatively small. Of the more than one hundred recognized reincarnations (*khuvilgaan*) in Mongolia, fourteen were awarded a seal by the ruling Manchus. Having a seal accorded these reincarnations special privileges. At the turn of the twentieth century, power was divided between the ruling nobilities and the monastic establishments. As Even writes: "Buddhist spiritual lineages were accorded a seal by the Manchu court: this privilege allowed them to rule the serfs piously offered to them as 'disciples' (šavi) by

Chinggisid rulers eager to accumulate religious merit. Administration of these serf-disciples was conducted by specific services of the incarnations' monasteries, separately from the internal monastic administration itself" (Even 2011, 628).

Those who were the disciples of monastic institutions were called *shavi*. As Kaplonski points out, until the 1920s the term could most aptly be translated to mean "ecclesiastical serf" (2014, 17). *Shavi* also referred to the land on which disciples lived and the herded animals owned by the ecclesiastic estates (Kaplonski 2014, 17). Accompanying the vast portion of the population who were *shavi* to the monastic institutes, the *khuvilgaan*s also held vast tracks of land and wealth. Laypeople, both wealthy and poor, paid tribute to the monasteries through gifts, especially during rituals and festivals, such as the Lunar New Year, Tsagaan Sar, and by sending members of their family to join the monasteries. It is estimated that at the beginning of the twentieth century around 17 percent of the national herd belonged to monastic institutions (Kaplonski 2014, 17). This estimate probably doesn't include the animals that were owned by lamas on an individual basis (Kaplonski 2014, 17).

In the 1920s the Eighth Javzandamba had the largest estate, known in Mongolia as Ikh Shavi, or "great Shavi," of around 90,000 disciples. This impressive estate was drawn from a population that, according to the 1918 census, numbered 647,504 persons (Even 2011, 628). The monastic population at this time was estimated to be around 110,000, almost half of the adult male population (Even 2011, 628). Given these figures it is hardly surprising that by the time the socialist government came to rule in the 1920s most Mongolian families had at least one lama in the family (Kaplonski 2014, 28). It is worth noting that not all of these lamas lived in celibacy within the walls of the monasteries. Only a third of the lamas in Mongolia in the early twentieth century lived a celibate life housed within monastic walls (Kaplonski 2014, 105–106; see also Lattimore 1962). Many had children and wives and families, a practice that is still common among Mongolian lamas today (see chapter 8).

Revolutions

The beginning of the twentieth century was a dangerous and bloody time for Mongolia. Chinese migrants, Russians, Mongolian nobles, laypeople, and Buddhist lamas alike found themselves negotiating a quick succession of invading forces and Mongol uprisings. The period from 1911 to 1921 saw five different ruling interests exerting control over Khüree (present-day Ulaanbaatar): the Manchus, the Mongols, the Chinese, a brief intrusion by the White Russian General Baron Ungern-Sternberg, and finally the Bolsheviks.

In 1911, Mongolia declared its independence from the Manchu Empire (Bawden 1968, 201). The Eighth Javzandamba became the head of the newly formed independent nation on December 29, 1911. The fledgling nation was run, for a brief period, as a monarchy under his rule. From an external perspective it seems strange that the Mongolian nobles and the decentralized Mongolian ecclesiastic establishments would have agreed to name a Tibetan-born reincarnate lama as their new king. While the Eighth Javzandamba was born in Tibet and was ethnically Tibetan, through his reincarnation lineage he connected the two most powerful elements in the country: the Buddhist and Chinggisid establishments. During his enthronement, the proclamation read by Sain Noyon Khan Namnansüren recalled the first of the Javzandamba lineage, Zanabazar. The First Javzandamba through his noble parentage and exceptional Buddhist accomplishments could claim an exemplary connection to the two most powerful groups in Mongolia (Even 2011, 630). As the son of Tüsheet Khan, a descendant of Chinggis Khan (Even 2011, 630), and an exceptional Buddhist scholar and sculptor, Zanabazar was able to pass to the man believed to be his eighth rebirth a continuity of connection between the Mongolian nobility and the Buddhist establishment.

After Mongolia's declaration of independence in 1911 some of the Manchu administrators gave up with almost no conflict, and others, such as those in Khüree itself, were pushed out with great ferocity (Bawden 1968, 197). During this early period of independence the costs of supporting military engagements along with the indulgences of the Mongolian nobility were taking a heavy toll on the lay population, causing widespread starvation and extreme poverty (Bawden 1968, 203–204). Buryat Mongols, living within Russian borders, assisted the Mongolian administration by introducing modern medicine and helping to set up mines, scholarships, and schools (Bawden 1968).

When tsarist Russian power collapsed in 1917, assistance from the north was withdrawn and forces from the south saw an opportunity to reassert their presence, on the pretext of "protecting" the Mongols from a Russian invasion (Bawden 1968, 204). In 1918 and 1919 this presence increased, and in February 1920, after negotiations to ensure the place of the Mongolian nobility were drawn up by the Eighth Javzandamba, Mongolia once again came under Chinese administration. After their authority was secured Chinese forces began abusing their powers. They robbed and assaulted men, women, and children, attacking them in their gers at any time during the day or night, and they insulted the Eighth Javzandamba by not following appropriate ceremonial etiquette (Lattimore and Isono 1982, 103–104) and by imprisoning him (Bawden 1968).

While the Eighth Javzandamba appealed to Chinese administrators to stop the violence perpetrated by their troops, a group of revolutionary Mongols from the capital traveled to Russia to get help. They obtained the seal of the Eighth Javzandamba who in desperation granted his permission to seek Russian aid. This group was made up of seven people, including the much-loved Sukhbaatar (who died shortly after the liberation of Khüree) and the man who later became known as Stalin's right hand in Mongolia, Choibalsan (Bawden 1968, 210). As Bawden writes: "The comrades who were to go to Russia to seek help were chosen by lot. This fell on Sukebator, Choibalsang, Danzan, Bodo, Losol, Dogsom and Chagdarjav: all of these, except for the first two, were to be liquidated on one pretext or another during the next twenty years" (1968, 210).

In October 1920, as part of this group were traveling on a diplomatic mission to Moscow, and Sukhbaatar and Choibalsan waited in Irkutsk, an invasion of White Russians was under way in the north of Mongolia. This invasion was led by the Baltic Baron Ungern-Sternberg, whom Lattimore describes as "a pathological sadist who was soon to make himself infamous as the 'Mad Baron'" (Lattimore 1962, 63). Seeing the Russian invasion as a chance to free themselves from Chinese rule, many Mongols joined the baron's army.

By February 1921 the baron had reached Khüree. He successfully removed Chinese authorities and returned the Eighth Javzandamba to his position as monarch (Bawden 1968, 216). However, it soon transpired that the baron was not someone with whom the Mongols wished to be allied. As Lattimore describes him:

> Of the Russians in Mongolia he killed every Jew he could find, shot any other Russian he thought might not be entirely one of his own men, and to maintain "discipline" among his troops would pick out men here and there in the ranks and have them shot, just to "encourage the others". He also had insane dreams of uniting Mongolians, Tibetans, Manchus—anybody who was not Russian and not Chinese (since he himself was a Balt not a Russian)—to sweep

the world with a conquest more devastating than the wildest exterminations attributed (not always correctly) to Chingis Khan. (Lattimore 1962, 64)

In March 1921, in direct opposition to the Javzandamba's administration, a provisional government was set up in Russian Khiakta. They published a letter that was sent to lamas and nobles in Mongolia telling them to desist in their support for the baron. The new Mongol-Soviet alliance entered Mongolia from the north and, under the command of Sukhbaatar, defeated Ungern-Sternberg's troops in the northern region.

Their army entered Khüree without any real obstructions or delays, excepting a magical protection ritual performed by the Eighth Javzandamba, on July 6, 1921. The government that was to develop from this victory remained, until the Democratic Revolution of 1990, a Mongolian one with very strong allegiances to Soviet Russia. As Bawden writes:

> The fact that . . . it was to the guidance and help of the Comintern and the Soviet communist party that the revolutionaries owed their success, meant that . . . those men who failed to conform to the pro-Soviet line as developed by Choibalsang and his faction, and reinforced from 1922 onwards by a department of internal security and a secret police force largely under Russian control, were to fall from power and most often be denigrated and liquidated as and when they ceased to serve the narrower purposes of the revolution and became an inconvenience to the "general line" of the party. (Bawden 1968, 237)

This debt to Soviet Russia at the cost of all other allegiances was the beginning of a difficult period for Buddhism in Mongolia, which declined precipitously over the course of the following years. This demise came partly because the government chose to follow the Soviet ideological agenda and, more importantly, because the Buddhist establishment commanded considerable power and resources, and this potential opposition proved too great to be tolerated under the new regime.

The Repression of Buddhism (1921–1940)

Over the course of the next two decades Mongolia followed along with Soviet anti-religious policy. According to Kaplonski's analysis, this period can be roughly divided into three distinct periods of dealing with what the socialist government labeled the "question/problem of the lamas" (*lamiin asu-udal*) (2014). The first begins in 1926, two years after the death of the Eighth Javzandamba. During this period the government used predominantly, though not entirely, nonviolent coercive means to discourage monastic power and influence. The second period from 1934 to 1937 saw the reinforcing of a nonviolent strategy to dissolve the power of the monastic institutions but focused more heavily on the idea of class, highlighting the feudal nature of the monastic institutions. The third, culminating in the latter half of 1937 and the first half of 1938, continued the class-based approach but drastically increased the use of physical violence (Kaplonski 2014). By 1940 a fifth of the monastic population had been killed. In 1936 there were 767 monasteries in Mongolia (Lattimore 1962, 137); by the end of the decade, there was only one.

At the beginning of the 1920s, the Mongolian People's Revolutionary Party (MPRP) was headed by fairly moderate members and took a relatively lenient approach toward the lama question. They sought to replace what they saw as the "superstitious" reliance on the Buddhist establishment by educating the lay population (Bawden 1968, 244). The government focused on decreasing the wealth and power of the monastic establishments rather than concerning themselves with questions of private belief (Kaplonski 2014, 66). In 1926, two years after the death of the Eighth Javzandamba, the party officially passed a law that separated religion from the state. In the same year they decreed (much like the Qing before them) that no more incarnations were to be found in Mongolia (Bawden 1968, 260–263).

The early period of socialist rule saw reform policies aimed at transforming Buddhism both within and outside of Buddhist institutions. In the 1920s a number of party members were lamas (Bawden 1968), and discussions about the lama question in Mongolia tended to focus on the purification of Buddhism from its current corrupt and superstitious forms, rather than its destruction. As Kaplonski writes:

> Until the Eighth Party Congress of the MPRP in early 1930, there would be attempts to reconcile Buddhism and socialism. "Purer Buddhism", as it was known, was about undermining the hierarchy and structures that could challenge socialist stability rather than a facing down of religion itself. It was an attempt to convince people that the actually existing Mongolian Buddhists had gotten it wrong . . . This purer Buddhism traced its roots to nineteenth century

Buryatia, which similarly sought a reformation of Buddhism and a return to teachings of celibacy and a renunciation of worldly pleasures and wealth. (Kaplonski 2014, 36–37)

At the same time as promoting a vision of a pure Buddhism free of feudal hierarchies and corruption, the socialist state promoted a new idea of modernity. For many of the members of the MPRP this new vision of modernity did not necessarily need to exclude Buddhism (Kaplonski 2014, 69). They argued for a brighter future set against the dark past of feudalism (Kaplonski 2014, 69). In order to further this goal they set up a ministry of education, literally the Ministry of Enlightenment (*Ardin Gegeerüülekh*), to educate the largely illiterate Mongolian population (Kaplonski 2014, 73).

While initially the government seemed to be taking a noncombative approach toward the monasteries, the lands, wealth, and influence of both the monasteries and nobles were slowly being eroded, beginning with the abolition of the Javzandamba's Ikh Shavi estate in 1925 (Kaplonski 2014, 67). This expropriation of wealth increased in its intensity. In 1929, 669 noble families had their property expropriated, and another 837 households, including that of 205 important religious figures, followed from 1930 to 1931. During this period the heads of 711 households were imprisoned or executed for "opposing the state" (Lattimore 1968, 122). The expropriated livestock from monasteries and the nobility were placed in newly founded (and often coerced) cooperatives that were very poorly managed. As a result, the total head of livestock decreased by a third from 1929 to 1932 (Bawden 1968, 311). This drop was exacerbated by the emigration of Mongols who fled into China to avoid the theft of their herds and the destruction of their property.

The end of the 1920s saw an increase in violence, a change from the previously financially oriented approach to the problem of the lamas. From 1929 to 1932, a period called the Leftist Deviation encouraged a more heavy-handed approach toward the lamas and monasteries. These policies began to provoke hostility from the general population. Bawden quotes an official letter sent out by the Youth League to its members in 1930 that implores them to desist in aggravating the populace. It reads:

> The arbitrary expulsion of young lamas from their lamaseries has taken place in almost every aimak [*aimag*], and other actions contrary to policy have occurred, offending the piety of the people and the lamas. Such activities include:

the destruction of stupas; the gouging out of the eyes of the statues of the Buddha, stopping people giving free-will offerings to the lamaseries, and so on. Offensive actions of this sort have proved a great hindrance to the work of getting the poor lamas on the side of the People's government, and attracting the people away from the lamaseries. (Bawden 1968, 314)

This letter apparently had little effect, not surprisingly perhaps, as earlier in the same year the Anti-Buddhist League, intending to copy the work of the USSR's League of the Militant Godless, had been formed (Bawden 1968, 313).

Toward the end of the 1920s a few small uprisings began to erupt in the countryside. By the beginning of the 1930s these uprisings became increasingly serious, and in 1932 there was so much resistance to the policies of the new government in the western *aimags* that a civil war began. These rebellions were most often led by lamas and nobles and included disgruntled members of the MPRP and the general population. Some estimates suggest that the uprisings were so widespread that up to 40 percent of the population were involved (Kaplonski 2014, 123). Were it not for the advice and intervention of the Russians the rebels had the real potential of usurping the MPRP's control over the population. As the USSR could not afford to have a weak Mongolia and lose its buffer against the invasion of the Japanese in the east, they intervened, and the Comintern came up with a strategy to calm the angst of the Mongols (Bawden 1968, 351).

After the 1932 uprisings in the west the government promised to change its direction. For a brief while the monasteries gained a reprieve under the New Turn Policy that the government employed after 1932. The government claimed to abhor the excesses of the Leftist Deviation, and people were assured that the policies, which had infuriated them to the point of civil war, were to be abandoned. The Anti-Buddhist League was disbanded, and it was announced that people were once again free to practice religion. Traditional medicine was allowed to be practiced, and people were assured that they would not be persecuted because they attended religious services. Lamas who had been forced to disrobe were told that they could rejoin the monasteries without any fear of harassment (Bawden 1968, 351–352).

After the failings of the policies of the government in the early 1930s, the period from 1934 to 1937 saw the government increase their efforts against Buddhist institutions through (mostly) nonviolent means. They focused on indoctrinating the often very poor lower lamas with class consciousness, exposing their exploitation at the hands of the "feudal overlords" or high lamas. They tried to attract the poorer lamas away from the monasteries with economic enticements. At the same time they crafted a taxation system that discriminated against high lamas. The rate of taxation went up steeply in a couple of years so that a young high lama who was paying 120 tögrögs in 1933 was paying 1,000 tögrögs in 1938 (Bawden 1968, 361). The new taxation rate factored in all private property in its assessments. This meant that lamas could not escape the cripplingly high taxation rate by keeping privately given donations. New laws were passed that forbade the teaching of religion in schools, and public religious services were prohibited. Furthermore, the government outlawed the recruitment of minors for the monasteries and banned any new building of temples (Bawden 1968, 364). The policies of this period like the one before it "led to an emphasis on law and sentences to handle counter-revolutionary activity, rather than the bare violence of the exception" (Kaplonski 2012, 76). This bare violence of exception was to follow, beginning September 10, 1937, with the arrests of one hundred Mongolian politicians—the majority being executed soon after (Kaplonski 2012, 84).

In 1936, Choibalsan, after purging the preceding prime minister Genden, known as the prime minister who opposed Stalin, took over as prime minister and started his own dictatorship. It was to be one more year before the politics of the country turned violently against Buddhism. Under Choibalsan, who closely followed the political advice of Soviet Russia, the annihilation of Buddhism became an important vision of the government, and this time it was an objective that could be achieved. The government had abandoned the unpopular collectivization policy, and they were assisted by the large presence of Soviet forces within their borders. By the late 1930s Buddhist institutions' resources and prestige had been sapped by the government's harsh economic policies, and the MPRP once again stepped up its propaganda campaign. This time the monasteries had no resources to counter the party's attacks. The MPRP would mobilize its military strength to close down monasteries (Bawden 1968).

In 1937 the campaign against the lamas, Buryats, intellectuals, and anyone else thought to oppose the will of the state intensified. Those who were ethnically Buryat were singled out because Stalin accused them of being allied with the Japanese invaders (Buyandelger 2013, 253). During the intensely violent period of the "third technology of exception" (Kaplonski 2014), around 15,000 Buryats were killed—approximately half of the adult population (Buyandelger 2013, 71).

During the period lamas (especially high-ranking lamas) were violently targeted: "About half of the 36,000 people killed between September 1937 and mid-1939 were lamas. In early 1938, Choibalsan (Mongolia's ruler, often called 'Mongolia's Stalin') pointed out that there were still 80,000 lamas in the country; this was at a time when there were less than 14,000 Party members" (Kaplonski 2012, 84).

Within a couple of years most of the country's monasteries were looted and burned and their lamas were forced to disrobe and join the laity. Many lamas of military age were required to join the army, and others were arrested and/or executed. "In September 1937, there had been 83,203 lamas in the monasteries. On 25 July 1938, there were 562" (Kaplonski 2012, 85). The strategies of the Choibalsan-led MPRP to eliminate Buddhism were so successful that in 1940 there were only 251 lamas left to pay the exorbitant taxes exacted upon them by the government (Bawden 1968, 362).

Implications

The history of Buddhism in the Mongolian cultural region has implications for contemporary Buddhist practice in Ulaanbaatar. Promotions of revisionist histories by the Fifth Dalai Lama that linked Chinggis Khan and his bloodline (the golden lineage, *altan urag*) to Buddhism are still used to naturalize Buddhism (at least for some) as the traditional religion of Mongolia. The Qing's policies of ethnic and religious purity, along with the centralization of religious power in Tibet, have encouraged certain trends and ambivalences in contemporary religious practice. Today the main liturgical language in Mongolian temples is Tibetan, and this is something that many lay Buddhists complain about (see chapter 8). The historical dominance of the Gelug lineage underpins the predominance of the "yellow religion" in the country. Mongolia's religious connection with Tibet continues, and many Mongolian lamas and laypeople travel for study and pilgrimage to India, where many Tibetans live in diaspora. Many Mongolian temples and individuals are connected to the Tibetan diaspora and their extensive global networks both religiously and financially (see chapter 5).

The repression of Buddhism during the socialist period is a very recent memory for many lay Buddhists. After the 1930s Buddhism in Mongolia was all but suffocated. Only one monastery, Gandan Khiid in Ulaanbaatar, was permitted to function after 1940, and this was done under the close supervision of the MPRP (Even 2012). Part of the temple was reopened in 1944 as a showcase for foreign dignitaries to demonstrate that Mongolia still enjoyed "religious freedoms." In 1977, Moses wrote:

> Significantly across the country outside the capital religion is rarely invoked, and an entire generation has grown up without an ecclesiastical institution in which it could be taught the religious heritage of Buddhism. Religion has survived in the minds of the older generation but it will continue to survive only as an oral tradition. It will not have the vital support of churches, monasteries and holy relics to reinforce its teachings, those have been destroyed. It will not have a tutorial clergy. They have been forced into secular life or exile. It will not have the daily ritual of prayer and example to demonstrate faith to the believers. Those acts have been foresworn or forbidden. Religion, in short, is no longer a social factor in the Mongolian People's Republic. (1977, 3)

For Moses in the 1970s, Buddhism had been all but completely destroyed, a residual memory left only among the stories of the older generation. Yet his projection that Buddhism would no longer be a social factor in Mongolia was erroneous. Forging a new identity from elements of pre-socialist history has become an important project in the definition of post-socialist Mongolian nationhood. The historical weight of Buddhism as the dominant religion prior to the socialist revolution propelled Buddhism back onto the nationalist agenda of the newly democratic Mongolia, just as religion has been mobilized elsewhere in post-socialist nations (Blazer 2005; Froese 2001; Goluboff 2001; Hann and Pelkmans 2009; Papkova 2008; Peyrouse 2007).

Chapter 3

Buddhism, Purification, and the Nation

The Mongolian People's Republic is perhaps unique in having
successfully eradicated almost all vestiges of religion, from the dogma
once taught to the people, to the individual monastic institutions that
once existed all across Mongolia.

—Larry Moses, *The Political Role of Mongolian Buddhism*

Everyone has faith in Buddhism. Since my childhood I have been exposed
to this environment. This is the traditional religion in Mongolia.

—Naranbaatar, 2010

I think that most Mongols are Buddhist. And I think from my birth
I have been a Buddhist.

—Bolormaa, 2010

Historically in Mongolia ideas of purity have been mobilized to encourage processes of anti-syncretism. Just as the Qing Dynasty promoted a form of purified Buddhism and the socialist government that followed "purified" Mongolia of what they saw as religious "superstitions," the era from the Democratic Revolution onward has been notable for the mobilization of narratives of national purity. This chapter will explore how ideas of national and ethnic purity relate to contemporary religious identities and practices. In order to understand the changes in public religious affiliation after 1990, along with contemporary contestations of light, purity, and pollution, one must look to the Democratic Revolution of 1989–1990 and the political, social, and economic reforms that followed.

During the socialist period in Mongolia (1921–1990), some foreign scholars believed that Buddhism in Mongolia was so close to being completely extinguished that it ought to be considered as such. Anti-religious state propaganda dominated public discourse, and only one monastery, Gandan Khiid, remained open. It survived as "proof" of religious tolerance and to illustrate the feudal stage of development necessary within the Marxist model of human evolution (Kaplonski 2004, 152). However, within twenty years of the Democratic Revolution, most Mongols that I encountered identified themselves as Buddhist, despite almost seventy years of anti-Buddhist propaganda. Many considered Buddhism to be the "traditional" and "natural" religion of Mongolia. When I asked how long people had been Buddhist, I was frequently told that they never "became" Buddhist but were "born Buddhist," even when they were born decades before the end of socialism.

During the Democratic Revolution, to construct a convincing alternative national narrative to socialism, the democratic opposition encouraged Mongols to look back to a time before the revolutions of the early twentieth century into their "deep past" (Humphrey 1992), to Chinggis Khan and old traditions. Mongolia, like other post-socialist nations,[1] reconstructed its national identity from images and ideas of its pre-socialist past. As Humphrey writes, "the Mongols are now in the process of rethinking their 'deep past', not only because this is for once their own, but because historical origin in Mongolian culture is the source of moral authority in the present. Thus the 'deep past' is being called upon to provide the inspiration for a discontinuity of the immediate past" (1992, 375).

According to Humphrey the history of prerevolutionary times is treated as a kind of "single other world" from which "images can be picked almost at random" (1992, 376). While there are disagreements about which aspects of the past should be emphasized, both Chinggis Khan and, more controversially, Buddhism are seen by many as core components of Mongolian identity.

Buddhism did not completely vanish during the socialist period and start anew at the beginning of the Democratic Revolution. Many Mongols practiced it in their homes, and most of my interlocutors had memories of hidden sacred objects and rituals that family members conducted in secret during the socialist period. When the opportunity was presented, Buddhism, along with other pre-socialist traditions, reemerged from the private sphere to become an important symbol of Mongolian identity and ethnicity. However, it is important to remember that not all Mongols were at home secretly practicing Buddhism during the socialist period; some saw and still see Buddhism as an imperial force or as superstition, and others have rejected it for different reasons.[2] Not everyone agrees that being Buddhist is a core component of being Mongol, and, as with any form of nationalism, there are always those who do not fit within delineated bounds.

Since my first visit to Mongolia, the historical periods emphasized to support nationalist identities have changed. In 2009, Chinggis Khan was commonly referred to when linking Buddhism to Mongolian tradition. However, during subsequent visits, earlier periods of history have begun to be highlighted. In 2015, an exhibition at Ulaanbaatar's Zanabazar Museum[3] contained Buddhist artifacts from and references to the Silk Road and the Hunnu Empire (third century BCE to first century AD). In 2016, a number of lamas that I spoke to linked the first period of Buddhist history in Mongolia with the Hunnu Empire and to archaeological sites such as the Dunhuang Mogao Caves (built from 366 AD) located in the Gansu Province of China. In 2016, the Naadam opening ceremony at the Central Stadium began with a homage to the Hunnu Empire, highlighting its growing importance in nationalist narratives. I have had conversations with some friends who believe that Mongols independently evolved as the first humans on earth, linking Mongols to the earliest moments of human evolution.

Some forms of Mongolian nationalism are linked to ideals of ethnic and racial purity and of "pure" bloodlines stemming from the golden lineage (*altan urag*) of Chinggis Khan. As Buddhism is entwined with post-socialist nationalist narratives, nationalism affects and is affected by Mongolian Buddhist power structures, Buddhist institutions' connections to other nations, and internal agendas. While some nationalist narratives promote ideas of Mongolian "purity," others advocate religious and ethnic cosmopolitanism. Both of these constellations are active within the contemporary characteristics of the post-socialist resurgence of Mongolian Buddhism.

Symbols of the Democratic Revolution

The first thing one notices on arrival into the Chinggis Khan Airport in Ulaanbaatar is that Chinggis Khan is associated with everything Mongolian. His face and name seem to be everywhere in the capital, from the white stone portrait on the southern mountain Bogd Khan Uul, visible during summer when it is not covered in ice and snow, to the adornment of vodka bottles. His face is printed on Mongolian currency, and there is an imposing

Chinggis statue outside the front of the parliament house. There is a Chinggis hostel and hotel, Chinggis wallets and souvenirs, Chinggis rugs and home wares. In 2013 the main square in Ulaanbaatar's heart, formerly known as Sukhbaatar Square in celebration of the revolutionary hero (see chapter 2), was renamed Chinggis Square. Ulaanbaatar's mayor implemented the change without public consultation, and in the controversy that ensued, many of my friends commented that it was a sign that some Mongols wanted to erase all other aspects of Mongolian history. Some saw it as a personal attack on the name of Sukhbaatar and the socialist revolution by the mayor, whose Buryat heritage caused him to be very sensitive to revolutionary history. This they said was because Buryats in Mongolia were disproportionately persecuted during the socialist purges (see chapter 2; Buyandelger 2013; Empson 2011). In 2016 the name was changed back, with a similarly low level of public consultation, to general approval.

Buddhism is conspicuous in the capital mostly due to the visibility of lamas and some landmarks, which are increasingly difficult to spot due to extensive construction works throughout much of the city. One fairly often sees lamas walking around, dressed in Mongolian monastic robes with striking sky blue cuffs and their upturned monastic hats. As one travels from the city center west to the Third and Fourth District, the trees neatly lining the boulevard that leads to Gandan Khiid's main gate is a noticeable change from the haphazard appearance of the rest of the city's streets. There are other monasteries nearby, like Betüv Khiid and the astrological monastery Tüvden-pejeelin Khiid. The FPMT's center, Shredrup Ling, is a notable landmark in the center of the city, with a white and gold stūpa and prayer flags marking its entrance. To the southeast of Chinggis Square, the Choijin Lama Monastery Museum's Manchu-era architecture sharply contrasts that of the modern buildings that now surround it.

Chinggis Khan's and Buddhism's revitalized presence in the capital indicate a strong departure from the histories sanctioned during the socialist period. Socialist historians portrayed Chinggis Khan in state-sanctioned histories as a "necessary evil" (Kaplonski 2004, 108). It was acknowledged that he had built the foundations of the Mongolian state and therefore provided the grounds for Marxist agendas of social evolution, but they emphasized his role as exploitative conqueror and oppressor. This idea of Chinggis as leader and conqueror remains, but most Mongols now see him as a lawgiver, world maker, and trader rather than an exploiter. Socialist historians likewise viewed Buddhist lamas as dominating and subjecting both the general populace and lower-status lamas to feudalism. The worst of these were thought to be the reincarnate lamas, or the *Khutagts* (*Rinpoches* or high lamas), notably the lineage of the Javzandambas. As Kaplonski writes, in socialist history books, "we find, as we may well have expected, the feudal lords scheming to control and oppress the masses, most effectively by means of religion. Class relations and ideology find their most perfect feudal expression: a feudal lord who was also a god" (2004, 148).

In addition to this portrayal of feudal oppression, the first of the Javzandamba lineage, Zanabazar, was seen by socialist historians as the Mongol who gave Mongolia to the Qing, an idea that no longer appears to have much social currency. In spite of these socialist histories, on the eve of Democratic Revolution in Mongolia, images of Chinggis Khan and of Buddhism started to appear throughout the capital.

In the mid-1980s, following the dismissal of Tsedenbal (prime minister: 1952–1974) and the rise to power of Batmönkh (prime minister: 1974–1984), the Mongolian People's Revolutionary Party (MPRP) started to implement reforms that reflected Gorbachev's policies of *glasnost* (openness and transparency) and *perestroika* (reform) in the Soviet Union. These reforms were aimed at addressing the inefficiencies of centralized planning and bureaucracy and increasing openness in governance (Rossabi 2005, 7–8). They weren't intended to dismantle socialism in Mongolia but rather were meant to be "ideological house-cleaning" in the socialist form (Kaplonski 2004, 51). By 1989, the state newspaper *Ünen* (truth) had occasional columns discussing the importance of both "renewal" and "tradition" for socialist governance (Kaplonski 2004, 56).

Taking advantage of the mood of openness facilitated by the government and informed by changes that were sweeping the rest of the Soviet world (as many among the opposition had studied overseas), a number of secret meetings were held by a group that was soon to call itself the Mongolian Democratic Union (MDU). On December 10, 1989, International Human Rights Day, around two hundred people gathered outside the Youth Cultural Centre, calling for a democratic system, respect for human rights, and a free press (Kaplonski 2004, 57). The group then issued a petition that, alongside other demands, requested that the government acknowledge the political repressions of the past, in particular the violence against Buddhism during the 1930s. The government responded positively to these initial demands, fearing, among other things, that any sign of domestic instability may have provoked interference from the Chinese (Rossabi 2005, 12).

The response of the government was not decisive enough to be accepted by the MDU and the movement continued, quickly gathering momentum. The next protest, held a week later outside the State Drama Theatre, attracted around two thousand people (Kaplonski 2004, 57). As the protests persisted, in spite of the harsh Mongolian winter, the crowds grew larger still. By January 21, 1990, the protest had moved to Sukhbaatar Square in front of a parliament house and attracted a crowd estimated to be twenty thousand by Mongolian sources (Kaplonski 2004, 61). At this protest, the grandson of the revolutionary hero Sukhbaatar, Sukherdene, spoke to the crowd, and a well-known Mongolian singer sang a traditional folk song that exalted the figure of Chinggis Khan. This protest effectively appealed to tradition, first in the proximate image of Sukhbaatar, hero of the socialist revolution, and second, in Chinggis Khan, the distant founder of the Mongolian state. Kaplonski writes that by exalting Chinggis Khan the protestors directly challenged the official state history that saw him as despot and oppressor. Through this they also defied Russian imperialism; after all, Chinggis Khan and his descendants had once conquered Russia (Kaplonski 2004, 62).

Following this protest, the mobilization of cultural icons became increasingly prominent in the opposition to the one-party socialist regime. Protestors carried banners with Chinggis Khan's portrait, Buddhist symbols, and Mongol *Bichig* (the Mongolian system of writing that had been used before Cyrillic was introduced in 1941). Socialist symbols were targeted, and on February 22, 1990, the large statue of Stalin that stood outside the state library was removed by anti-government protestors in the middle of the night (Rossabi 2005, 18).[4] The much less controversial statue of Lenin remained in a prime location outside of the Ulaanbaatar Hotel until it too was removed by the council in the middle of the night in 2015. To date the large statue of Choibalsan remains outside the National University of Mongolia as he, while certainly acknowledged as an aggressor during the purges of the 1930s, is viewed with ambivalence by many Mongols as he is thought to be the reason that Mongolia was not invaded by China.

On March 7, 1990, still unhappy with the government's response to the demands made by the protestors, ten men started a hunger strike in Sukhbaatar Square (Rossabi 2005, 19). Several hundred workers from Ulaanbaatar stopped work to express their solidarity with the hunger strikers, and workers from the smaller cities of Erdenet, Darkhan, and Mörön also went on strike. As the government met inside a parliament house, they knew that they were losing control over the population. The following day, as the hunger strike continued into International Women's Day (which was a public holiday in Soviet countries and Mongolia), the crowds continued to increase in the square. At this time it seemed like the MDU were losing their grip on the crowd, and the policy of nonviolence was not being ubiquitously upheld. Estimates of the size of the crowd vary from tens of thousands to ninety thousand people. Finally on March 9, amid growing pressures from the crowd and encouragement from the Soviet Union, an agreement was reached. Batmönkh and the Politburo announced that they would resign, and the hunger strike ended (Rossabi 2005, 22–23).

The demonstrations continued, as the opposition were still unsure that fair elections could be possible due to uneven access to funds and the media (Rossabi 2005, 24). On March 11 and April 2, the MDU held religious rallies at the Choijin Lama Monastery Museum. Kaplonski writes, "These rallies were an adroit move, for people link Buddhism to a wider conception of 'Mongol-ness', viewing it as the traditional religion of Mongolia. To hold a rally for Buddhists then was to play a trump card, linking even further the opposition to some (vague) concept of traditional Mongolia, which was rapidly being constructed in opposition to socialism" (2004, 64).

By March 21, 1990, amendments were made to the constitution ending the legal right of the MPRP as the only party able to form government. Shortly after, in July of the same year, the first democratic elections in Mongolian history were held. The vote from 98 percent of eligible voters elected a parliament of which the MPRP held 84.5 percent of the positions (Kaplonski 2004, 68–70).

Since the Democratic Revolution, Mongols have continued to actively reimagine the Mongolian traditions that predated socialism, commonly invoking Buddhism as a national characteristic. In the early 1990s, television shows tested people's knowledge about Mongolian customs and proverbs (Marsh 2009, 121). People began to widely celebrate the old Mongolian Lunar New Year, Tsagaan Sar, which was banned by the socialist regime in the 1950s and permitted later only in the countryside as the "herders holiday" (Kaplonski 2004, 177). Shamanism has become increasingly popular in

Figure 5. One of the many ovoos that top Bogd Khan Uul's mountain ridges.

the country and is used by some as a way to connect with their ancestral past (Abrahms-Kavunenko 2016; Buyandelger 2013). Many people I spoke to now have calendars that include auspicious Buddhist astrological dates that tell them when they should carry out even fairly mundane tasks, such as cutting their hair or cleaning their house. Lamas are consulted surrounding the more important dates of children's hair-cutting ceremonies and marriages. It is common for lamas to give blessings after weddings, to visit people's homes to conduct rituals, and to advise people about the best name for their newborn child (see chapter 7). Lamas are increasingly involved in state-making activities (Sneath 2014), and they are often called upon to consecrate the sites of new buildings and mining digs. Important loci in the countryside and in the mountains surrounding the city have been resacralized with *ovoo*s, stūpas, and statues dotting the landscape. Old monasteries are being restored, and people now travel long distances to visit sacred sites in the countryside, such as Eej Khad (Mother Rock), Amarbayasgalant Khiid, and the Energy Centre at Sainshand in the Gobi Desert.

Nationalism and Ideas of Purity

Anderson defines the nation as a political community "imagined as both inherently limited and sovereign" (1983, 6). For Hobsbawm, nationalisms are "dual phenomena, constructed essentially from above, but which cannot be understood unless analyzed from below" (1990, 10). The symbols of nationalist discourse must be understood through the relationships that people have to them on a personal level and how they affect individuals unevenly along gender, ethnic, and economic lines. Nationalist symbols come from somewhere: to be effective they must also have resonance with ideals already embedded in the minds of the populace.

Bulag argues that nationalism in contemporary Mongolia can be separated into three distinct ways of imagining the nation: *pan-Mongolism*, *civic nationalism*, and *Khalkha-centrism* (1998). Pan-Mongolism, the most inclusive of these visions, imagines the boundaries of the Mongolian nation extending beyond the boundaries of the state. Within the concept of the Mongolian state, pan-Mongolism includes ethnic Mongols who live in the nation-states of Russia (i.e., Buryatia) and China (Inner Mongolia). This is the most marginalized of nationalist discourses partly because Mongolia has made a political commitment to respect the sovereignty of both Russia and China (Batbayer 2002, 333) and partly because of the popularization of ethnic boundaries to distinguish the Mongolian nation.

The second of these is civic nationalism, propounded by Mongolian intellectuals and politicians such as Baabar, a well-known former politician and public intellectual. Civic nationalism imagines the boundaries of the nation to be the same as the boundaries of the Mongolian state. It identifies the members of the Mongolian nation by formal citizenship rather than primarily in terms of ethnicity (Tumursukh 2001, 126–128). As Tumursukh describes it:

> This discourse maintains ethnic characteristics and, just as in the other two versions of national identity, subscribes to the powerful heroic image of Chinggis Khaan and the unique, and therefore valuable, nomadic heritage. However, their interpretations of Mongolian historical and cultural attributes stress the commonalities (real or imagined) between Mongolian and western liberal states and differences between Mongolia and other Asian states. (2001, 128)

The democratic success of Mongolia relative to other nearby states is emphasized by proponents of civic nationalism, and it is argued that democracy's success in Mongolia has its roots in its traditional nomadic lifestyle.

The third form of nationalism that Bulag identifies is *Khalkha-centrism*. Khalkha-centrism centralizes ethnicity and "racial purity" as the defining feature for membership within the Mongolian nation. While the Khalkha ethnic group only constitutes around 80 percent of the Mongolian population within the state of Mongolia (Kaplonski 2004, 15), proponents of this form of nationalism consider Khalkha ethnicity to be the sign of true Mongolian identity. Within this conception, other ethnicities and people of mixed heritage (*erliiz*) are marginalized and are seen as being Mongol in name only (Billé 2015; Bulag 1998; Kaplonski 2004).

The search for identity retold through the reimaging of tradition has not been positive for all members of Mongolian society. In circumscribing a nation there will almost certainly be those who do not fall within its ideological boundaries: "The most powerful image of the nation, the voice that wins out in the competition of identities, is most likely to project and protect the self-image of the most privileged societal group that is able to institutionalize its own vision of national identity and impose it on others through the use of state apparatus or the mass media (or both). Such domination results in an internal cultural imperialism" (Tumursukh 2001, 122).

Ideas of racial purity and the centrality of passing on Mongolian bloodlines have been mobilized to marginalize people that don't fit within nationalist discourses. These include ethnic minorities, those in intercultural relationships and marriages, those of mixed ethnic parentages, those who don't fit into heterosexual norms, and women that have not had or are not able to have children. Within the more extreme nationalist narratives, those in "mixed" relationships are seen as muddying the purity of Mongolian bloodlines. Those who do not reproduce heterosexually are seen as thwarting the reproduction of Mongolian gender identities and the next generation (Billé 2015).

National Purity and Fears of Hybridity

While it is common for my interlocutors to identify as Buddhist due to nationalist narratives, Buddhism's role as the traditional religion of Mongolia is contested. Most Mongols see Buddhism as one of the traditional religions of Mongolia. The other "traditional" religion is shamanism. Postulating either Buddhism or shamanism as an essential part of the national character denies certain people and groups access to the imagined community of the nation on the basis of ethnicity and individual religious preferences.

Kazakhs, one of the other major ethnic groups that live in Mongolia, are Muslim and account for over 4 percent of the population (Kaplonski 2004, 16). Most, but not all, of the Kazakh minority live in the western *aimag* Bayan-Ölgii, although an increasing Kazakh population travel to Ulaanbaatar for study and work. When I interviewed a Kazakh woman living in Ulaanbaatar about her religious beliefs and practices I was surprised to discover that the government had only recently given permission for the Kazakh community to build a mosque in the city. This was in 2009, and in 2016 the mosque was still only half built, apparently due to a funding shortage. As my interlocutor put bluntly, the reason that the government had not initially given their approval to the project was because they were concerned that it might attract terrorists to the capital.

Although most Mongols demonstrate an open-mindedness toward other religions, fears of invasion and cultural assimilation were common. In an interview in the basement of Jampa Ling with one of my young students, Dorj, a tall twenty-four-year-old who lived in the ger districts, he told me that he had been reading literature written by Lama Pürevbat, a popular artist and well-known Mongolian lama (see also chapter 2). According to Dorj, Lama Pürevbat predicted that in 2012 the Chinese would invade Mongolia and cause great suffering to those who do not have "clean" karma. The year 2012 was a period usually attributed to the end of the Mayan calendar and popularly predicted among conspiracy theorists worldwide to bring radical and potentially catastrophic change to the world. The film *2012*, a Hollywood apocalyptic action movie, was released in 2009 and shown in cinemas in Mongolia. After 2012 had passed and there was no evidence of an apocalyptic event, one of my friends told me that there had, indeed, been a shamanic showdown in the city. This she told me was due to the great number of shamans, some of whom she said were charlatans, operating in the capital. After this "shamanic war" the "energies" within the city had settled, and the shamans in the capital were now able to operate in harmony with one another. Dorj, in 2010, was very worried about the impending date and was following the book's advice on ways to "clean" his karma through meditation.

Saskia: Do you read Buddhist books?

Dorj: Yes, I last read *Prophecies from the Wisdom of Greater Mongolia* by Lama Pürevbat.

Saskia: Has it changed the way that you think?

Dorj: In general, yes, it has. I have thought about preparing and purifying myself. Some of the things mentioned in the book are happening now as well as what will happen in the future. Something will happen in 2012; many people will die.

Saskia: What will happen in 2012?

Dorj: I do not know that much about it, but it is said that the Bogd Tsongkhapa[5] prophesied that two people will arrive here from China to create suffering.

Saskia: Is this something that a lot of people have heard about?

Dorj: I think the people that read those books have heard about it, but it is not very common.

Saskia: Is there anything that you can do to avoid this from happening?

Dorj: Yes, there are many possibilities, but if you are supposed to suffer, you will suffer. You will experience the suffering . . . as a result of your karma. There will be suffering for those who survive . . . I do not know much about it, but it is said that there are two people that are being trained for nine years to be sent to Mongolia to make Mongols fall out with each other and start fighting. The book suggests that we should keep peace among the nation without fighting each other to prevent this suffering. I saw the movie [*2012*].
    It will be very similar to that.

This fear of an imminent Chinese invasion (though not generally related to 2012 or to Buddhist prophesies or practices) was almost ubiquitous among the Mongols I spoke to during my fieldwork. A number of my well-educated inner-city-dwelling friends have told me that their hatred for the Chinese was "in their blood" and that it was something that all Mongols felt (see also Billé 2015).

Many Mongols link this hatred of China to the Manchu period when Mongols were indebted to Chinese merchants (Delaplace 2012). In theory, because Mongolia was a suzerainty of the Qing Empire, China could consider itself to have a historical claim to Mongolia, though this is highly unlikely to be acted upon due both to Mongolia's northern neighbor and China's diplomatic recognition of the Mongolian state. China already occupies Inner Mongolia, and Inner Mongols, like other ethnic minorities, suffered disproportionately during the Cultural Revolution (Humphrey and Ujeed 2013; Sneath 1994). In addition, there is a strong line of communication between the Tibetan diaspora and the Mongolian *Saṅgha* (*khuvrag*),[6] as most of the Tibetan lamas that visit Mongolia are part of the Tibetan diaspora living in India or elsewhere. There is surprisingly little interaction with Chinese Buddhism, and when I started to see feng shui objects appearing in Ulaanbaatar in 2015, people who I spoke to told me variously that it was a tradition from India, Taiwan, or Korea. Taiwan and Hong Kong are not generally considered by Mongols to be part of China.

Although many Mongols do travel to China for trade, study, and work, Chinese pop culture in the forms of fashion, film, and television are notably absent from the cosmopolitan mix one finds in Ulaanbaatar, wherein Japanese, Russian, Indian, American, and, increasingly, Korean popular culture are prevalent. I did find one exception to this among the followers of the Supreme Master Ching Hai, whose group has been banned from practicing in China. As these students are vegan and vegetables are often associated with Chinese diets, and they maintain a global orientation toward ethical and peaceful coexistence, they tend to have a more positive attitude toward Chinese people and products (see chapter 9). One of the Supreme Master's followers had learned "fire healing" while visiting China and was happy to acknowledge its Chinese origins, something that I have not noticed among other new religious practitioners (see chapter 9). Another of my friends often referred to how her grandparents were healthy because they ate a lot of "Chinese foods" (by which she meant vegetables), as they were cosmopolitan urbanites at the beginning of the century. On one occasion she told me that her friends asked her how she was so healthy given that she ate only vegetables, many of which were imported from China.

While I was shopping at the *Ikh Delgüür* (the State Department Store), a middle-aged woman approached me to tell me not to buy an apple as it was poisoned (*khortoi*) with Chinese chemicals.[7] I initially assumed that she was giving me a warning about the high levels of pesticides and suspect farming practices that are the result of massive monoculture farms. This may have been part of her intention, but it was not the whole story; as Billé points out, the interpretation of Chinese foodstuffs as poisoned links Chinese food products to "evil intent" on behalf of the Chinese government (Billé 2015, 23–24). "Fruit and vegetables are seen as harmful not because China does not adhere to good farming practices; they are harmful because the Chinese government is believed to be actively trying to poison the Mongols and drive them to extinction" (Billé 2015, 24).

When visiting herders in the countryside it is customary to accept and eat foods given by the family receiving guests. To not do so causes great insult to the family you are visiting, as it indicates that you think they are trying to poison you—a practice that friends told me dated back to the time of Chinggis Khan. This relationship with food seems to be amplified in Mongolian perceptions of and at least ideal rejection of Chinese agriculture. Rather than interpreting issues with food quality as the result of systemic tribulations, problems with Chinese food products are regarded as being the result of malevolence on behalf of the Chinese government.

I had many arguments with friends and acquaintances about whether or not *all* Chinese people were bad people. An acquaintance tried to convince me that the 1989 protests in Tiananmen Square were protests by the Chinese people demanding the invasion of independent Mongolia. I heard that because the Chinese one-child policy had meant that there were more men than women in China that Chinese men were going to invade and start marrying Mongolian women. This links to concerns about reproductive purity that are frequently found in nationalist narratives (see Billé 2015; Bulag 1998; Tumursukh 2001). In the winter of 2009–2010 when a "Chinese" bus driver hit and killed twins on an icy road because his brakes didn't work, the Mongolian media emphasized that he was from China. Delaplace writes that Mongols tend to see Chinese people as "parasitic," living off Mongol resources and threatening their "ethnic integrity" (2010, 129). According to Bulag, many Mongols are suspicious of children of mixed marriages with foreign fathers, imagining them to be "hidden moles, gradually transforming themselves to expose more of their patrilineal bone, so that they may stage a quiet *coup d'etat* in Mongolia" (1998, 159). Billé discusses conspiracy theories about Chinese men impregnating Mongolian women so that they will give birth to Chinese babies (Billé 2015, 25). When Mongols from Inner Mongolia came to Mongolia after the end of the Sino-Soviet dispute, many were disappointed to find that the people who they considered to be kinsfolk did not, in turn, consider them to be Mongols (Bulag 1998). In 2015, when a group of Mongols from Inner Mongolia came to worship at Burkhan Khaldun Mountain and were attacked by neo-Nazis who humiliated and taunted them, it took two weeks for the mayor of the region to issue a public apology (Zoljargal 2015).

As a result of international trade relationships there is an imbalance between exports and imports that is weighted in China's favor. Mongolia exports its mineral and pastoral wealth and imports Chinese products. Because the imported Chinese products are often very cheap they tend to be of low quality (Rossabi 2005, 237–239). Mongols often refer to Chinese products as "new rubbish" and prefer to buy products from Russia when they can (Billé 2015).

Fears of Chinese invasion have, in their most extreme cases, given rise to the neo-Nazi movement in Mongolia. These extremist groups have built upon anti-Chinese sentiment to put pressure on the government to remove Chinese writing from Chinese businesses (Billé 2015, 31). They have used the example of the employment of illegal Chinese workers by mining companies and on building sites to incite hatred against Chinese migrants. They have been known to use violence against these illegal workers as a kind of vigilante law enforcement. They oppose interethnic marriages and especially relationships between Mongolian women and Chinese men. One friend told me that once, when she was walking on a street in Ulaanbaatar with a white western male colleague, they were threatened by a car full of young men who then chased them down the street. Hip-hop songs by popular musicians, such as Gee, frequently contain anti-Chinese lyrics that express violent sentiments against Chinese people, who they derogatorily call *khujaa* (Billé 2015).

Religious Hybridity

Compounding the potential difficulties of naturalizing a single religion as the traditional religion of Mongolia, and unlike trends in Buryatia (Amogolonova 2015), there is no single figure responsible for Mongolian Buddhism (or shamanism). The Khamba Lama Choijamts, the Abbot at the main temple Gandan Khiid, is just that, the Abbot of Gandan. While he plays an important role within Mongolian Buddhist hierarchies (see Jadamba 2018), he does not give permission for the opening of new temples or grant permission for Buddhist activities within Mongolia more broadly. Each temple has a head lama, with the more popular institutions' heads being held in higher esteem. The government gives permission for new buildings or associations. This continues patterns of decentralization from the pre-socialist period. During the Qing Empire the Javzandamba, undoubtedly the most powerful lama in Mongolia, did not control the other temples (Kaplonski 2014). Elsewhere where Vajrayāna Buddhism is practiced, certain high lamas, such as the Dalai Lama, while held in high esteem among the Buddhist community, are not responsible for building new temples or for controlling the activities of other high lamas and their students.

Along with, and potentially superseding, the decentralized prestige of the most frequented temples' head lamas (Gandan, Dashchoilin, and Erdene Zuu, among others) is the identified but unnamed rebirth of the Javzandamba lineage. The Tibetan-born Ninth Javzandamba died in Ulaanbaatar in 2012 after living in exile in India for most of his life. Before he died he stated that he would be reborn in Mongolia and that his reincarnation would be identified by the Dalai Lama (Jadamba 2018). In late 2016 it was announced by the Dalai Lama that the Javzandamba had been reborn in Mongolia. However, it is important to note that even this reincarnation (who will almost certainly be an important political and religious figure), when named, will unlikely become more than the figurehead of "Mongolian Buddhism" (see chapter 5).

Due to Buddhist and shamanic institutions or individuals remaining largely independent of one another, no one figure is able to define religiosity in Mongolia and with it a restricted sense of religious identity. The power that the Khambo Lama has in Buryatia (Bernstein 2013; Amogolonova 2015) is not reflected in any single person that defines religion and ethnicity in Mongolia. This may contribute to the general open-mindedness most Mongols that I spoke to have toward religion. Yet there does remain one authority that most people invoke in discussing religion. When I explained that I was researching religion in Mongolia, a number of my interlocutors referenced Chinggis Khan when relating their position on religion. When I interviewed Sarantuya, a forty-one-year-old economist, in the middle of winter in 2010, she told me: "As you know Chinggis Khan respected all religion. I think that he liked to say, 'We are living under the one sky.' It means, I think, that he means that there is only one God. But the approaches are in different ways. They are talking about the one thing from different sides."

In this quote, Sarantuya uses Chinggis Khan as an exemplar who gives Mongols a moral impetus to be tolerant toward other religions.[8] This attitude was common among my interlocutors, who tended to exhibit a form of polytropism (Carrithers 2000), at least in the sense that they viewed religious practices and beliefs from different religious traditions as complementary rather than exclusive (see chapter 9; Abrahms-Kavunenko 2015).

In most cases, a concern with national integrity does not translate into a dislike of all things foreign. When I first arrived in the capital I was surprised by how cosmopolitan Ulaanbaatar was. Most middle-class urban Mongols are quick to embrace global trends, and this is evidenced by changing fashions, restaurants, and media. Mongols are always proud of their ability to speak other languages, and wealthy Mongols often travel, work, and study overseas. South Korean melodramas are the most popular shows on television, and the Japanese martial arts of sumo and judo are well loved throughout Mongolia. When the Mongolian judo player Tüvshinbayar won a gold medal at the Beijing Olympics, a public holiday was declared in celebration. Hip-hop and indie music are very popular among young people, and fashion trends tend to follow those of the ex-Soviet bloc, the United States, and Korea. Mongols have embraced new religions as well as traditional ones. Alongside Christianity there has been a rise in New Religious Movements in Ulaanbaatar (see chapter 9). Many Mongols now go on pilgrimage to India for religious teachings (see chapter 5), and some young middle-class Mongols travel there to study English. I was visibly foreign, yet the majority of Mongols that I met were very friendly and were more than happy to talk to me about religion. On the few occasions that my husband and I were mistaken for Russians by older (and most often intoxicated) people, it was almost always an amicable interaction.

Buddhism was one of the symbols used to promote a reimagining of Mongolian identity during the Democratic Revolution. While the symbol of Chinggis Khan is unassailably connected to most people's sense of national identity, Buddhism with its decentralized temples and contentious position as the "traditional" religion of Mongolia is a symbol but not *the only* symbol of religion in Mongolia. Shamanism has become increasingly popular, and due to the historical relationship between shamanism and Buddhism, there is sometimes animosity between shamans, Buddhist lamas, and their followers.

There is no one public figure that defines religion in Mongolia and, as such, no authoritative determination of which religions fit and don't fit within contemporary ideas of the nation. While there are many practices within Mongolian Buddhism that are related to purification and purity, these ideas were not (at least in my research) explicitly connected to concerns about "pure" bloodlines common within nationalist narratives. However, as Sinophobia is pervasive among Mongols, it is also found within Mongolian Buddhist institutions. A distrust of Chinese religious elements and Chinese political interests are certainly factors in the resurgence of Mongolian Buddhism. As I will explore in later chapters, Buddhist transnational networks of funding and education (chapter 5), as well as engagement with the New Religious Movements that have become common in the capital (chapter 9), are influenced by the attitudes and fears that many Mongols have toward China.

Chapter 4

IGNORANCE AND BLUR

I would say that I'm a Buddhist, but sometimes I'm not sure, because if
I say that I am a Buddhist then I should have a good knowledge of
Buddhism. In fact, I don't have enough knowledge on Buddhism to say that
I am a Buddhist. But still, I say I am Buddhist. So I want to know more
about Buddhism to say proudly that I am Buddhist.

—TSEVELMAA, 2009

Most Mongols say they are Buddhist. But for me I can say that I am a *real*
Buddhist. Not a blind faith one. Not like most of them . . . [For] less than ten
years I [can say that I] am a real Buddhist. Before that I was a Buddhist,
but not a real one. When I grew up at home, we had an altar . . . and *thang ka,*
we lit a candle and prayed. But the real one? Less than ten years.

—DAWAATSUREN, 2015

During my fieldwork in Ulaanbaatar I have often heard Mongolian Buddhists express concerns about religious ignorance. It has been explained to
me that after over fifty years of socialist religious repression, knowledge about
Buddhism in Mongolia has been lost, monastic lineages have been broken,
and most laypeople no longer understand Buddhist rituals and ideas. Narratives surrounding religious experiences are infused with uncertainty and
doubt, and most feel unsure about which religious practitioners to trust.
Interactions with religious institutions often expose feelings of dissatisfaction rather than providing spiritual consolation.

At the same time, religions of all kinds are discussed with great enthusiasm. Most people that I spoke to have met with numerous religious specialists, read a variety of books on spirituality, and attend a diverse range of
religious rituals, sacred places, and retreats. Instead of being overwhelmed
by frustration and uncertainty, religious ignorance has enabled exploration,
improvisation, and creation. For some, ignorance about the meaning of

objects, rituals, or philosophies leads to religious objects, rituals, or people with "special information" being infused with extra significance and power. For others, ignorance creates a desire to know and provides a space into which a bricolage of ideas and practices can flow. For most, religious ideas and practices combine all of the above: frustration and uncertainty, mysticism and power, and an impulse to learn or fill in perceived gaps in religious knowledge.

My urban interlocutors discuss religious ignorance in three main ways. First, feelings of ignorance and uncertainty frequently lead to the mistrust of public religious figures. When this mistrust occurs, people looked for other sources of religious guidance, often in the private sphere or from alternative public religious figures. Second, ignorance surrounding sacred objects or rituals can increase their perceived power. This perception of power leads some to engage with religious specialists or rituals, while pushing others away: fueling ambivalence, fear, and/or apathy. Finally, ignorance is sometimes seen as a space that can be filled, that encourages a desire for knowing. This fits within the broader democratization of knowledge from the pre-socialist period. Religion is now no longer entrusted to religious specialists only; instead, religion is discussed as though it suggests a sphere that could be enlightened but at present remains unclear. By constantly referring to religious ignorance, my urban interlocutors indicate that religious unknowing is a site of importance. Ignorance about Buddhism is being collectively identified as a conspicuous site among an infinite set of possible unknowns.

Metaphorically, light in Mongolia is often linked to knowledge, contrasting with obscuration, which indicates a lack of understanding. Yet the way that my interlocutors describe religious ignorance demonstrates not an absence of light but a kind of fuzziness, much like the metaphor of dustiness that friends use to describe the struggling economy in 2015 and 2016 (see chapter 1). Interestingly, while ignorance about Buddhism is often discussed by those Mongols who irregularly visited local temples, those who regularly attended Buddhist educational classes do not foreground talk of religious ignorance—indeed, among them discussions of religious ignorance are mostly absent. As such, the focus of this chapter is on those who irregularly visit local temples and their perceptions of religious ignorance.

The Anthropology of Ignorance

Anthropologists have traditionally tried to elucidate cultural knowledge within a culture's own internal logic. Due to the emphasis placed on knowledge formation, very little attention has been paid to a culture's self-identified gaps in knowledge (High, Kelly, and Mair 2012). The anthropologist positions herself or himself as an outsider explaining the inner logic of a culture's actions and beliefs. It was generally assumed that a culture's ignorance is beyond the informants' abilities to comprehend. When Evans-Pritchard (1937) described the Azande, he attempted to explain how the Azande's religious beliefs about witchcraft were rational within the group's own cultural beliefs. As High, Kelly, and Mair contend, Evan Pritchard's ethnography "depends on attributing two orders of ignorance to the people he is describing: they are unable to think outside of the web of belief that provides the categories of thought, and they are also unable to recognize the arbitrary nature of these categories because they can only think within them" (2012, 13).

As anthropologists have become increasingly aware of the porous nature of cultural boundaries (Appadurai 1996) and the limitations of cultural translation (Rosaldo 1980), this focus on culture-bound knowledge production has been replaced by investigations about how certain groups are disempowered through their exclusion from knowledge (Bourdieu 1977) or how increases in certain types of knowledge may be constitutive of hierarchies of power (Foucault 1978). Drawing attention to the cultural awareness of ignorance has recently become a topic of interest for anthropologists both in Inner Asia (Buyandelger 2007; Højer 2009; Mair 2007) and elsewhere (Berliner 2005; Gershon and Raj 2000; High, Kelly, and Mair 2012).

Knowledge, as theorized in the social sciences, tends to focus on what we know rather than those things that are known to be unknown or are believed to be unknowable. New ethnographies of ignorance attempt to examine this gap by investigating fields of ignorance that are culturally mobilized. As High, Kelly, and Mair write of culturally elaborated ignorance, "they are often valued states produced and sustained intentionally, sometimes as the result of significant effort; sometimes people work to produce these states of ignorance in themselves, sometimes they produce them in other people.

They combine metacognitive aspects—essentially theories of ignorance—with emotional, habitual, and social ways of relating to a body of knowledge that is not known" (2012, 7).

These unknowns are considerable sites of importance. High (2012) explores ignorance as a positive social value among the Waorani of the Amazon. To deny knowledge about shamanism is also to deny being a shaman: the position of a shaman being loaded with antisocial bias among the Waorani, as the human-animal relationships that shamans develop can interfere with established social relationships (High 2012). Flora (2012) discusses discourses of ignorance as a means of replacing negatively valued talk about suicide causality in Greenland. In Greenland, the speaker's words, as well as the speaker, have agency and can cause terrible results. Flora (2012) writes that in order to avoid potential cycles of harm, Greenlanders avoid discussing the reasons why someone may have wanted to take their own life. In Inner Asia, Buyandelger (2007) has discussed the generative relationship that concerns about shamanic ignorance have on the proliferation of shamanic rituals among the Buryats in Mongolia; Højer (2009) has written about the compelling nature of religious ignorance in Mongolia; and Mair (2007) has described how ignorance and detachment is an important part of Buddhist practice in Inner Mongolia.

Early anthropological explorations of Buddhist societies tended to focus on how the lived experiences of lay Buddhists demonstrated knowledge or ignorance about Buddhist doctrine. Buddhist societies were measured against core Buddhist texts, and lived experiences were often seen through the lens of how they deviated from those texts (Gombrich 1971; Southwold 1978; Spiro 1982; Tambiah 1970). As Cassaniti writes, "there had been a tendency in scholarly work to isolate Buddhism as an objective system that only elites can understand" (2006, 59). The expectations that middle-class lay Buddhists have about religion in contemporary Ulaanbaatar challenge this assumption. One of the continuities from the socialist period has been the educational aspirations of the middle class. Most middle-class interlocutors are self-conscious about their own religious ignorance and tend to be dissatisfied with attending religious rituals that they do not understand. After decades of state-sponsored atheism and high levels of literacy, approaches to religion involve expectations about religious education that challenge the idea that all religious practices are inherently mysterious and beyond their reach as non-monastics. Ideas about what can be known and what should be known are changing, at least among Ulaanbaatar's educated urban middle class.

This post-socialist epistemological transformation seems to have arisen contemporaneously with the syncretic and heterodox nature of religious beliefs and practices among lay Buddhists. Ignorance is generally not discussed with explicit reference to the contents of Buddhist, shamanic, monotheistic, or New Religious Movements' religious doctrines or soteriologies. Instead, lay Buddhist elaborations of ignorance are typified by improvisation, something that tends to be characteristic of Mongolian religiosity in general. While lay Buddhist relationships with religious ignorance form discernible patterns, in each of my conversations these were presented in unique ways. Just as religious knowledge is collated, interacted with, and transformed, so too ignorance, as a form of culturally elaborated unknowing, is understood in multifaceted and often contradictory ways.

For my interlocutors that regularly visit Buddhist organizations for education about Buddhist doctrine, being ignorant is an essential characteristic of those who are not yet enlightened. However, these lay Buddhists do not identify Buddhist ignorance as a site of importance in the same ways as those who irregularly visited Buddhist temples. Discussing her interlocutors' perceptions of the Buddhist concept of *anicca* (impermanence), Cassaniti writes:

> If a man says to me that he feels distraught when his daughter leaves for Bangkok, the textual accounts might claim that he does not understand the Buddhist idea of impermanence because if he did he would understand that nothing is permanent, and he would be calm and unemotional. This conclusion seems problematic at best, because if someone truly understands impermanence he or she will have attained release from the very thing that the Buddha said was the core of human suffering. The person would not just be Buddhist, he or she would be enlightened. (2006, 83)

Within Buddhist philosophy, unless one is enlightened, there is a necessary degree of religious unknowing. Enlightened realization comes only after countless lifetimes of committed religious practice. Like those of my interlocutors who visit educationally oriented Buddhist centers, Cassaniti's informants' sense of unknowing is a demonstration of their understanding of Buddhist philosophical concepts (Cassaniti 2006).

The significance of ignorance *about* Buddhism, rather than *within* Buddhist philosophical and soteriological concepts, is mentioned by Buddhists that regularly attend Buddhist centers only as it relates to their frustration about other lay Buddhists or religious specialists in Mongolia. As regular attendants at global Buddhist educational classes, they are apparently not disturbed by the kinds of uncertainties that characterize other people's ideas of ignorance. The topic of ignorance as it relates to doctrinal understandings requires a level of understanding about Buddhist doctrine that those who visit temples primarily for ritual efficacy continually state that they do not possess. I contend that the types of religious ignorance that most lay Buddhists who irregularly visit Buddhist temples speak about is qualitatively different from the ways that Cassaniti (2006) and Mair (2007) describe religious ignorance and from those Buddhists that I spent time with that regularly attend educational classes. For many lay Buddhists, religious ignorance is seen as a complex but potentially temporary condition rather than a state of unknowing inherent in religious practice.

Trust and Religious Practitioners

Like other parts of the Soviet world, the socialist period in Mongolia was characterized by heavy restrictions on religious activities (see chapter 2). As a result of this fierce oppression, religion was forced out of the public sphere into the private sphere. Dragadze described this shift as the "domestication of religion." "On the one hand it embodies the idea of shifting the arena from public to private, from outside the home to its interior. On the other hand, it also signifies the harnessing and taming of that which seemed outside the control of ordinary people" (Dragadze 1993, 144). As public religious institutions were suppressed, religion moved into the private domain of the home where ideas, practices, and objects were either passed down from generation to generation, hidden, rejected, or forgotten.

In the early 1990s, after the shift to a democratic system, the growth of Buddhism led to a rapid increase in the number of Buddhist institutions and lamas in the capital. Yet, for most Buddhists, religious education still happens in the private sphere. While visiting temples is a key way that many Buddhists confirm their religious identity, the relationship between most lay Buddhists and Buddhist institutions is somewhat strained. Most feel unsure about the quality of the education that religious practitioners have received, and more than a few are cynical about lamas' motivations. While some lay Buddhists have a particular lama that they regularly visit, most do not, and there is a sense among most of my interlocutors that, while some lamas are very good, not all can be trusted. Like Buyandelger's (2007) Buryat interlocutors, people told me that they are concerned about the motives for becoming a monastic, whether lamas have learned from a proper lineage, and whether they can perform rituals properly (Buyandelger 2007; 2013). In addition to these concerns, some of my participants worry about the relaxed attitudes toward monastic vows, which mean that most lamas are married or have girlfriends, and there are few restrictions on the consumption of alcohol, which is occasionally used as payment for ritual services (see chapter 8).

In addition to these concerns, my interlocutors tend to be self-conscious about their own ignorance in religious matters, and the activities at temples have done little to ameliorate this feeling. At temples, prayers are read in Tibetan and personal visits to lamas focus on astrological or practical advice for help with worldly problems rather than for soteriological matters. Many of my interlocutors feel ambivalent toward their experiences at Buddhist temples. Some say that they do not understand the rituals, that religious knowledge is poor among monastics, and that there is a feeling among some that the religious experience in temples is, in some ways, detracted from by the fiscal interactions between monastics and laypeople (see chapter 8). As a result, most lay Buddhists learn about religious matters from alternative sources. Friends and family members, living or dead, are frequently referred to in discussions of religious concepts and practices. Many of my interlocutors when describing core religious concepts refer to alternative religious doctrines and practices sourced from Christianity and New Religious Movements, such as those headed by Sri Sri Ravi Shankar. These New Religious Movements tend to be approached primarily as assemblages of personal development techniques rather than as exclusive religious affiliations. The three most popular of these teach meditation and yoga, preach the value of vegetarianism, and explain core Buddhist concepts such as karma, reincarnation, and enlightenment in their own ways (see chapter 9).

The uncertainty surrounding religious specialists reflects the general feelings of uncertainty in the post-socialist urban context of Ulaanbaatar. While many aspects of the city could be seen to be thriving, since the socialist period ended the capital has seen a dramatic increase in population, inequality, unemployment, corruption, crime, alcoholism, and domestic violence (Højer and Pedersen 2008; Rossabi 2005). In this context, it is hardly surprising that many Mongols are searching for alternative forms of stability. The rupture that occurred in the 1990s was not just marked by political changes, it also profoundly shifted the Mongolian socioeconomic landscape and undermined the moral imperatives that people had accepted during the socialist period.

Mysticism, Ambivalence, and the Power of the Past

Concerns about ignorance and mistrust of public religious institutions are generally not due to a lack of belief in the power or efficacy of religion. The public destruction and desecration of religion by the state has not always led to a weakening of belief in religious power (Berliner 2005; Højbjerg 2002; Højer 2009; Pedersen 2011). As Højer argues, in Mongolia, the socialist government's persecution of religion in some ways strengthened people's belief in it.

> Socialism's attack on its imagined enemy backfired, because not only did so-cialism's imagination of superstition serve to eradicate such superstition, but it did—while eradicating it—bring it into existence as superstition: that is, as something which was important and powerful enough to necessitate destruc-tion. The point is that the force of destruction and the sheer amount of energy expended on superstition mystified "mystification". It fashioned an entity and gave it potential life. Much "superstition" was lost, surely, but simultaneously an imagined space of absence was created. People were made to know that certain things existed of which they did not, and should not, know, and the negative came into being and gained power by virtue of being subject to destruction. (Højer 2009, 579)

By taking religion and repressing it, the socialist government made of re-ligion a powerful and unknown entity that must have been worthy of repression. While many Mongols told me that their families had practiced Buddhism in secret during the socialist period, religion was negatively val-ued, obfuscated, and rejected and construed as powerfully lurking, by the socialist government.

Lay Buddhists told me stories about how the improper treatment of sa-cred items or places had led to ill effects. Solongoo, a small, smartly dressed government employee, aged thirty, told me in an interview in a university classroom in 2010 that in the Zavkhan Province, the mountain called Otgontenger was inhabited by the Buddhist deity of Vajrapāṇi. In the past, the mountain's river was used for Buddhist prophecy, and people threw gold and silver cups into the water to determine whether or not they had good karma. As she described, "in 1990, some people took the bowls that people put out for the gods . . . Afterwards this province had difficulties for four years." Tampering with sacred sites or religious objects is considered to be dangerous, and stories about the fates of people who tried to, or successfully, destroyed religious sites are common among lay Buddhists (Humphrey 1993).

While the negative consequences to those who damage places or objects of religious significance are often reported to be the result of greed for power or money, ignorance about the proper treatment of sacred objects can also cause misfortune. As Oyunbat, a short middle-aged man who was born in the countryside, recalls:

> When I was a child my younger sister had a problem. She was one year old but she had a serious illness. My parents went to many hospitals many times for about one year. But she wasn't well. One time my aunt went to a Buddhist lama who *mereglekh* [divines]. You use coins. This lama said that they had some Buddhist *burkhan* [Buddha, deity, god] at home but that the *burkhan* was not in a suitable place. After that my aunt came to my home she said that to my parents. We found a *burkhan* picture. About two years before my grandmother died, and she had some *burkhan*, some pictures. But we didn't have any religion so after she died we put them in there [gesturing to indicate a cupboard]. We searched and we found them and we relocated and renewed them. After that my younger sister was well. I was young, about ten years old, but I thought that this is not ordinary. This is not simple. The lama has powers. The lama knew about this. So I believe in religion, I believe in Buddha.

Many people report that a story or experience of a religious practitioner's extra-normal powers caused them to believe in Buddhism. Yet belief in the potential powers of religious practitioners did not always result in people engaging with religious specialists.

As Højer (2009, 578) describes, in Mongolia, strong beliefs are often characterized by avoidance rather than engagement, especially in relation to shamanism. Most of my lay Buddhist interlocutors describe shamanism as a strange and powerful religion that they do not understand. The fifty-year-old mother of a friend, who is a successful bank administrator, told me sitting in her office inside the centrally located Golomt Bank:

> I'm afraid of shamans because very recently I read a book about the healing of the horse boy. In this book, in Khövsgöl Lake, this reporter says that they went to the number one shaman . . . And this shaman said, "After I make this ritual you should leave after my performance because many other elements that we cannot see will come and they might hurt you. I can protect myself." This shaman said, "But you cannot. That's why it is better for you to leave very soon." This is my understanding. Shamans—they call many other elements, and then I cannot protect myself. (Odgerel)

Odgerel said she would rather be cautious in religious matters than expose herself to powerful religious practices that she does not understand. This quote also provides an example of the diverse ways that lay Mongols educated themselves about religion. *The Horse Boy* (Isaacson 2009), which Odgerel had read in English, is a nonfiction story and documentary written by an English-born author based in Texas whose child has autism. Upon discovering that his son's condition appeared to improve around horses, the family travels to Mongolia in order to combine shamanic healing and horses. This book and the descriptions of shamanism that it contains provide Odgerel with the foundation for her interactions with Mongolian shamanism. While connection with shamans is very rewarding for some of my interlocutors (Abrahms-Kavunenko 2016), during fieldwork in Mongolia in 2015 and 2016 many Mongols told me that they avoid attending shamanic rituals for fear that they will be asked to become a shaman. Some people told me that the practice of singling out a person during a ceremony to become a shaman is becoming increasingly common in the capital and is one of the reasons for the proliferation of shamanic practice. Friends that attended shamanic ceremonies told me that while there were some charlatans trying to make money out of shamanic rituals, the reason for the growing number of shamans is due to the need that every family has to communicate with their own ancestors.

Occasionally ignorance of religion lends itself to apathy and ambivalence. Sarangerel, a slender middle-aged professional originally from Bayankhongor, told me that she went to a shaman after her husband left her and her three children. Looking for some "extra help" with the problem she sought advice from a domestic female astrologer who divined with Tarot cards, an unusual medium for divination among Mongols, who usually use coins or anklebones. During the session she was advised to go to see a shaman. As she recounts the experience: "He was wearing interesting clothes and jumping and doing many things. I was surprised. Then he read this book and is singing words slowly, slowly. I couldn't catch the words. And after that my friend said, 'Did you hear the words?' And I said, 'No, why? Did I have to hear?' And she said, 'Yes, he tells you everything that you have to do.' But I didn't hear [while laughing]." Encouraged by her friends she later visited another shaman because her son was ill with jaundice. When I asked her if the shaman helped her that time she responded, "Did it help or the doctor help? I don't know."

This uncertainty about the efficacy of people in positions of religious authority also extends to lamas and other religious figures. While a number of people said that they asked lamas for advice, most said that they would only follow the lama's suggestion if they thought that it was correct. A young banking professional in his mid-twenties, Nergui, told me that he would only listen to a lama's advice if he believed that it was right and if he already knew that the lama could be "trusted." This was especially important if he asked them for specific advice, which he believed the lamas were more likely to get wrong. This kind of religious pragmatism is common among the people I speak to. People seek advice about problems, but if it contradicts what they already think, especially if they do not know the lama well, they will decide for themselves. As Nergui said, not all lamas are good or tell the "truth," so lamas need to be tested before they can really be trusted.

Unlike Buyandelger's Buryat interlocutors, whose search for authentic shamans led to an increase in shamanic rituals and the ongoing search for more ever-more powerful shamans, uncertainty surrounding lamas has led to a kind of religious pragmatism that encourages laypeople to seek information and ritual efficacy from a variety of religious specialists and nonspecialists. Most Buddhists mention interactions with an assortment of religious traditions when explaining their religious beliefs and practices, and it is common for people to visit many religious specialists when a problem occurs, as a way of hedging their bets. As Solongoo said later in the interview: "You know, last year my mum died and people said, 'You need to visit the lama or the shaman and they will help your mum go to heaven.' And me and my dad visited everyone, Buddhists, Christians, everyone, but now I don't know if it's true or not."

Like Sarangerel, who visited allopathic medical centers, lamas, astrologers, and shamans when her son was sick, Solongoo wanted to make sure that she had the best possible chance of helping her mother, so she visited numerous religious specialists. This religious pragmatism, as well as promoting diversity in the kinds of religious specialists that one can access, resulted in highly divergent and syncretic religious exegeses among my Buddhist interlocutors (see chapter 9).

Creativity and Syncretism

> Ignorance is seen as a resource, or at least a spur or challenge or prompt: ignorance is needed to keep the wheels of science turning . . . The regenerative power of ignorance makes the scientific enterprise sustainable . . . We need ignorance to fuel our knowledge engines. (Proctor 2008, 5)

Given the dominant conceptual thrust of the anthropology of ignorance it may seem strange to be using the above quote to elucidate Mongolian Buddhist ideas of ignorance. Yet this feeling of a gap that can be filled, as discussed by Proctor, dominated my discussions with middle-class lay Buddhists. This represents a change in Mongolian epistemologies from pre-socialist times. Prior to the socialist period, when lay Buddhists felt that they could rely on the ritual efficacy carried out by ensconced religious specialists for religious matters, I doubt that the same kinds of concerns about religious ignorance would have featured in discussions about Buddhism. However, through transforming the meaning of *gegeerel* from religiously enlightened to educated during the socialist period, the government effectively transformed a term that was previously reserved for high lamas to one that was available to people at all levels of society.

Decades of Soviet-style education, religious disconnection, and repression, along with the importation of new religious groups each with their own understandings of religious education, have transformed the very nature of what it means for middle-class urban Mongols to be religious. There is a feeling among my interlocutors that Buddhism is presently unknown but that it could be known. Just as the uncertainties embedded in religious ignorance reflect the uncertainties in the city, this aspect of religious ignorance repre-sents the feeling of vibrancy and hope, which, in spite of the myriad difficul-ties in Ulaanbaatar, pervades city life (Pedersen 2012).

Interestingly, these findings contrast those of Mair's (2007) work in Inner Mongolia. Among his Inner Mongolian interlocutors, religious ignorance was explained as an essential part of religious understanding, not as something to be overcome. His lay Buddhist informants acquiesced their desires to know through a discourse of Buddhist detachment: as only enlightened beings can be truly knowledgeable about Buddhist doctrine, laypeople's ignorance is seen as part of the essential nature of ignorance that we ultimately have about all things. Ignorance, for his participants was seen as an expression of humility and passivity, along with a deep understanding and trust in religious authority.

This style of relationship to religious ignorance is not something that I find among my Buddhist interlocutors. In general, ignorance is discussed in a negative way, while those family members or friends who are considered knowledgeable about religion are positively described. In the cases where ignorance is preferred, like Odgerel's relationship with shamanism, it is due to the fear of the power of religion. Most of the informants who spoke about the inevitability of unknowing as it related to Buddhism were those who spent a significant amount of time learning about Buddhist doctrine. For these lay Buddhists and lamas, their knowledge about Buddhism is limited because they had not yet reached enlightenment. Yet these Buddhists spoke very little about and seemed unconcerned with their own personal religious ignorance.

In some of my conversations, an active attitude toward religious educa-tion was linked to global religious organizations or religious figures. In others, it seemed to come from the pedagogical ideas imbedded in secular education, itself influenced by decades of socialist-enforced atheism. Saran-tuya confidently discussed her dissatisfaction with the low levels of doctrinal education at temples when she explained: "Now I'm improving. I want to follow Buddhism in a more practical way. Because Mongols, as you know, approach this issue without theory. When the Dalai Lama came to Mongo-lia several years ago he said to Mongols, 'You should study the theory of Buddhism. Without theory you can't pray.' He found that Mongols just pray without any theory. But my understanding of religion is more scientific."

In order to follow the Dalai Lama's advice, Sarantuya attended two week-long retreats run by Sri Sri Ravi Shankar's Mongolian group, was reading books about Christianity and books by the Dalai Lama, had attended a couple of classes run by a Thai Theravāda monk (who had visited Mongolia for a short period), and was visiting local temples once or twice a month, at the time of the interview. She was seeking astrological advice from a "red" lama (see chapter 5) and read the mantra of Avalokiteśvara and the Medicine Buddha (Manal)[1] every morning and evening before eating. Knowledge about religion, for Sarantuya, did not have to be gained exclusively through Buddhist sources, a trend that I noticed among most of my informants.

Most of the people I interviewed presented a tolerant attitude toward other religions, and these were frequently seen as potential sources for rituals or education. Because religions are often thought to be the same thing from different perspectives, most participants were happy to educate themselves about Buddhism through multiple different sources. The most common of these are from New Religious Movements, in particular, Sri Sri Ravi Shankar's group, and books about monotheistic religions (the Bible and the Kabbalah) or self-help psychology (see chapter 9). The tendency to access numerous sources, along with infrequent temple visits, creates diverse responses to questions about core Buddhist concepts and ritual practices. As education at public Buddhist institutions tends to be limited and people are often uncertain about public religious specialists, most lay Buddhists learn about religious practices and doctrine in the private sphere. Because of attitudes toward religious education, the gaps that most people have in their religious understandings are filled with ideas from friends and family members or ideas from other religions.

Religious ignorance influences and is influenced by historical and contemporary phenomena in the city. First, the uncertainties and mistrust that surround lamas and public religious institutions mirror apprehensions about capitalism, corruption, lost tradition, and education. Second, beliefs in the potency of religious rituals, sacred landscapes, and artifacts were made more powerful by the socialist state's attempts to destroy religious traditions. Third, by creating the sense of a possible space of knowing, talk about religious ignorance encourages religious exploration as a way of "filling in" knowledge gaps. Due to the ambivalence that many of my interlocutors feel toward public religious institutions, this learning is often done in reference to ideas and practices that they have learned from the domestic sphere and from a wide range of Buddhist and non-Buddhist religious mediums.

The resulting diversity of religious exegeses reflects the increasingly polyvocal and cosmopolitan city that Ulaanbaatar has become.

By frequently discussing their own and other people's ignorance of Buddhism, my interlocutors identify Buddhism as a site of importance. Rather than being a city emptied of religious interest, Ulaanbaatar is effervescent with religious and spiritual activity. Discussions of religious ignorance highlight feelings of uncertainty and mistrust, while simultaneously providing a space that allows enthusiasm, creativity, and improvisation. Though most lay Buddhists identify Buddhism as part of their cultural tradition, they are heavily influenced by the alternative religious philosophies that are flowing into (and out of) the capital. Because of the perceived spaces created by discourses of religious ignorance, local and translocal ideas of all kinds are combined into new religious understandings. Religious ignorance, rather than dispossessing Mongols of religion, is encouraging a flowering of religious improvisation and syncretism in the context of fuzziness and blur.

Chapter 5

Networks and Visibility

The contemporary buildings that make up Züün Khüree Dashchoilin Khiid are a small part of what remains of the once extensive monastic complex. Inside the administrative office there are a number of illustrations portraying Dashchoilin in the pre-socialist period. The pictures depict Dashchoilin's prominence next to Ulaanbaatar's surrounding northern, southern, and eastern mountains. Given the complex's size one can imagine that the merchants, traders, and administrators would have felt peripheral to the large complex of temples and monastic residences. In a picture drawn in 1913, the complex of Dashchoilin dominates the nearby buildings of Gandan Khiid. Together they form the two great monasteries, accompanied by smaller temples and residences, such as the Choijin Lama Temple[1] and the Bogd Gegeen's Winter Palace. The two main complexes balanced one another: Gandan Khiid to the west housing the great statue of Avalokiteśvara, the image of compassion, and Dashchoilin Khiid with its grand depiction of Maitreya (Maidar),[2] the coming Buddha, rising from the east.

Ulaanbaatar owes its founding to the presence of monastic residences. The old name for its predecessor was Örgöö, meaning palace, and referring to the collection of gers that formed the First Javzandamba, Zanabazar's, itinerant monastic institute (Campi 2006). In 1778, after being nomadic for around 139 years, the encampment then named Ikh Khüree, meaning "great frame" (referring to the walls that enclosed the complex), settled near the Tuul River (Campi 2006). This encampment became known as Ikh Khüree Khot, *khot* being the Mongolian word for "city." The city's name changed again in 1924, after the Bogd Gegeen (the Eighth Javzandamba) died, and the city was renamed Ulaanbaatar, "red hero," to emphasize the country's transition to socialism (Campi 2006, 39).

When I met with one of the lamas from Dashchoilin in 2016 he pointed to a small section of the picture and told me that this is what remains of Züün Khüree. Most of the monastery was destroyed or repurposed during the socialist period, and the unique, brightly colored ger-shaped domes that now form Dashchoilin were used during the socialist period to house a circus. In the intervening time what was left of the great temple complex was demolished. Today, the temple is surrounded on all sides by tall apartment blocks and businesses. Like a canopy with trees competing for sunlight, the gray and beige high-rise buildings crowd the edges, in every available spot, overshadowing the temple.

Later in the conversation the bespectacled lama told me that there is now nowhere to house the young lamas who train at the temple. Dashchoilin doesn't charge for the young students who come from the countryside (and elsewhere) to become educated about Buddhism. However, the training lamas must provide for themselves from their own resources for housing and food. They, like most other lamas in the city, must support themselves and live as any other urbanite does in accommodation outside the temple. "This is the greatest problem facing Mongolian Buddhism today," he says.

From this interaction one can distinguish some of the central challenges for those who wish to revitalize Buddhism in Mongolia. The urban landscape no longer physically or metonymically centralizes Buddhist institutions as it did before socialism. In the pre-socialist period, the temples that physically dominated the city's landscape were home to shimmering representations of tantric deities and housed high lamas who were considered by many to be enlightened beings. In contemporary Ulaanbaatar, religious architecture does not have a strong physical presence. Most lamas are unable to live within temple walls, causing them financial hardships and generating fiscal imperatives that are criticized by many lay Buddhists (see chapter 8). Most of the major temples, the rebuilt and the new, are now tucked away in between the crowded multistory buildings that shoot up in what used to be old parks, green spaces, and former ger districts. This lack of central architectural visibility is reflected by and reflects the somewhat marginal presence of Buddhism for most Mongols in their day-to-day lives.

As the initial renewal of Buddhism in Ulaanbaatar saw new and old temples and statues being built and rebuilt, the city's landscape was fast undergoing major transformations. Since I first lived in the capital, the city's high-rises have expanded at a rapid rate. This expansion has obstructed the visibility of the mountains that surround the city and has obscured some of the imagery associated with Buddhism's resurgence. As new high-rises appear (sometimes left unfinished) on every available space in the city and as the ger areas expand, the southern sacred mountain Bogd Khan Uul has become increasingly obscured by buildings and the seasonal air pollution. In 2009, when one drove to the base of the southern mountain, one was able to see a tall, newly built golden Buddha statue backed by trees on the slope. Along with the central statue of Chinggis Khan at the parliament house, this is one of the key sites that people visit for pictures and blessings after they get married. In 2009 it seemed symbolic to me that the Zaisan socialist memorial and Chinggis Khan's face inscribed in white stones on the side of Bogd Khan Uul both overwhelmed the smaller, lower, but still quite prominent statue of the Buddha. In 2016 when I revisited this site, I found that Zaisan, the image of Chinggis Khan, and the Buddhist statue were all more or less obscured by the new apartment blocks and shopping malls that were spreading up the sacred mountainside to the south.

In spite of the growing physical obscuration of Buddhism in Ulaanbaatar, there are extensive networks that visibly and invisibly connect urbanites to Buddhist institutions and Mongolian institutions to teachers, funding, individuals, ideas, and practices overseas. These connections have, in recent times, been a source of support and critique for local formulations of Mongolian Buddhism. As most of the overseas networks interconnect Mongolian Buddhists with Tibetan Buddhists in diaspora, the changes that have occurred within international Tibetan Buddhist lineages have significantly influenced the resurgence of Buddhism within Mongolia. Tibetan high lamas (Mong., *Khutagt*; Tib., *Rinpoche*), who are believed by many Mongols to be enlightened,

Figure 6. The statue of the Buddha that stands at the foot of Bogd Khan Uul,
now obscured by new high-rise building developments.

visit the capital at different times in the year, reinvigorating lay Buddhist practice and establishing key links with Mongolian Buddhist institutions. While
there are a number of Mongols who have been identified as rebirths of reincarnation lineages, when I talked to people about enlightened people, most referred to Tibetan-born Rinpoches, the Khamba Lama Choijamts of Gandan
Khiid, scholars, or foreign new religious teachers (see chapter 9). Visits by

Tibetan Rinpoches have a significant impact on local understandings of *gegeerel* (enlightenment, knowledge) and purification (*ariulakh*) in the capital. This chapter will describe the rebuilding of Buddhist institutions in Mongolia after the Democratic Revolution. It will look at the networks that have formed between local and translocal institutions as they attempt to once again centralize Buddhist institutions and *gegeerel* in the minds of urbanites.

Rebuilding Temples

After the end of the socialist period, many Mongols were enthusiastic about rediscovering their Buddhist past and reaffirming their Buddhist identities as an alternative or complement to socialist ideals of citizenry and progress. In the early 1990s, old men who had been lamas during the socialist period began to reinhabit old temples and build new Buddhist temples. They reinvigorated rituals that they remembered from their youth and/or began to publicly practice rituals that they had carried out in secret during the socialist period. These old lamas took on students, some of whom gravitated toward a religious vocation. Others were encouraged to become lamas because they were good at school or were born in fortuitous years according to local astrological systems. Some of these young lamas now hold key positions at Ulaanbaatar's major temples. Old lamas formed a link from past memories to present-day Buddhist practice. Many young students studied with Mongolian lamas in the early 1990s before traveling to India to learn more about Buddhism from translocal lineages. Others received Buddhist education at temples in Mongolia or individually from Mongolian teachers.

In their 2007 survey, Majer and Teleki estimated that there were around two hundred Buddhist institutions in Mongolia (Majer 2009, 542). Due to the advanced age of the old lamas and the difficulties of maintaining young students, particularly in remote locations, by the time of their survey around half of the temples that had been rebuilt and reinhabited in the early 1990s had shut down (Teleki 2009). It was easier for the temples that were close to populations in regional centers and those in Ulaanbaatar to sustain themselves, as they were close to the lay populations upon whom they relied for support (Teleki 2009). Without counting each of the separate temples that can be found within Gandan and larger temple complexes, about thirty-six of these two hundred temples were in Ulaanbaatar (Majer 2009, 53).

Following the traditional layout of the Mongolian ger, the entrance for most Mongolian temples is at the south. As laypeople enter the temple they tend to circumambulate the inside of the temple or stop to sit for a while on wooden benches that are placed around the temple walls. A person entering should always walk to the left side and circumambulate in a clockwise direction (*nar zöv*, the correct way of the sun). Reflecting the symbolic structure of a ger, the northern side of the temple houses the major shrine. This is where one finds the temple's most sacred statues and images. If the temple has pictures of teachers that they consider to be important within their lineage, they are frequently placed next to the northern wall of the temple (see Empson 2011 for descriptions of shrines and photographs in gers). In front of the northern shrines, lamas and laypeople place offerings such as food, money, incense, candles, water, and vodka. The central part of the temple usually contains low wooden benches on which lamas sit when they recite their daily prayer readings. These benches face inward toward one another, to the east and west. Toward the northern end of the temple are higher seats reserved for visiting high lamas. In many Mongolian temples these are symbolically left vacant during the morning *khural* (prayer readings, meeting). Rather than serving as a seat for a lama of low rank, these may display the picture of a high lama, such as the Dalai Lama, or the image of the recently deceased Ninth Javzandamba.

Within some temple complexes there are universities or schools for Buddhist education. Gandan Khiid, Betüv Khiid, Dashchoilin Khiid, the Sakya Pandita Dharma Chakra Monastery, and the FPMT's nunnery the Dara Ekh Khiid all provide comprehensive monastic education. Most temples provide some form of Buddhist education for their *sangha* (Majer and Teleki 2008), though this education depends on the temple's resources and orientation. Some temples, such as Tüvdenpejeelin Khiid, have a stated astrological or medical focus. However, astrological predictions and soothsaying of various kinds are carried out in most Mongolian temples. In Majer and Teleki's survey, six of the temples recorded were housed in gers (Majer 2009, 57). It was not uncommon for ger temples to be run by only one lama (Majer and Teleki 2008). Only one of the temples that Majer and Teleki recorded in Ulaanbaatar chanted in Mongolian; all others used Tibetan as the liturgical language (Majer 2009, 55). A small number of temples in Ulaanbaatar are occupied by female religious specialists. In 2007 there was only one Gelug nunnery, two Gelugpa women's temples and one Nyingma women's temple (Majer

2009, 54). Three of these female temples and at least seven more temples were founded or cofounded by women (Havnevik 2015).

In 2007, twenty-five Buddhist institutions were in the Gelug lineage, eleven were Nyingmapa, and one center (which runs out of an office) was Kagyupa (Majer 2009, 54). In 2013, a new Sakya temple, the Sakya Pandita Dharma Chakra Monastery, was built to the east of the city. The categories of Nyingmapa and Gelugpa tend not to be exclusive categories in Mongolia. There is often a significant overlap between Gelugpa and Nyingmapa temples (Havnevik, Ragchaa, and Bareja-Starzynska 2007). In Mongolian these schools are referred to as the "yellow hat" (*shar malgaitan*) and "red hat" (*ulaan malgaitan*), or "yellow" and "red" religions, respectively. These classifications are unclear among religious specialists and are inconsistently understood among laypeople. Some laypeople that I spoke to thought that the yellow school was only found in Mongolia and Tibet and that all other Buddhist schools were red, including the traditionally "black hat" Kagyu and the Theravāda schools (Havnevik, Ragchaa, and Bareja-Starzynska 2007). Adding to this confusion, the term *shashin* itself can be used to refer to Buddhism specifically, rather than religion in general (Even 2012, 255). Buddhism can also be referred to as the "yellow religion" (*sharin shashin*), the Buddhist religion (*buddin shashin, burkhani shashin*), or the lamas' religion (*lamin shashin*).

In 2007, there were around 1,000 lamas in Ulaanbaatar, and around 660 were associated with the predominantly Gelugpa temple complexes at either Gandan or Dashchoilin (Majer 2009, 57). In 2016, Lama Munkbaatar from Gandan Khiid estimated to me that there were around 800 lamas associated with Gandan. Located slightly to the west of the city center, Gandan is the largest temple complex in Mongolia, and many lay Buddhists that I spoke to considered it to be the center of Buddhism in Mongolia (see Jadamba 2018). While most lay Buddhists consider the largest temple complexes of Gandan and Dashchoilin to be the result of local assemblages, they are very much connected to translocal networks of funding, teachers, pilgrimage, and ideas.

Translocal Buddhism

As old Mongolian lamas and their young students were reimaging local practice in the early 1990s, global Buddhist organizations began to take an active role in the reinvigoration of Buddhism in Mongolia. Several globally funded Buddhist individuals and organizations have impacted the reemergence of Buddhism in Ulaanbaatar. Some have sponsored young Buddhists to receive religious tuition in India. Others have been involved in rebuilding Buddhist temples or have created new temples and Dharma Centers. Others have created charitable projects, seeing poverty as the major issue restricting Buddhism's proliferation in the country.

These global Buddhist organizations tend to be connected to the Tibetan diaspora living in India or elsewhere. As such, the reformulations of religious practice that have occurred among Tibetans living in diaspora have influenced the resurgence of Buddhism within Mongolia. When global Buddhist organizations arrived in Mongolia after 1990, their focus had transformed from monastic-lay relationships and ritual efficacy to lay and monastic religious education, the translation of Buddhist literature, and charity. This shift in focus is a reflection of broader religious reform movements that have been transforming Buddhism[3] throughout the world.

Before the late eighteenth century in Burma, many monastics believed that too much time had passed since the Buddha's lifetime, and, as such, it was no longer possible to become enlightened. Buddhism, it was thought, had become so degenerate that the best a person could hope for was to make merit in this lifetime so that they might be reborn as a human being to hear the teachings of the future Buddha, Maitreya (Pranke 2010, 445). In the eighteenth century, a few charismatic monks challenged this idea and started to practice Vipassanā meditation. This style of meditation slowly became more and more popular, exponentially growing within and outside of Burma's borders among both monastic and lay populations (Pranke 2010). Among those who advocated the practice of Vipassanā, enlightenment became a possibility in this lifetime for both laypeople and monastics, albeit a very difficult one.

In the late nineteenth century in Sri Lanka, a globally influential reform movement, subsequently labeled as "Protestant Buddhism" by Gombrich and Obeyesekere (1988), began. This movement was born from the interaction between British colonialism, Protestant ideas about religion, and Sinhalese society. One of the movement's key proponents, Anagārika Dharmapāla, encouraged a new model of experiential and textually fluent lay Buddhism. Dharmapāla lectured on the importance of textual and ritual understandings, along with centralizing meditation practice. He de-emphasized the relationship between lay Buddhists and monastics and advocated the importance of the education of laypeople above ritual and donative relationships between laypeople and the Buddhist *saṅgha* (Gombrich and Obeyesekere 1998). He also encouraged the moral purification of Sinhalese society and an anti-syncretic approach to religious practice and despised what he saw as the "popery"-like adornments of the northern Mahāyāna schools of Buddhism (Gombrich and Obeyesekere 1998).

As Dharmapāla founded a new reform movement in Sir Lanka, Thailand saw the growth of its own meditation movement in conversation with other reform movements in the Buddhist world arising from a combination of pressures, including the potential loss of sovereignty due to colonial activity in the region and Christian missionary activity. Thai Buddhist reformers, like Dharmapāla, wanted to demonstrate to Protestant colonialists that Buddhism was not a mystical practice; rather, it was a rational religion based on the scientific method (Cook 2010).

Informed by Protestant ideas about religion, these reform movements in Southeast Asia challenged the idea of monasteries as places for quiet contemplation and renunciation, suggesting a different role for monastics and Buddhist organizations. The roles of monks living in monasteries have now changed in many places across Asia. In China, monastics are sometimes seen as being a "burden" on the laity and are encouraged to support themselves financially rather than relying on the lay population (Caple 2010). As reform movements have challenged lay-monastic relationships, a number of Asian charity organizations have proposed new approaches to charity. These include the Mahāyāna Taiwanese organization Tsu Chi (Chien-Yu and Weller 1998) and Theravāda Sri Lanka's Sarvodaya Shramadana (Hayashi-Smith 2011), which, in conversation with Christianity, see the role of Buddhist institutions as active in charitable works.

The style of teaching that translocal Buddhist organizations advocate in Mongolia is the result of decades of interaction between European, North American, and Australasian contacts with the Tibetan diaspora. While foreign scholars initially viewed the lineages of Buddhism practiced in Tibet and Mongolia unfavorably, Vajrayāna Buddhism has become increasingly popular around the world. As a result of its popularity internationally, new expectations about religious tutelage have influenced the Tibetan diaspora's style of religious instruction.

In the twentieth century Tibetan lay-monastic relationships, which were already undergoing internal changes, radically transformed following the exodus of high-ranking religious teachers from Tibet. Those that resettled in the Americas, Europe, Australasia, and India were exposed to the new teaching expectations of interested foreigners. These new students, already having expectations about Buddhism that were derived from the global export of Theravāda "Protestant" reform movements, expected to understand doctrine and to learn transformative practices, such as meditation.

For centuries scholars referred to the Mongolian and Tibetan variant of Buddhism as "Lamaism" in spite of it never being a term used by either to describe their own religion (Lopez Jr. 1996). According to Lopez Jr., in the last half of the nineteenth century, when Protestant scholars described "Lamaism," they presented it as an inferior devolution of the "true Buddhism" of Theravāda (Lopez Jr. 1996, 13). Theravāda Buddhism, considered to be more pure and rational and less mystical, was likened to Protestantism while "Lamaism" was likened to Catholicism. Unlike Protestantism, which had grown out of Catholicism, "Lamaism" was viewed as degeneration from the "true Buddhism" from which it supposedly descended. Protestant expectations about religion in the late nineteenth century dismissed Tibetan Buddhism as hierarchical and esoteric in contrast to the "religion of reason" (Lopez Jr. 1996, 18) that they saw in Theravāda Buddhism.

Obeyesekere writes that these attitudes toward the "Tibetan" style of Buddhism began to change with the Theosophical society's esoteric explorations of Vajrayāna Buddhism in the late nineteenth century (Obeyesekere 2006, 77). They transformed again when the occupation of Tibet by China in the 1950s brought a once mysterious and remote religion onto the global stage, where it then began to attract a more diverse series of interpretations. The first Tibetan-Mongolian Buddhist institution was built in the west in New Jersey in 1955 and was started by a Kalmyk Buddhist, Geshe Wangyal, who had escaped the persecutions of religion in Soviet Russia during the 1930s (Ignacio Cabezón 2006, 97). This was soon followed by an increase in Vajrayāna Buddhist institutions internationally after Chinese troops reached Lhasa in 1959 and many high-ranking Buddhists, including the charismatic Fourteenth Dalai Lama, fled across the Himalayas and were granted asylum in India. Several high-ranking Buddhist lamas, such as Namkhai Norbu and Deshung Rinpoche, were invited to participate in scholarly projects in western countries as early as the 1960s (Ignacio Cabezón 2006).

Since then Vajrayāna Buddhist institutions of all of the four major lineages (Gelugpa, Nyingmapa, Sakyapa, and Kagyupa) have spread around the world. International pilgrims travel to parts of India, such as Dharamsala, where the Tibetan government in exile resides, to receive teachings from Buddhist lamas and the Fourteenth Dalai Lama. Film stars, including most notably Richard Gere, who visited Mongolia in 2010, now practice Vajrayāna Buddhism. The charismatic presence of the Dalai Lama, who was awarded the Nobel Peace Prize in 1989, has added to the growing attraction of this style of Buddhism (Ignacio Cabezón 2006). As a result of its popularity internationally, international students have influenced the Tibetan diaspora's style of religious instruction.

While it seems strange to apply the label "Protestant" to Buddhist organizations connected to the Tibetan diaspora, because of its imputed historical associations with Catholicism, the styles of teaching that global Buddhist organizations encourage, with their emphasis on understanding and translation, are similar to the ideals of knowledge acquisition found among Protestant-derived educational traditions. These Buddhist institutions encourage textual knowledge and experiential practices among the laity, and these, in turn, influence Mongolian ideas about what Buddhism is and "ought" to be (see chapters 4 and 8).

However, the term "Protestant Buddhism," as Gombrich and Obeyesekere describe it, does not elucidate the ethnographic realities in Mongolia. As they describe it, "Protestant Buddhism" has the characteristics of being polemic, fundamentalist, anti-religious, and dependent on English-language concepts (Gombrich and Obeyesekere 1988, 218). Translocal Buddhist institutions in Ulaanbaatar are none of the above. For instance, when I asked Lama Zorigt about the efficacy of shamans, he replied that they are powerful but that their efficacy is limited to the troubles of this lifetime. Mongols and Tibetans working within global Buddhist organizations tended not to undermine the efficacy of other religious practices. When one of the Irish volunteers at the Buddhist center was having problems reconciling her Buddhist practices with her Catholicism, Panchen Ötrul Rinpoche told her that she should continue her prostrations while thinking about the Father, the Son, and the Holy Ghost.

The idea that lamas are not practicing in an ideal way in Mongolia does not—like Sri Lanka, a former colony of the British Empire—have Protestant roots (Gombrich and Obeyesekere 1988, 225). Rather, the idea of monastic "degeneration" reflects the historical relationship between Tibet and Mongolia, where the Tibetans have considered Mongolian Buddhism to be under the religious tutelage of Tibet (see chapter 2; Elverskog 2007). It is the deviation from the practices of central Tibetan Buddhist institutions (now in diaspora) that invokes degeneration narratives. Additionally, the translations of religious concepts do not come from English but instead are being translated from Tibetan to Mongolian or from old translations written in Mongol *bichig*. Unlike Sri Lanka, Mongolian lamas have not taken on the roles of Protestant priests, with whom they have had little or no contact. While my interlocutors all interact with "modern" ideas of education, these ideas have not originated exclusively in the Protestant west. Years of Soviet-style education still have an influence on lay understandings of religious education. Indeed, many Tibetans in diaspora have ended up in Catholic, Orthodox Christian, or Hindu countries. Notable figures from the early diaspora, such as Namkhai Norbu, live in Catholic countries, such as Italy. Jampa Ling is run not by an organization based in a Protestant country but by an Irish NGO.

As the teaching methods and philosophies at Dharma Centers are largely informed by Tibetan Buddhist institutions in diaspora, the teachings that I came into contact with at these centers did not seem to vary much in content from other global Buddhist institutions around the world. What makes these Dharma Centers unique is the specific ways they are being integrated (or not) into Mongolian society and how they interact with local temples and practices.

Local and Translocal Networks

A number of key translocal Buddhist figures have been particularly influential in the resurgence of Buddhism in Mongolia. Some of these have cemented their relationship in the sponsoring of building projects, the provision of resident teachers, and the establishment of NGOs. Others are connected to local institutions through intermittent visits or through hosting Mongols that travel overseas. Some have helped to rebuild or revitalize Buddhist practice in Mongolia, and others, including the Javzandamba lineage and the Dalai Lama, are important both as "enlightened" spiritual leaders and as part of complicated geopolitical networks.

One of the early international figures instrumental in the reinvigoration of Buddhism was the Nineteenth Kushok Bakula Rinpoche. Born in Ladakh, he was the Indian ambassador in Mongolia from 1990 and played a key role in connecting Mongolia's reemerging Buddhist community to the Tibetan diaspora. Believed by many Mongols to be enlightened, he was responsible for building Betüv Khiid, a temple to the northwest of the city, which trains young Mongolian lamas residentially from the age of fourteen. According to one of the translators at the temple, Betüv Khiid was built in an area of the city that was once notorious for prostitution and poverty. By building a temple in a poorer section of the city, Bakula Rinpoche wanted to bring hope and religious faith to an afflicted area. Along with its focus on monastic discipline, Betüv Khiid carries out several monthly pūjās (*sar tutmi khural*) and reads daily prayers (*ödör tutmi khural*) for laypeople. It also provides regular education activities for the public, such as weekly dharma teachings. The building of Betüv Khiid was finished in 1999, just before Bakula Rinpoche died in 2003.

The Ninth Javzandamba, along with his identified but unnamed reincarnation, has also influenced the revitalization of Mongolian Buddhism. Although the Mongolian socialist government outlawed the Javzandamba lineage in 1924 following the Eighth Javzandamba's death, in 1936 the Tibetan-born Fifth Reting Rinpoche identified a boy believed to be his reincarnation. By the 1950s the reincarnation of the lineage, Jampal Namdol Chökyi Gyaltsen, had disrobed to become a householder. Although a layperson when the Chinese army made incursions into Tibet, there were concerns that the presence of the Chinese Communist Party would reveal his identity, and in 1959 he fled Tibet to reside in India, where he lived for most of his life. His recognition was publicly revealed in 1990 after Mongolia's Democratic Revolution.

The Ninth Javzandamba followed in the reincarnation lineage of Zanabazar (see chapter 2), one of the most influential figures in Mongolia's Buddhist history. Zanabazar's Buddhist statues are some of Mongolia's most revered artworks, and his Soyombo symbol from the Soyombo script (*soyombo bichig*) now forms part of the Mongolian flag. The eighth reincarnation in this lineage, the Bogd Gegeen, briefly headed an independent Mongolian nation from 1911 (see chapter 2). Though ritually enthroned in India in 1991, the Ninth Javzandamba did not visit Mongolia until 1999. After his first visit he was refused permission to visit again for ten years due to Mongolian political controversies surrounding his rank and its effect on Mongolian Buddhism (Jadamba 2013, 31). As noted in chapter 3, Mongolian Buddhist temples are not administered by a central Buddhist organization. However, the

Javzandamba lineage, with its historical prestige, does pose a potential threat to the power of key lamas and politicians in Mongolia. As his previous incarnation was the former head of an independent Mongolian state, some politicians think that the new incarnation could potentially pose a challenge for the country's political leadership.

In 2010, in spite of these controversies, the Ninth Javzandamba was granted Mongolian citizenship. He was ritually enthroned in Mongolia in November 2011 and was visited by the Dalai Lama within a week of the ritual (Jadamba 2018). He died four months after his enthronement and was subsequently embalmed, a common Buddhist practice. His mummified body remains at Gandan Khiid in a locked area, where his son, also a Rinpoche, lives and conducts regular rituals over his body. The Abbot of Gandan Khiid, Khamba Lama Choijamts, made this public statement following his death: "'The Ninth Jebtsundamba said before his passing away that he would be reborn in Mongolia. His next reincarnations would not be involved in political affairs.' This was the summary of the deal made between the Ninth Jebtsundamba and the government of Mongolia; namely that a) his next reincarnation would be Mongolian and not Tibetan and b) that the next incarnation would not be involved in Mongolian political affairs" (Jadamba 2013, 31).

In late 2016 the Dalai Lama visited Mongolia, causing trade and diplomatic problems with China. During his visit he made an announcement that the rebirth of the Javzandamba had been found but that the child was currently too young to be named. Who the next reincarnation of the Javzandamba lineage is, the translocal connections they maintain, and how they will be trained is a matter of geopolitical import and internal politicking. Although the Dalai Lama renounced his political position within the Tibetan government in exile in 2011, he still represents an unwelcome opposition to Chinese policies in Tibet. As the Dalai Lama grows older, the question of who will be his next reincarnation becomes increasingly politicized. The Chinese government has supported their choice of the Panchen Lama, a lineage that was historically involved in recognizing the Dalai Lama. The Tenth Javzandamba, as a high-ranking reincarnation, could be influential in the choice of the next Dalai Lama. Who the search party chooses will have ramifications for Buddhists across the country.

The Fourteenth Dalai Lama himself is popular among lay Mongols, lamas, and the nonreligious alike. He has visited Mongolia on many occasions. His first visits to Mongolia were in 1979 and 1982. During these visits his presence was monitored by the socialist government. One of my interlocutors, who was a student helper organizing the Asian Buddhist Conference for Peace in 1979, recounted: "When the Dalai Lama came, we were not allowed to come to him to just pray or get some blessing or something. The people from the KGB[4] would watch who was coming up to him."

Since the renewal of strong ties between Mongolia and China after 1990, the Dalai Lama's visits to Mongolia (and there have been several) have been the source of diplomatic tensions. During his 2002 visit, the Chinese government shut down the railways that connect China and Mongolia for two days (Campi 2012). Each time he visits, there is a strain on Sino-Mongolian relations. Some Mongols told me they are worried that the next Dalai Lama will be reincarnated in Mongolia and that this would strain Sino-Mongolian relationships. In 2009 I was berated by a young man at a party about what he saw as the damaging influence of the Dalai Lama on Mongolia's geopolitical situation. Most other people I spoke to were disparaging of the Mongolian government when they restricted the Dalai Lama's visits as they were seen to be demonstrating their political weakness (see chapter 3 for Mongolian perspectives on China).

During conversations and interviews many people referred to the Dalai Lama's teachings and visits to Mongolia. Some described his recommendations for Buddhism in Mongolia, particularly when discussing religious education among laypeople and lamas in the country. Others told me of his moral teachings, for instance that people should care for one another and that they should not drink vodka. For others he is a compassionate figure who is relatable and has a good sense of humor. Some Mongolian lamas discussed his views on stricter monastic vows (see chapter 8). Most of my interlocutors have read a book by the Dalai Lama, visited his teachings, or seen his teachings on the Internet or on television.

Another important figure in the rejuvenation of Buddhism in Mongolia is Lama Zopa Rinpoche. His organization, the Foundation for the Preservation for the Mahāyāna Tradition (FPMT), has been responsible for several projects in Ulaanbaatar, including assisting the rebuilding and funding of an education temple for young lamas, Idgaachoinzinlin Datsan within the complex at Gandan Khiid. The temple building was completed in 1999 and is one of the few that contains residential dormitories for training lamas. The FPMT continues to support the funding of hot meals for resident monastics and the funding of their electricity bills. It is in this building that they carry

Figure 7. Lay Buddhists read the mantra of Avalokiteśvara inside Idgaachoinzinlin Datsan.

out their annual monthlong "100 million *mani* retreat." During the retreat, laypeople and some monastics read prayers and attempt to collectively read the mantra *om mani padme hum* a hundred million times. This is the mantra of Avalokiteśvara and is believed to generate *bodhicitta*[5] and to bring blessings to wherever it is read.

In 2000 the FPMT repurposed a building in the center of the city on Juulchin Street, naming it Shredrup Ling. It continues to offer educational classes to laypeople, teach Tibetan, translate texts into Mongolian, and carry out monthly rituals, such as the Tārā and Medicine Buddha pūjās. The center funded the restoration of the old Dara Ekh Khiid, an abandoned monastery to the southeast of Ulaanbaatar. In May 2003 several Mongolian nuns who were ordained in 2001 began to live in the restored temple. In 2009 it had nine resident Mongolian nuns along with two Tibetan nuns from Nepal's Kopan Nunnery, a number which had dwindled to two nuns in 2016, with an additional nun being sponsored to study in India.

Many local temples receive teachings from internationally based Rinpoches or lamas. Some are given funding from translocal Buddhist organizations for heritage purposes or with an interest to seeing Buddhism grow. While the major translocal centers are all part of the Gelug lineage, there have been other lineages of Buddhism both within the Vajrayāna tradition and more broadly with the Mahāyāna and Theravāda schools that have influenced Mongolian Buddhism. Some Theravāda monastics have visited and taught in Mongolia and funded large rituals, such as the lamp celebration in 2009 and 2010. Connections with Taiwan, Hong Kong, and, less visibly, mainland China have created funding avenues for new temples, statues, and *stūpa*s (*suvarga*) in Mongolia. Visiting Rinpoches and teachers come from many different Buddhist and non-Buddhist lineages.

Along with translocal Buddhist organizations in Mongolia, Mongols have contact with translocal Buddhist organizations through pilgrimage. Just as Buddhists from all over the world travel to India to receive teachings from high Tibetan lamas in diaspora and other religious teachers, so too do many Mongols. Those who study in India retain connections to friends and teachers overseas. These connections reach back to the early 1990s when some young Buddhists left to study in southern or northern India.

Mongolian lamas, sometimes with sponsorship from translocal Buddhist organizations and sometimes raising their own funds in Mongolia, frequently travel to India on pilgrimage and for Buddhist education. There is now a Mongolian Buddhist temple in Bodh Gaya, the pilgrimage site in Bihar, India, where the Buddha is believed to have attained enlightenment. Most Mongolian lamas I spoke to that had studied in India studied at one of the three main Gelugpa monasteries in southern India—Sera Jey, Drepung Gonang, and Namdroling Monastery—or at the Buddhist university at Sarnath, near Varanasi. Those who have returned from studying overseas now have an impact upon the teaching styles and aspirations of the Mongolian saṅgha (see chapter 8).

Visiting Rinpoches and Purification

> On the one hand, a *tulku* is a spiritual system embodied in a concrete person. On the other hand, he or she is a metaphor . . . where one encounters the naked, unmediated state of enlightenment . . . Meeting a Nyingma *tulku* is not meeting a person, but rather meeting *Dzogchen* or the Great Perfection itself. (Smyer Yü 2012, 48)

When Rinpoches visit Mongolia, lay Buddhists enthusiastically attend their teachings and rituals to learn more about Buddhism and/or to receive blessings and purification. For many lay Buddhists, being in the presence of a *Khutagt* is spiritually important, as they believe that being in the presence of an enlightened being will bring them great benefit, renew vital energies, and provide purification. Every summer at Jampa Ling, Panchen Ötrul Rinpoche, the center's spiritual head, visits for around three months and teaches, gives blessings, and conducts ritual transmissions. His arrival at Jampa Ling during the summer of 2009 signified the start of a break from the ordinary weekly classes taught by Lama Zorigt. During his visit, Jampa Ling was buzzing with activity. When he stays at the center, people come at all times of the day to receive personal blessings, sometimes after traveling great distances.

In 2009, to mark Panchen Ötrul Rinpoche's arrival, Jampa Ling was filled with around two hundred lay Buddhists dressed in their finest *deel*s. Panchen Ötrul Rinpoche took his place on the (usually empty) ornate chair that is reserved for him or other high-ranking lamas that visit the center. Lama Zorigt and another lama began the ceremony by participating in a debate. They spoke in Tibetan, while seated laypeople present patiently watched them pacing and smacking their fists into their open hands. According to Lama Zorigt, this gesture represents the intention to empty the hell realms (as you smack your palm with your fist) and as you raise your hand you express your intention to bring all beings up from the lower realms to the higher realms. After the debate, the audience calmly formed a line to receive a blessing. Each person offered a *khadag* (prayer scarf) folded three times, with the fold pointed toward the recipient, as they received a blessing. Friends told me that if I faced the fold toward myself it meant that I wished the recipient injury. While people waited to receive their blessings, the older students chanted mantras led by a laywoman who frequently leads the chanting at Jampa Ling, a somewhat unusual lead as in most Mongolian Buddhist rituals, chanting is normally led by male lamas. As people offered their sky-blue (*tsenkher*) *khadag*s, Panchen Ötrul Rinpoche touched their hands and then their heads and gave them a red thread with a knot tied in it (representing blessing and protection) and some incense for purification.

Throughout the summer months the excitement surrounding Panchen Ötrul Rinpoche's visit is punctuated by visits from a number of other high-ranking teachers. These are mostly, but not all, Tibetans. Upon arriving at the center, most begin by prostrating to the shrine three times, demonstrating their humility to the Buddha, the dharma, and the *sangha*. Some of the more confident laypeople follow along, doing prostrations before taking their seat. When I asked Enkhtuya, a bright twenty-one-year-old university student living in the ger districts, what the benefit of doing prostrations was, she said that she felt as though she was helping other sentient beings and herself.

Enkhtuya:	The benefit of prostrations goes to all sentient beings. Basically you have to think that you are bringing all the sentient beings up from the hell realms. I feel like I absorb them, like a magnet.
Saskia:	How does that make you feel?
Enkhtuya:	When I am praying, I think that my bad deeds are getting thinner and that I am making good deeds.

Some lay Buddhists prostrate toward shrines and teachers or images of high lamas, as they are thought to be emanations of the Buddhist teachings. While prostrating at home is believed to have benefits, I was told that prostrating in sacred spaces or to living teachers is believed to intensify the activity of purification and to multiply the blessings.

In the summer of 2009, the head of the Sakya lineage, Sakya Trizin, visited Jampa Ling and gave the tantric initiation for the popular Bodhisattva Green Tārā (*Nogoon Dara Ekh*).[6] This ritual was translated from Tibetan into Mongolian to clarify its meanings to the participants. The event at Jampa Ling was for those with invites only, as rituals by Rinpoches can attract a lot of people. To mark his arrival, the road to Jampa Ling was lined in anticipation by participants waiting with symbolic offerings of sky-blue *khadag*s. As he arrived he was rushed forth to plant a tree and then hurried inside the building, flanked by security.

Sakya Trizin sat on the golden, raised ornamental chair where Panchen Ötrul Rinpoche had been seated some weeks before, with Panchen Ötrul Rinpoche sitting on a slightly lower seat to his right. Lama Zorigt and another lama began the ceremony by debating Buddhist texts in Tibetan. After this the tantric initiation of Green Tārā began. Tantric initiations connect Buddhist practitioners to the living and dead masters of esoteric practices and to the powers of the figures that they instantiate. After receiving this initiation, reading the mantra of Green Tārā is believed to have greater effect. The imagery present during the initiation helps practitioners to visualize and connect with Green Tārā while reading the mantra.

As well as energizing one's practice, a blessing from an important lama is believed to help purify one's karma and to connect a person to the dharma so that in their next lifetimes they will be reborn as a human with the opportunity to study the dharma. The expanding numbers of visitors during the summer period at Jampa Ling indicates that being in the presence of high lamas perceived to be enlightened is considered meritorious by many Mongols. One friend told me that during one of the Dalai Lama's visits to Mongolia so many people were pushing to get themselves into the stadium that she thought she was going to be crushed to death. Many lay Buddhists told me that the benefits of having contact with a high lama stem from their capacities to purify the harmful consequences of the recipient's previous actions. When I spoke to a herder from the Töv aimag about his reasons for attending regular classes at Jampa Ling, he replied: "I come to Asral to reduce my karma." Later he told me, "Our teachers pray for us and do readings to reduce our karma." While he explained that he was not powerful enough to affect someone else's karma, he thought that the teachers at Jampa Ling did have that capacity.

Enlightenment in the Capital

The resurgence of Buddhism within the capital has coincided with the radical physical transformation of Ulaanbaatar. This has meant that even as old temples have become reinhabited and new ones have been built, the skyline of the city has increasingly crowded them over with new high-rise buildings. Due to the rising height of the buildings packed into the city center, the old architectural presence of temples has not reinstantiated its centrality in the capital. The growing ger areas and their associated pollution further shroud low-lying temples from view.

As the built environment overwhelms the architecture of local and global Buddhist institutions and the air pollution blurs their place in the city's landscape, translocal networks continue to grow. Donations from foreigners help rebuild temples, set up charities, and fund printing presses and translations. Foreign teachers exchange knowledge with local Mongolian lamas, and many Mongols travel to India for pilgrimage or monastic education. Other foreign donors have funded the building of *stūpa*s and statues that are visible throughout the country. Accompanying funding, ideas about education have entered the capital through reform Buddhist networks. These ideas and practices favor a more "Protestant" version of Buddhist practice, wherein laypeople are expected to understand Buddhist philosophy and carry out transformative practices.

If enlightenment in the pre-socialist period was housed in the many temples that were dotted around the country, in the post-socialist city foreign enlightened figures shine brightly during brief visits, and local figures of enlightenment are increasingly obscured by a rapidly changing skyline and the buzz of urban living. The next Javzandamba will be an important figure internally for the lay Buddhist population and externally for the Tibetan diaspora (with its global following) and Mongolia's geopolitical relationship with China.

Chapter 6

Karma and Purification

Wednesday night classes at the FPMT's Ulaanbaatar Dharma Center, Shredrup Ling, teach meditation and visualization practices. Shredrup Ling is tucked between apartment buildings and a Mormon church, across the road from the centrally located Zanabazar Museum, which houses some of Mongolia's most impressive Buddhist artworks sculpted by the First Javzandamba, Zanabazar. The building is three stories high, overshadowed by larger apartment buildings to the south and west. To the northern front of the building stands a white *stūpa*, which, along with what remains of the old temples and the new Buddha statue to the south of the city near the Zaisan Soviet war memorial, is one of the few Buddhist symbols visible within the largely physically secular capital city.[1] Occasionally elderly Mongols can be seen praying to the *stūpa*. Next to it a flagpole is adorned with brightly colored prayer flags, spreading blessings as they catch the wind. On the ground floor there is a vegetarian café, which in 2014 changed hands, for fiscal reasons and due to personal relationships, from being run directly by the FPMT to housing the Luna Blanca. This restaurant, which was formerly located down the road, is one of the most popular vegan restaurants in the capital, and its employees are predominantly practitioners of the Supreme Master Ching Hai's Quan Yin method (see chapter 9).

Buddhist classes take place on the first floor of the building in the *gompa* room, which is ornately decorated with colorful *thang ka*s, Buddhist statues, and offerings. On the main shrine rest pictures of the Fourteenth Dalai Lama, Bakula Rinpoche, the recently deceased Ninth Javzandamba, and the center's own teachers, Lama Zopa Rinpoche and his teacher, the now deceased, Lama Yeshe. Sitting cross-legged on the carpeted floor of the gompa room after walking through a late May snowfall in 2016, I am one of around fifty laypeople attending the meditation class led by Australian nun Ani Gyalmo. After meditation practice, with help from the center's translator Khulan, she leads a purification visualization. "Imagine," she tells us, "that your body is filling with black smoke. This smoke represents your negative actions formed from your body, speech, and mind." The visualization continues until the body is slowly filled with smoke right down to one's toes. "Now," she instructs us, "as you exhale, empty the smoke from your body through your breath." We each picture the smoke being slowly cleared, released from every part of our body. "As you imagine the smoke leaving your body, visualize the defilements of body, speech, and mind leaving with it." After the smoke is gone and our bodies are (imaginatively at least) free of the dark smoke and, with it, all impurities of body, speech, and mind, she asks us to envision our bodies filling with light. "Imagine," she instructs us, "that white light is coming from all directions and that it is coming into the body, filling up every aspect of our being." Smoke is as an allegory for obscuration and defilement. Bright light both cleanses and represents illumination, one of the key properties of Buddhist enlightenment.

In Mongolia and elsewhere visualization practices and tantric images, such as those of the Bodhisattva Vajrasattva,[2] are used to purify one's present motivations and one's previous actions. Vajrasattva, a white androgynous figure, is often pictured next to clear flowing water and a clear blue sky. Vajrasattva's image is associated with the diamond for its unsullied and adamantine qualities. The imagery of pure water and pure air are frequently used in tantric initiations, Buddhist iconography, and daily offerings. Ani Gyalmo's use of smoke to symbolize obscuration is used in Mongolia and elsewhere. These metaphors have strong resonance in a city plagued by chronic air pollution.

The above visualization metonymically instantiates negative spiritual elements, which are believed to cause unfavorable repercussions for a person's future, predominantly in this case bad karma as environmental pollutants. When I discuss the city's environmental pollution with my interlocutors, many connect environmental pollution with the blockage or worsening of people's fortunes. There are two main ways that environmental pollution is thought to be connected to fortune in Ulaanbaatar. First, as this chapter will explore, through karma (*üiliin ür*). Karma is accrued through the activities of body, speech, and mind, which are believed to have results in this lifetime and in the next. The repercussions of karmic actions can be felt by individuals and collectives, and, in some cases, it can be passed from one family member to another. Karma is somewhat distinct from, though often interwoven with, other systems of causality in that it stresses explicitly moral dynamics. Second, people link environmental pollution (*bokhir*) to spiritual contamination (*buzar*) through causalities that are external to intentional action. Spiritual contamination, as chapter 7 examines, generally involves external pollutants, bad energy, blockages, or a nonhuman force or agent, such as an angry spirit. In my discussions I noticed that the categories of karma (*üiliin ür*) and spiritual contamination (*buzar*) are not mutually exclusive and that the means by which people attempt to eradicate the ill effects of both are often similar. Sometimes people's explanations of ill fortune include both a karmic causality and an external contaminant. Some types of pollution, for instance earning money through dubious means (see chapters 1 and 8), are morally operative but affect a person's fortune both karmically and through spiritual contamination—in this case, carried physically by the money itself.

A number of my interlocutors explicitly tell me that physical pollution (*bokhir*) is the result of bad karmic actions carried out through body, speech, and mind. When discussing the air pollution in Ulaanbaatar over beer with a former monk, Ganbaatar, at the Ikh Mongol brewery, he told me: "People pollute the environment because they are polluted in their minds. When I was a boy, the Tuul River [the river that runs through Ulaanbaatar] was clean, and it ran freely. But now the Tuul is polluted and hardly runs at all. It smells very bad and people throw rubbish into it. If we look at the pollution in the river we can see the pollution internally within people."

As Ganbaatar (who is around forty) explains, the city's environment has transitioned from a relatively carefree period characterized by clean air and an untainted flowing river to a polluted one in his lifetime. "The city is polluted," he continues, "because our minds are polluted." This statement has the implication of linking environmental pollution (*bokhirdol*) and spiritual pollution (*buzarlal*) with moral inadequacies. As a former lama, Amaraa, who now works at Shredrup Ling, told me during an interview in 2016: "Polluting the river and not polluting the river . . . these two actions are completely different. Countless other creatures use the river. So, if you pollute the river, your action brings a lot of damage. We are all interconnected. I believe that at the time we die, there will be judgements about our actions. The good will go to heaven [*divaajin*], and the bad will go to hell [*tam*]." In this case environmental pollution and bad fortune are connected through karmic action. As all creatures, human and nonhuman, are interconnected, harming other beings by creating pollution has negative results, and these extend beyond one's current lifetime.

The purification of karma—along with purifying contamination, clearing obstacles, and refreshing one's internal energies (see chapter 7)—is one of the main reasons that lay Buddhists attend dharma classes and visit local temples. In spite of the general uncertainty around what Buddhism *is* and what one should actually *do* at a temple (see chapters 4 and 7), the notion of karma and the possibility of its purification are persistent elements of contemporary Mongolian religious practice. Although karma was one of the most consistent religious concepts that I discussed with Buddhists in Ulaanbaatar, there are different ways in which it is thought to be accrued, and a variety of practices are prescribed for its purification. For most lay Buddhists, being a good person and making merit, broadly conceived, is the best way to avoid the accumulation of bad karma. For those that seek ritual efficacy at temples, lamas' rituals are thought to assist with the karmic fruits of one's previous bad deeds.

As this chapter will explore, karma is a model of causality that has a moral aspect to it. In karmic discourses causality is not limited to the random linear knock-on effects of actions creating reactions through time. How a person thinks, feels, speaks, and acts influences their situation both in the immediate and distant future. It affects the unfolding of one's current life and the possibilities of future rebirths. Thinking, speaking and acting influence a person's future, along with their family's prospects and sometimes the destiny of an entire region. Its ephemeral and tangible potentials cause karmic reverberations that yield either positive or negative results. Most of the lay Buddhists and monastics I spoke to told me that the repercussions of karma can be mitigated by a person's own religious practice, interactions with sacred objects or high lamas, and/or with the assistance of religious specialists. While a small number of lay Buddhists told me that one couldn't change the outcomes of a bad deed, most did think that there are ways that a person can purify their karma.

Individual Karma and Purification

Karma stood out as the most consistently described Buddhist concept among both the Buddhists and non-Buddhists that I spoke to during my research. In the sixty-one formal interviews that I carried out, only two participants said that they did not believe in karma. The Mongolian word for karma translates literally as "action-result," *üiliin ür* (*üil* meaning "deed" or "action" and *ür* meaning "seed" or "result"). Karma, as it was described to me, was the result of an action that was created in this life or previous lifetimes. Likely, the term's very literal meaning, unlike Buddha (*burkhan*) or enlightenment (*gegeerel*), increased the consistency of peoples' explanations.

Karma was generally explained by my interlocutors as a law of cause and effect that comes back to the self, in this lifetime or the next, either as a natural law or something that is mediated by deities and/or a monotheistic god. Most people thought that they themselves were at the nexus of karmic action and reaction and that a person would receive back what they created. As Chimeg, a female retired factory worker aged seventy-five, described:

> If I do bad things, the karma will be bad. If I do good things, the karma will be good. It depends on the action. During my lifetimes, I have experienced both good and bad results, and I might have done more bad things than good ones, which might be the reason for my suffering. I suffered because I have done bad actions. But I have the opportunity now to receive the teachings. This is because of the good karma from my previous life. If my actions are bad, then my karma will be bad. If my actions are good, then my karma will be good.

Because the results of karma can come back to you in this lifetime or in the next, good people who seem to experience unjust suffering may be considered to have carried out negative actions in the past. As Chimeg said later in the interview, she considered being born as a human and one that was able to hear the Buddhist teachings to be the result of the good karma that she accrued in her previous lifetimes. However, the suffering she has experienced in this lifetime, she thought, was the result of the bad karma she had accrued in this and her previous lifetimes. One did not neutralize the other.

Most Buddhists that I spoke to told me that their present and future rebirths are the consequence of their present and previous lifetimes. Karma is thought to invisibly ripple through space, time, and mind, affecting this and future lives. The outcome of an action can manifest in a person's next life, far removed from physical causal chains. When I asked about the reasons for economic inequalities, most lamas told me that the reason some people were rich and others were poor was due to karma. However, for those that answered in this way, bad karma was not measured through wealth alone. These lamas told me that wealth could be a hindrance to spiritual advancement and that there were other aspects of one's life, such as being able to connect with good Buddhist teachers in this lifetime, that were far more valuable. At Dharma Centers students are taught that being born in a time and place where one can connect to the teachings of Buddhism and practice those teachings is of highest value and hence that everyone present, to some extent, has very good karma.

At Jampa Ling, during my fieldwork in 2009 and 2010, Lama Zorigt focused on the teachings of the Bogd Tsongkhapa's central text, the *Lam Rim Chen Mo*. From this text he taught students that there were three ways that one can create bad karma:[3] through one's body, speech, and mind. A few of my interlocutors referred to the concept of the ten black deeds, or ten black nonvirtuous actions (*arvan khar nügel*), when I asked them about what created bad karma. Instead of translating *nügel* as "sin," I have translated it as "action," as sin is a supersaturated concept in English. Three of the ten black actions are carried out through the body: killing (*amtni am taslakh*), stealing (*khulgai khiikh*), and engaging in sexual misconduct (*ariun bus yavdal*). Four are carried out through one's speech: lying (*khudal yarikh*), gossiping (*khov ögüülekh*), harsh words (*shirüün üg ögüülekh*), and meaningless chatter (*demii chalchikh*). And the last three occur in the mind: being covetous (*khüsel shunal*), having poisonous thoughts (*khor setgel*), and holding false views (*buruu üzel*). Lama Zorigt taught his students that holding wrong views consisted of denying the Buddha's teachings (Tsong-kha-pa 2000, 226–227).

At Jampa Ling the evening practice of acknowledging (*naminchlakh*) wrongdoing was taught to be the most effective way of eliminating bad karma. Students were taught that if the seeds of bad karma were not acknowledged they would multiply and, much like the effects of spending money made through dubious activities on durable items (see chapter 1), bring forth ever larger negative results. As such, every night they should take refuge in the three jewels: the Buddha, the dharma, and the saṅgha. Students were told to think through the actions of the day and acknowledge their deeds that may have created bad karma. They were taught to promise not to do those things again until they reach enlightenment, to pray, and do prostrations. Lama Zorigt lectured that if someone did these practices with absolute sincerity and commitment, the results of bad karma would be mitigated. Some of my interlocutors, especially the older ones, do this practice every night. As a young female university student who regularly attended classes at Jampa Ling described:

> We are taught in Buddhism that bad consequences of an action can be avoided if you acknowledge it . . . There are three levels of acknowledgment. If you acknowledge your action to a lesser extent, the karma will not proliferate. If you acknowledge it to medium degree, your karma will be reduced. If you acknowledge it . . . thinking that you never will do such acts again, you have the possibility of not suffering the bad consequences of what you have done. However, this does not mean that you just say, "I am sorry for what I did." If you think . . . about what you did and you acknowledge it genuinely, you can avoid the bad consequences. (Oyuntsetseg)

Lama Zorigt lectured to students that a good way to understand one's personal suffering was to think of it as purifying one's negative karma. In his Buddhist classes, students were instructed that if they learned how not to react to suffering and did not perpetuate the negative cycle of karma (such as a poor person becoming a thief), the experience of suffering would deplete the bad karma they had accrued in previous lives. If a person was unwell, Lama Zorigt counseled that they should imagine their store of bad karma reducing, instead of focusing on their illness. They should, as he said, imagine their bad karma burning away through the pain of illness.

While black actions, black smoke, and smog are associated with impurities, fire is used ritualistically as a vehicle for purification. At the southern entrances of some temples, incense is left burning inside a large metal brazier, and as people pass they place their hands, heads, hats, and sometimes wallets

Figure 8. A visitor passes a metal brazier burning incense at Gandan Khiid.

next to the incense to let the smoke pass over them. Burning incense is often incorporated in Buddhist and non-Buddhist rituals to purify contamination, such as in prosperity ceremonies (*dallaga avakh*). In a popular ritual element of the reinvigorated Tsam (Tib., Cham) ritual at Dashchoilin Khiid, a cone-shaped construct, previously placed at the center of the Tsam dancers, is burned in a large bonfire. Before the lamas ignite it, laypeople throw

Figure 9. The audience rushes to catch sweets handed out by the lama dancers during the reinvigorated Tsam Dance at Dashchoilin Khiid. (I was told that these sweets, when ingested, act as purification.)

pieces of paper on which they have inscribed their bad deeds onto the pyre. As the fire burns it is believed to act as ritual purification for the bad deeds and thus dissipate their potential accompanying results.

Some of my interlocutors extended this idea of burning through and dissipating negative karma to include thoughts of reducing the world's suffering as they experience adversity. When I asked Enkhtuya, a regular student at Jampa Ling, to explain *orchlon* (Sans., *saṃsāra*) she said: "About *saṃsāra*, in books it says that it is an eternity of suffering. But, instead of seeing everything as hard or as suffering, I try to see the side of peace. It feels like it's not suffering. If I am sick, I think that I am carrying the suffering of other people. It is like I am blocking the suffering of other people by experiencing it myself." Here Enkhtuya is referring to practices in Buddhism (such as *gtong len* [Tib.]) where practitioners try to take away the suffering of others by enduring it themselves.

When I asked Lama Sükh from the Idgaachoinzinlin Datsan at Gandan Khiid if it were possible to purify (*ariulakh*) karma, he replied that it must be, as otherwise it would not be possible for the great masters, such as Milarepa (*Myal Bogd*), to have been able to reach enlightenment in a single lifetime. The popular story of Milarepa, which is translated into Mongolian and available at most bookstores, begins with Milarepa's youth. As a young man he was encouraged to become a sorcerer to get revenge on the extended family members that had caused his family to be impoverished after his father's death. He became so powerful that he was able to kill thirty-five of his family members and cause a hailstorm that destroyed the village's barley crops. After committing these acts he felt great regret and sought the help of an accomplished master to help him eradicate the bad karma he had created. Under the tutelage of Marpa, he was able to extinguish the seeds of bad karma that he had sown in his life and reach enlightenment. Lama Sükh told me that as Milarepa had been able to purify his bad karma, it was possible for others to do so. The way to purify one's bad karma, he told me, was to acknowledge (*naminchlakh*) one's wrongdoings and to promise to never repeat the deed again.

Avoiding Bad Karma

For most of the lay Buddhists that I spoke to, avoiding the accrual of bad karma was the best way to avoid unwanted karmic ramifications. The personal practices that students of Dharma Centers do at home and in class are thought to strengthen a person's morality and therefore reduce the accrual of negative karma. These are carried out both formally and informally and include meditation, reading mantras, saying prayers, chanting, doing prostrations, acknowledging wrongdoings, attending tantric initiations, and making offerings. For some meditation is something they do on a bus, while others have a formal time set aside every day (sometimes twice a day) for meditation. All meditated in classes, even if they do not continue the practice during the rest of the week. The level of commitment to these practices mostly increases with age, which reflects the commonly held belief that people should become more religious as they age to prepare for death. In spite of this tendency, I interviewed a number of young people (in their early twenties), such as Enkhtuya, that did extensive daily practices.

A common practice used during meditation practice is to focus on the incoming and outgoing air. Ani Gyalmo and Lama Zorigt both taught students to calm their minds by focusing on the feeling of air coming and going through the nostrils. Focusing on the air around the nostrils helps one to focus, and the air that is breathed is a reminder of interdependence with the outside world. Meditators are taught to disengage from extended discursive reactions that accompany troublesome feeling states and to observe, rather than react to, the physical states that arise within the body. As Narangerel recounts:

When I'm concentrating on my breath, I feel calmer and more relaxed. It gives me a chance to think about the other side of things. Just breathing, just concentrating on my breath. And then after meditation I feel relaxed and calm, and I start to think about why I became angry: what was the reason? Why did that person do that? Why did I start to feel angry? And then it's over. Otherwise, after a bad thing has happened it's not very nice for me to think about the reasons for it. At that time I was just thinking about myself. It's quite different [after meditation]. I'm not just thinking about myself; I'm thinking about others.

When Mahmood writes about the importance of *salāt* (daily prayer) within the Egyptian piety movement, she explains that *salāt* is not just an expression of being a pious Muslim; it is how one *becomes* a pious Muslim (2001, 828–829). Likewise, meditation and other Buddhist practices assist in the transformation of individuals toward Buddhist moral ideals. Narangerel explains that through meditation she can distance herself from an event that caused her to be angry. She is able to detach herself from her anger and see the "wider picture" of cause and effect. As a result she is better able to avoid reacting in anger, which would lead to the accumulation of bad karma. As another one of my interlocutors, Ariunaa, a medical student in her early twenties who regularly attended classes at Jampa Ling, described:

> People are very busy with their everyday lives. Mornings and evenings are always passing by. They do not have much time to think through different processes and actions . . . When you are in a peaceful state after meditation, you see your actions in the past more clearly, what you did wrong and how you should act in the future and so on. As long as you understand that you can be in a peaceful state when you treat others well, you will have more awareness of your past actions. If a person previously argued every time that someone said something unpleasant or did something to make them angry, they may realize the consequences of their actions and stop behaving in that way. The more they become aware and stop repeating these actions, the more their karma will be reduced.

According to Ariunaa, by calming the mind and emotions one can become nonreactive in difficult situations. By not reacting to unpleasant things they are able to avoid repeating emotions, thoughts, and actions that sow the seeds of bad karma.

Like those that regularly attend Dharma Centers, many lay Buddhists who irregularly visit Buddhist temples tell me that in order to avoid bad karma one should behave in a moral way and be a good person. Being a good person is thought to generate merit (*buyan khiikh*). Narantsetseg, who occasionally visits local temples when she has a problem in her life, told me that when she was studying at university she had some problems with friends spreading malicious gossip about her (*khar khel am*) (see Swancutt 2012, 127–153 for further discussion). She was doing very well in her studies, and this (along, no doubt, with her good looks) attracted the envy and ire of five of her closest friends. One day she arrived at university to find that malicious gossip had been spread about her. As she described:

> It was really hard to study in that university . . . I knew it was lies. I was crying a lot . . . So at that time I just said OK. I don't want to be friends with you anymore. Let's finish our friendship. But now . . . my life, my career, my studies, my family, everything is better than them . . . Their life isn't so good. For example three of them have really bad husbands. Their husbands some-

times hit them and they drink alcohol and it's difficult to find a good job . . .
I know they had bad activities when they were young. That is why karma is
working for them in their lives.

Narantsetseg attributed her former friends' present tribulations to the
effects of immoral speech. Instead of seeking out a ritual intervention, as
Swancutt describes among the Buryats that she lived with (2012, 154–184),
Narantsetseg felt that she could avoid the results of malicious gossip by being
a good and moral person. Rather than reacting to what was said, she enacted
being a good person. She told me on a number of occasions about how she
worried about the effects of people talking about her, both as praise (*tsagaan
khel am*, literally "white speech mouth") and gossip (*khar khel am*, "black
speech mouth"), both of which are believed to have detrimental effects on
both the subject of discussion and the speakers, causing problems both karmically (for the speakers) and non-karmically (for the subject of the speech).
In spite of these potential threats she believed that she was protected from
the negative repercussions of praise and gossip because of her moral conduct.

This idea that broader spiritual forces would not affect a "good" person
was reinforced by conversations that I had with lamas. When I asked lamas
whether or not other-than-human beings could negatively affect people's fortunes, all of the lamas I spoke to replied affirmatively. A number of times
after asking this question, the lamas replied with something like: "Yes, they
can affect people's fortunes, but you don't need to worry. What you really
need to worry about is rebirth into the eternal cycles of *samsāra*." After a while
I started to wonder why this was their response to me, even though they provided ritual efficacy for others. In a conversation with Lama Amaraa in
2016, I asked why he thought that I would not be affected by nonhuman beings. His reply was that Buddhists who have taken refuge do not need to
worry about these forces as the Buddhist pantheon of Bodhisattvas and
Dharmapālas will protect them. It is those who have not taken refuge (a practice that few lay Buddhists do in Ulaanbaatar) that have to seek ritual
efficacy from lamas. Because they have not taken refuge, he told me, they cannot enlist the help of the Buddhist pantheon on their own. As a result, Lama
Amaraa said that these people need help from lamas who would try their
best to assist them. Just as Narantsetseg told me that she didn't need to be
worried about karmic repercussions because she was a good person, Lama
Amaraa told me that other-than-human beings would not affect Buddhists

that had taken refuge. Taking refuge is believed to protect one from creating future bad results and from the harm caused by nonhuman forces.

Enlightenment, Rebirth, and Karma

Lay Buddhists that regularly visit Dharma Centers tend, when asked to reflect on the teachings given in Buddhist classes, to state that there are six possible realms into which one could be reborn. These are the hell realms, the realm of the hungry ghosts, the animal realm, the human realm, the realm of the *Asuras* (jealous gods), and the realm of the *Devas* (the long-living gods). The Choijin Lama Monastery Museum, built at the beginning of the twentieth century to house the Mongolian state oracle, contains within it grisly depictions of the various realms. One wall depicts hell through illustrating an inversion of normal life, with human beings being eaten and defecated out by Mongolian herding animals (*mal*) and human tongues being ploughed, presumably to grow grain from. Cloth representations of the skins of wild animals and humans are hung from the interior of the walls, and on one ceiling there are graphic depictions of humans in various states of dismemberment. Alongside the depictions of hell are illustrations of the realm of the hungry ghosts, where it is said that beings roam with unquenchable desires, unable to fulfil their intense cravings. Cosmologically, above the animal and the human realms are the *Asuras*, a type of demigod, who, though powerful and capable of experiencing more pleasure than humans, are driven primarily by their passions and are therefore never satisfied. Above the *Asuras* are the *Devas*, or the long-living gods. This is a realm of bliss where beings with very good karma, such as the Buddha's mother, are reborn. While this is considered to be a good rebirth, beings here are so blissful that they forget to work toward enlightenment, and, after many eons of untold delight, they use up the last of their good karma and are reborn once more into the lower realms. A human rebirth is considered to be the most fortunate of all, as its midway position between abjection and bliss provides the greatest possibility for the recognition of the true nature of suffering that leads one to awaken.

Many of the people that regularly attend Buddhist centers explained to me that a person's rebirth is related to the type of impurity with which an individual struggles (see also Carlisle 2008). A couple of my interlocutors said that killing an animal had the result of shortening your present life.

Others told me that if you were very generous, you would be reborn as a wealthy person. Another told me that if you cheat on your partner, you will have relationship troubles in your next life. As Ganbaatar described to me in 2009:

> After a person is dead they will get another body. What kind of body? It depends on their karma. In this life, if I always do good deeds, make good karma, and I collect good karma, then that karma will take me to a good body. Maybe to a good realm, so you can find a human body. That next life depends on your karma. There are three types of karma, but mostly two, good and bad karma. In this life, if you keep yourself very pure in your mind then you are always collecting good karma. If you keep your mind very impure then you are always collecting bad karma. For example if you are always very angry then you are always collecting bad karma . . . The result will be that in the next life you could become a wolf or a lion or a tiger.

According to Ganbaatar, impurities are generated through one's thoughts, speech, and actions, and these impurities relate to specific kinds of karmic reactions. The kinds of impurities that one has in this life will be reflected in the conditions one is born into in the next.

One's motivations and thoughts are just as important as one's speech and physical actions. All have karmic consequences. As motivations and intentions are the basis of moral action (Heim 2003), their transformation is of central importance. As Gombrich writes, "Buddhist doctrine agrees with Kant that what counts is intention, not effect" (1971, 246). In Mongolia it is commonly thought among my interlocutors that if an action is accompanied by a strong negative or positive intention (*setgeleer*), the karmic results of that action will increase significantly. In conversations in both 2009 and 2015 a friend described karma to me by referring to the same Buddhist parable about a selfish woman living in India. Throughout her life the woman did not give to anyone in need and was considered by her fellow villagers to be stingy. In her later years, while going for a walk, she saw a calf that was so hungry it was about to die from starvation. The old lady suddenly felt such compassion for the calf that she lactated and was able to feed it with her milk, which she collected with an old cloth and wrung into the calf's mouth. Because of her actions the calf did not die from hunger. Shortly after this event the old lady died. To decide her next rebirth, all of the bad actions (of body, speech, and mind) that she had carried out during her life were weighed against the positive things that she had done. Because of her selfishness she was about to descend into the hell realms. However, as she began to descend the piece of cloth that she used to feed the calf blocked her descent. Due to the intense compassion and purity of this one action of making merit (*buyan khiikh*), she avoided the fate of a lower rebirth and instead was reborn in another (higher) realm. In this case one pure action borne from a positive intention enabled her a better rebirth in spite of a lifetime of selfishness.

Some of my interlocutors linked enlightenment to rebirth. Among those who did not regularly attend Buddhist classes, the idea of enlightenment varied considerably. For some, enlightenment was a concept heavily influenced by New Religious Movements (see chapter 9). For others, enlightenment referred to the acquisition of knowledge, and an enlightened person was one who, influenced by socialist understandings of the term, was highly knowledgeable. For others the idea of enlightenment was affected by Christian concepts. A few people told me that to become enlightened is to be reborn into a heaven that, mirroring Christian ideas, is eternal. When I asked a friend, Sükh, a bank worker in his mid-twenties, what enlightenment is, he replied:

> I've heard it's the same in every religion. I heard in Christianity when you believe in Christ you will get excused for your sins . . . and that when you're excused you can go to heaven. In Buddhism they think the same; also in the Kabbalah in the Jewish religion, they think the same thing. Everybody—every person who believes in God can get enlightened. If you clear away all the sins you've done before and do good things, you can get enlightened. But I've heard in Buddhism and also in yoga and things when you get enlightened sometimes you can make rain fall and sometimes you can fly and things like that. I think enlightenment is just becoming pure, getting ready to go to heaven. I think it's not really different from any other religions.

Enlightenment, as he describes, is connected to purification and going to heaven after death. His family regularly invites lamas to their house to purify obstacles for the coming year. When I talked to him about what happens after a person dies, he replied that they either go to heaven or to hell and that these were places from which a person could not be reborn.

Enlightenment was connected to death in other ways by a number of my interlocutors. In one interview, Munkhtsetseg, a twenty-four-year-old professional, explained that reincarnation as a human being *is* enlightenment. She told me that if you accumulated too much bad karma, you cannot be reborn as a human. Instead, you will go to hell. Being reborn as a human was the best possible rebirth, and if you became a human again, you had become *gegeerel* (enlightened, educated, bright).

Saskia:	What happens to you after you die if you are a good person?
Munkhtsetseg:	You'll be born again. Maybe you heard before about in Mongolia if someone has died and you put black points on the body and then if someone is born again in this family, these points come on the opposite side of the body, and then people realize that this is the person who died and he or she has been born again . . . In different provinces it can be different, but in Bayankhongor [a province to the southwest of Mongolia] they put black spots.
Saskia:	And do you know anyone who has these marks?
Munkhtsetseg:	I've seen someone. Someone who had many points here [pointing to her back]. It was when I went to the countryside and the grandfather of this child told us that his daughter had died in a storm. She was under a tree and it was raining very heavily and she died, and then they put some spots, some black spots. Then another daughter of his had a baby, and this baby had these points on the other side. I was thinking, "Wow, really?"

In many parts of Mongolia it is customary to mark a person's body after they die with the charcoal from the underside of a cooking pot (or with pen or milk) so that if they are reborn back into the family they can be recognized by the appearance of birthmarks in the same places (Humphrey 2002, 78–79). Most families that I spoke to consult lamas after the death of a family member, even those that follow the advice of shamans or attend Christian churches. Lamas' predictions often relate to specific details of how the person will be reborn, and many lamas predict that rebirths will occur within the same family. A number of my interlocutors described how a family member is the rebirth of a deceased relative. One friend told me that she is the rebirth of her well-loved great-grandmother. This practice marks continuity from practices during the socialist period when, according to Humphrey, lamas would give very specific information about a person's rebirth, including which part of the family the person will be reborn into and what kind of life that person will lead (Humphrey 2002, 76).

At Dharma Centers the attainment of enlightenment is the explicitly stated goal of religious practice, albeit a goal predominantly intended for future lifetimes. Enlightenment is explained by those who regularly attend these centers in fairly consistent ways. Many use metaphors of light or talk about it as the release from impurities. Some describe it as the release from saṃsāra and the cycles of rebirth. For others it is positively described as a state of being: illumination, peace, and tranquility. Others emphasize compassion (Mong., *bodi setgel*; Sans., bodhicitta). As Ariunaa told me at Jampa Ling in 2009: "It means understanding and recognizing causes of actions and things. The one who is enlightened has compassion for others, not for themselves. They are illuminated."

Enlightenment is often explained as a state free from defilements, trouble, and distress, wherein one has freed themselves from saṃsāra and its attendant suffering. As Enkhtuya described, "In my opinion it is to eliminate all the harm of the *nisvaanis* [Sans., *kleśa*], to make or collect good karma. It is the person who has reached *bodi setgel* (bodhicitta)."

At Jampa Ling, Lama Zorigt taught his students that the origins of suffering were rooted in *nisvaanis* (Sans., *kleśa*). *Nisvaanis* are defilements of the mind and body that bring about suffering in the form of desire, anger, pride, ignorance, doubt, and holding wrong views. According to his teachings, in order to be released from suffering one must rid oneself of these negative aspects. Enlightenment is believed to be the purification of the negative elements of *kleśa* and the development of compassion for all beings through the development of bodhicitta. Developing bodhicitta helps one develop into a Bodhisattva to help all sentient beings be released from the endless cycles of saṃsāra.

Saṃsāra (orchlon) was described in apparently paradoxical ways as being both emptiness and everything. This paradox reflects the Mongolian term that has been used to describe saṃsāra and the underpinning philosophical concepts from the Mādhyamika strain of Buddhist philosophy that, along with Yogācāra philosophy, heavily influenced the Tsongkhapa's teaching. When I interviewed Mendbayar and Chimeg, two students in their seventies at Jampa Ling, they described orchlon (saṃsāra):

Chimeg: From what I have understood from the teaching, orchlon is emptiness.

Mendbayar: Orchlon is me. Orchlon consists of insects and other animals. Like the universe is broken into different nations such as Australian, Mongol, and Kazakh people. Orchlon consists of all of these things like insects, horses, and human beings and so on. I think orchlon is the system of air.

Neither of my interlocutors saw a contradiction in their interpretations of Buddhist doctrine. Indeed, within Buddhist philosophical systems there does not have to be a contradiction in these two positions. Within Mādhyamika Buddhist philosophy there is nothing to point to that underpins reality, no foundations. This philosophy propounds that the nature of phenomena is *śūnya*:

> "śūnya" is often translated as "void," but it is not empty space; the term may be better understood as "relative," i.e., "devoid of independent reality" or "devoid of specific character." "Thus śūnyatā [voidness] is nonentity, and at the same time 'relativity,' i.e., the entity only as in causal relation . . . It is simply the negation of an independent reality or the negation of specific character" (Takakusu 1956, 109–110). Śūnya is not to be interpreted ontologically. It is an unattached intellectual position, rather like a raft for crossing a river. Once the river is crossed, the raft is to be discarded . . . Śūnya is complete nonadherence and nonacquisition. (Ahmed 2003, 170)

Saṃsāra is the state of misrecognizing the *śūnya* of all phenomena and may be used as a descriptor for the universe at large, including its constituent elements, in so far as these macro and micro phenomena are not correctly recognized as being devoid of inherent thingness or isolated existence. It is not a contradiction to define saṃsāra as both "emptiness" and "the entire universe." For lay Buddhists that do not regularly attend Buddhist classes, the secularized meaning of orchlon as "universe," emphasized during the socialist period, tends to be used in its nonreligious understanding.

Karma and the Collective

In Mongolia the person who creates negative karma is not necessarily believed to be the one who exclusively endures the consequences of their actions. A number of interlocutors told me that they thought that karmic reverberations could affect a family member, and a couple described situations in which the bad morality of a group could cause negative repercussions for a region (see also Empson 2011, 186–188; Humphrey 2002). In this way, karmic consequences are not always thought to have been created by the individual but could also be the consequence of another's misdeeds.

Karmic results are sometimes thought to be inherited from a person's ancestors or received as the result of a living family member's actions. One middle-aged woman told me that she believed that the death of her male work colleague's eighteen-year-old daughter, who had been killed in an accident, was the result of her colleague's womanizing past. Other examples that referenced karma being passed down through families referred to people that benefited from corruption, such as politicians, and those making money from the mining industry.

> In Mongolia there are a lot of—not just in Mongolia but everywhere, you know, there's corruption. You get rich with bad money, you know, dirty money and things like that. So for yourself, doing bad things, you could get rich and lead a good life. But still after that the consequences and the karma I think goes to your children, and if it doesn't go to your children then maybe it goes to your grandchildren, and then I heard once that if you do a bad thing it goes to seven generations. So, yeah, I kind of believe in that. And also there is a saying like in my age there are a lot of young guys who say that if you have a small child and then if you cheat on your wife then it will really influence your small child. So maybe it's kind of similar to karma. (Sükh)

Households both as a collective and as individuals can be seen to suffer from other family members' actions. As Sükh explains, small children are highly susceptible to the negative reactions created by bad actions, an idea that was also present among Empson's Buryat interlocutors (2011). She writes that a child's subjecthood is particularly unstable before their hair-cutting ceremony, occurring for girls at age two or four and for boys at age three or six (Empson 2011, 174–175). It is thought that a young child's soul has not yet become fully attached to their body. As such, people go to great efforts to make sure that spiritual pollution is not carried into the household from outside: "Seemingly ordinary actions outside the home, like that of a girl pulling off small shoots from a bush near to the stream, for example, can aggravate the land masters and spirits of surrounding rivers and landscapes . . . When she returns home, it is an infant, the most vulnerable person in the house, who would be affected by such an infraction" (Empson 2011, 157–158).

The difference between these two examples is that in Sükh's response the karmic effects are born from negative intentions and the selfishness of an individual. In Empson's example reactions are not caused by negative intentions but rather arise from ignorant actions that cause offence to local spirits (also see Højer 2009; Mills 2004). Both karma and unintentional contamination are reasons to seek ritual efficacy from a lama, and sometimes these causalities can be thought to be interlinked (see chapter 7).

Some people told me that karma could affect a collective, even an entire country (see chapter 1). A friend, Turuu, discussed this with me in an interview in 2015:

> When I watch a plane accident I think is it possible that all of these people had some bad karma all together at the same time? I don't know. But I know that most politicians or . . . bad people—some things happen to their family, bad things . . . One business guy who always bribed everyone to have a gas station everywhere, like near a school, his son was killed because his son was involved in some criminal activity . . . The general prosecutor, there was some case that a businessman paid two million US dollars just to be in charge . . . so his daughter drowned in Turkey . . . So like in her case, in the daughter's name there was like one million pounds in a Swiss account . . . There was a lot of sayings going around on social media—like that's the karma. You can do bad things but it's your kids maybe [that suffer].

Karma is morally framed, yet it is not always the individual in karmic schemas that bears the brunt of karmic retribution. In this case karmic causality passed onto the daughter from her father and spiritual contamination from the money in her Swiss bank account are both potential causes of her untimely death. Collectives in the form of families and entire nations can be thought to carry karmic debts and suffer from their repayment. In this way one is not necessarily responsible for one's circumstances; one may, for instance, have a relative whose greed has blocked an entire family's wealth from accruing.

Karmic Causality and Purification

Karmic causality ripples through space-time, body, and mind, influencing cause and effect. It can be multiplied and purified yet is morally contingent. A ripple can become a wave if not properly attended to. Karmic fluctuations extend from body, speech and mind invisibly altering possible futures both for oneself and (potentially) other human subjects. A person does not exist decoupled from their surroundings. If they cause environmental pollution, they may experience bad karmic ramifications. People are embedded in a world in which the flowing movements of karma run from and through them. As such, people are linked by subtle causalities to potential future events in this and coming lifetimes.

Karma is used to explain personal predicaments and a collective's circumstances. Karma influences the potential unfolding of one's future and present. Thoughts and feelings, like those of body and speech, create reactions. When tangible actions are connected to strong intentions, the results multiply. If negative actions or speech are connected to bad intentions, the negative results will become even more onerous. This works in the reverse, as good intentions can create powerful positive reverberations. One's (morally culpable) previous actions have effects in the present. They can cause you to be reborn as an animal or to be in a bad relationship. You may even have to endure the positive or negative effects of the actions of your kin.

Most of my interlocutors thought that it is possible to cleanse bad actions and purify bad karma. Alongside the desire to remove obstacles that may be inadvertently causing blockages or contamination (see chapter 7), people visit temples to purify problems that are caused by bad morality. A person's religious practice, morality, and interactions with sacred sites can all work to purify previous wrongdoings. One can come into contact with a sacred object or acknowledge their own wrongdoings to purify the latent results of previous actions. The fluidity between self and world allows possibilities to compensate for one's past and to create actions with compassionate intentions, shifting the pattern of one's own and perhaps others' future karma.

Ulaanbaatar's air pollution is broadly seen as a sign of moral degeneration, as the inability to combat the problem is linked to bad motivations and corruption (see chapter 8) and causes harm to human and nonhuman beings. Interestingly, while air pollution is associated with impurities and broader narratives of decline, fire and smoke are also thought to cleanse and purify. In the beginning vignette, black smoke imaginatively represents the moral impurities of body, speech, and mind, and the smoke is in need of purification through light. Yet fire and smoke, when used in specific ritual contexts, can also cleanse. Incense is frequently present in temples, Dharma Centers, and at sacred sites. People enthusiastically place objects that are broken, wallets, heads, and hats toward the purifying smoke of incense. The metaphor of burning can be used to understand suffering as the burning out of one's negative actions (see also chapter 9). Although black smoke can represent impurities, fire itself contains the possibility of purification.

There are categorical differences between small ritual fires and incense burning, and the chronic or acute generation of choking air pollution. When Ulaanbaatar's skies were clouded by smoke blowing in from the north in the summer of 2016, I asked friends and acquaintances about the smoke's origins. The smoke, though receiving very little media attention from the international press, was blowing in from a distressingly vast collection of wildfires that were burning across Russia. The fires were so extensive that the smoke from them spread the breadth of Russia from Moscow on into Mongolia, creating an immense cloud that was visible from space. When I asked people about what was causing the smoke, most told me that the fires that were burning in Russia were due to corruption. Burning forests was thought to have some fiscal benefits, either through procuring partially burned wood for sale or for the land that these trees were previously occupying. One acquaintance told me that because of this corruption the pristine waters of Lake Baikal (which was once part of Mongolia) were turning black. Likewise, corruption, in addition to collective negligence, is often blamed for the continuing environmental crisis that grips Ulaanbaatar's winter months.

Chapter 7

Removing Blockages, Increasing Energy

On a cold February day in 2009, along with thousands of other Mongols, I visit Gandan Khiid to have prayers read for my family for the coming year. It is the third day of Tsagaan Sar, and for most lay Buddhists visiting the temple after the Lunar New Year is a key part of their Buddhist identity. For some people I speak to, it is the only time of year that they will make the trip to the temple in their otherwise busy urban schedules. The main entrance to the Gandan temple complex is to the south. I walk into Gandan through the southern gateway and face the large white-walled, green-roofed northern temple that houses the giant statue of Avalokiteśvara. Many people are standing in front of this iconic temple to take photos, wearing their spectacular, richly colored silk *deel*s and warm winter hats. Many go inside to circumambulate (*toirokh*) the sacred statue, spinning the prayer wheels and stopping in front of the image of Avalokiteśvara for silent prayer.

Tsagaan Sar, along with the summer festival of Naadam, is the most important festival of the year. Held during February or March, the lunar, winter festival is when one demonstrates respect for their elderly relatives, while Naadam is a festival of masculinity, strength, and youth. At Tsagaan Sar people visit the homes of their elderly relatives to eat and drink as much as possible at each household. Guests bring a small gift to the elderly relatives, who in return host the young people (*zaluuchuud*), encouraging them to eat as many *buuz* (steamed mutton dumplings) as they can. In the hosts' house the central table supports a large stack of flat fried bread biscuits (*kheviin boov*) arranged in a circle. Each odd layer represents happiness and each even layer burden, so the arrangement must always be odd (generally five, seven, or nine stacks high). Sweets and white foods (*tsagaan idee*) are placed between, on, and around the stack, which, like everything else at Tsagaan Sar, is supposed to be overflowing with abundance, in the hope that this will presage the family's fortune for the coming year. As with other celebrations, such as weddings, families with enough money will place the most expensive cut of sheep, the fatty tail (*uuts*), on the table. Young family members leave the houses of older relatives with their bellies full of food and carrying gifts.

Like Christmas in Christian countries, Tsagaan Sar, while being a joyful occasion, is associated with overspending and family pressure. Many young people complain to me about the amount of steamed dumplings (*buuz*) they are expected to eat at each relative's house. Some tell me that if they don't eat enough, even though they have visited many relative's houses, that it will be taken as an insult by the hosts. A couple of unmarried ladies explain that Tsagaan Sar is one of the times that they receive pressure from their extended family regarding their marital status. This causes them to dread the coming festival, with one even planning to be away at this time of year. Elderly relatives, often living off savings or their pensions, will go into debt to be able to host their younger relatives. In 2016, as the economic crisis is worsening, the financial burden is increasingly felt by elder people. As Empson writes: "The older you get the more people you receive to your home. The more prestige you are granted, the more of a financial burden you have to shoulder" (2016b). Aware of the pressure placed on families during this period, the Buddhist NGOs that I did fieldwork with give low-income families extra support during Tsagaan Sar.

During the festival, on what will be for many lay Buddhists their only visit to the temple for the year, most people frequent the southeastern temple complex at Gandan. This temple complex, surrounded by a wall, contains within it a number of smaller temples, some connected and some freestanding.

In 2010 this was one of the main locations in which people would feed pigeons, a demonstration of generosity and one of the most accessible practices at the complex. However, due to health concerns and difficulties maintaining the buildings, this practice had been moved by 2013 to the area immediately outside of the southern temple gates. Within the complex there is a large incense burner, the likes of which is typically placed to the southern side of Mongolian temple entrances. When passing this cauldron of incense, people bow their heads to the incense burner so that they can circle the smoke toward this respected part of the body. Some wave their hats and sometimes their wallets over the smoke, as smoke is associated with purification and blessings. Some then circumambulate the temples, spinning the gold-colored prayer wheels and praying to religious statues, and most enter the prayer shop to the southeast of the complex to pay for particular prayers to be read for the coming year.

This prayer shop is the busiest in Ulaanbaatar, and throughout the year anyone can pay for prayers to be read for themselves, their friends, and their family members. At Tsagaan Sar this prayer shop is full of people jostling for attention from the lamas who sit behind the desks collecting money and printing off receipts. While at other temples lay Buddhists collect donations, at Gandan it is lamas who collect the set price for the prayers. Each person is given an itemized receipt after they pay for their prayers. A wash of voices and the punctuated chattering of cash registers characterize the soundscape of the shop. During the winter festival many people tell me that they seek out divinations and astrological advice from religious specialists to prescribe for them the appropriate prayers that they should have read for the coming year. The religious specialists that laypeople consult are often lamas but can also be diviners, such as housewives reading tarot cards or aura readers—a practice that is becoming more popular in 2015 and 2016.

On the third day of Tsagaan Sar I meet with my friend Baaska who has a list of prayers for my family and for herself to purchase that her mother has procured from a lama. Following her advice I choose three prayers from the prayer list and, like everyone else, jostle my way to the front of the queue to pay for them. Altogether the prayers cost 1,600 tögrögs (around 80 cents). After paying for my prayers and explaining how to spell my husband's name and mine, we are given a receipt with our names and the prayers printed on it. We are told that the prayers will be read for us in a service (*khural*) the following morning. Afterward we go to the Avalokiteśvara temple to spin

Figure 10. Laypeople touch the Güngachoiliin pole at Gandan Khiid during Tsagaan Sar.

the prayer wheels. Like the prayer shop, this activity involves some elbowing, and a number of impatient teenagers push into my back to try to get in front of me in the freezing temple. At one point a fight breaks out between two drunken men. Undeterred, everyone continues to circumambulate, saying their prayers and lighting candles in front of the overawing representation of compassion. As we leave the temple we feed the birds, take some photos, and ponder the year to come.

This experience is representative of the activities of many lay Buddhists at local temples during Tsagaan Sar and at other times during the year. Most, when they attend temples, do some number from a prescribed set of activities: lighting candles, feeding the birds, circumambulating sacred objects and temples, praying at sacred objects, paying for prayers, praying to the wishing tree (Güngachoiliin pole) at Gandan, donating to individual lamas, receiving blessings, receiving advice, and carrying out prosperity ceremonies (*dallaga avakh*).

Following on from the "domestication" of religion during the socialist period (see chapter 4), most people still heed the advice of a trusted family member or friend about when, where, and how to carry out public and private religious activities. The light of Buddhism that was kept alive during socialism within people's homes and memories is still largely maintained in the domestic sphere. As Buddhist institutions are now free to operate publicly, many seek out religious specialists for public rituals and advice. Due to the limited amount of time that most Buddhists spend engaging with temples, sometimes as little as once a year, ritual exegeses tend to vary greatly. Yet most lay Buddhists I speak to report that after visiting temples and carrying out rituals they feel lighter, that their energy has increased, and that some kind of obstacle has been removed. Ritual activities, carried out by lay Buddhists, frequently incorporate Mongolian ideas about light, energy, and obstacles.

Following Others

Most lay Buddhists go to temples at important times during the year and make additional visits if they have problems of their own or in their family's lives. Some tell me that they go to temples if they have an illness in the family, supplementing their visits to allopathic medical centers. Some also meet with other public religious specialists for rituals or advice regarding health and healing. Many ask advice from a lama when they or someone in their family is about to make an important journey for work or on a holiday. It is common for students to study in temple grounds or travel to pilgrimage sites immediately before exams, as these activities are believed to improve their results. Most Buddhists and non-Buddhists seek out a lama's advice before a coming wedding, to get dates for a child's first hair-cutting ceremony, and when they have problems with relationships. After a death in the family, it is common for a family member to meet with a lama to have their "golden box" (*altan khairtsag*) opened to see how the person's body should be treated and to make sure that they died at the astrologically predicted time.

Those that I speak to who are under forty, even when they have their own young children, tend to follow the advice of their parents or grandparents, rather than initiating rituals themselves on behalf of their family. At sacred sites and temples it is common to see Mongols improvising ritual activities by following the advice of a confident layperson. While Buddhist religious specialists tend to be men, it is often middle-aged (or older) ladies that instruct other laypeople on proper conduct at pilgrimage sites and temples. Family members instruct one another about which days to light a candle and on which days that they should eat vegetarian food. A number of my interlocutors told me that their mothers would call them when it was the Buddha's birthday (*Burkhan Bagshiin lagshin mendelcen*) to tell them to eat vegetarian food. This day, widely celebrated in Buddhist communities around the world, marks the celebration of when the Buddha is believed to have been born, to have reached enlightenment, and to have attained *parinirvāna*.

In many ways, this practice of listening to others is a continuity of the type of religious practices that were carried out during the socialist period. Just as my friend and I listened to her mother's advice about which prayers to have read at Tsagaan Sar, most of my interlocutors said they had learned which rituals to carry out from knowledgeable friends or family members. This could be from a family friend or from their mother, grandparent, uncle, aunt, or father. The advice might be given by a person who was newly enthusiastic about religion, an older relation, or relatives that are currently public religious specialists or were lamas before the purges of the 1930s. In 2015 Dawaatsuren, a thirty-eight-year-old IT consultant originally from Khovd, explained how his grandfather, who had been a lama before the socialist purges, had kept Buddhist practices alive during socialism:

My grandpa was secretly reading spiritual books and doing secret spiritual practices. They just closed the top of the tent and lit the candle and then read the book in the light of the candle. They read Buddhist *sūtra*s in the ger and if they heard something unusual they put everything in a hiding place. No one could see the light from outside . . . If there was a light [visible] from outside someone could come and see what they were doing. Maybe they would bring them to jail. They destroyed the temple. There was a big temple in our village. They destroyed the *sūtra*s and the books . . . But during the nighttime my grandfather brought a camel and loaded as much as he could on the camel and then hid them in the cave. And then during the daytime he herded sheep around that place. And without anyone knowing what he was doing he took the *sūtra*s and practiced . . .

My grandma said a lot of unbelievable stories about my grandpa . . . Before his passing, he told my grandma what to do and what was going to happen . . . He foretold his own death, when he was going to die—the exact date . . . He was taking some food with his children and it was around 4:00 PM. Then he asked his oldest daughter, "What day is it?" She checked the calendar . . . and said it was a full moon . . . And then Grandpa said, "It's the day, it's the day." Then he asked his daughter to bring some water and to clean his hands and face. Then he told her to bring some *sūtra*s from the hidden boxes. And he told them to put them on the top of his head, on the roof of the ger. And then he just sat there. He closed his eyes. If somebody saw him, it was like he was sleeping. But he passed away right there.

For Dawaatsuren, as he grew older, the stories that he had heard from his grandmother about his grandfather, who had died before the end of the socialist period, had a big impact on his now active interest in Buddhism. He lamented that as his grandfather had died before he was an adult and was not able to directly advise him about religious activities. For many other lay Buddhists that I spoke to, their grandparents or other family members considered to be knowledgeable about religion were able to give advice about the religious practices that they should carry out.

As Humphrey has argued, many Mongols refer to exemplarily moral figures when discussing morality (1997). These exemplars may be family members or teachers or historical figures, such as Chinggis Khan. Sitting in a classroom at one of the main universities I interview Chuluun, a short and slender government worker in his forties. When I ask him if he is a Buddhist he enthusiastically replies:

Chuluun: I think I am a Buddhist because my grandfather was
            Buddhist. He was a good Buddhist. Even though he
            participated in the Second World War before 1946
            against Japan, when Japan came to Mongolia . . . When
            he retired . . . he told me that when he was a child he was
            a teacher [a lama] . . . When he retired he . . . believed in
            Buddha.

Saskia: Did your grandfather practice Buddhism before 1990?

Chuluun: A little bit. During this time it was prohibited by the
            government, but he made some Mongolian traditions at
            home . . . For example, during Tsagaan Sar, we should
            make something. We lived in the city and this festival
            was prohibited. But we had this festival every year.
            We woke up very early and offered some things to God
            and made a candle and burned incense and read the
            books. When he died I got one type of sūtra. It is in
            Tibetan. He wrote it down in old Mongolian [Mongol
            bichig]. But I don't know old Mongolian . . . Most things
            came to me when my mother died . . . I have a bell from
            my grandfather and an *ochir*[1] . . . Before Tsagaan Sar or
            before Naadam . . . I try to read the sūtra from my
            grandfather . . . I can't read it but my grandfather
            recommended that I should make this [gestures as if
            turning the pages of the sūtra]. The wind will go
            through it and it is the same as if you read it.
            Even though you can't read it, please do this.

Another middle-aged man that I interview tells me that he practices the
same ritual at home. They both received sūtras from their grandfathers, and
both believe that even though they cannot read the texts the wind blowing
through the turning pages of the sūtras, just like the wind blowing the flags
dotted around the country, will spread the benefits contained within.

One does not need to understand the meaning of the prayers for them to
have efficacy. The prayers that lamas read in *khurals* are believed by most of
my interlocutors to have effect. On mountain passes prayer flags attached to
ovoos are blown by the wind and carry prayers to the surrounding areas.
As an Australian monk visiting Shredrup Ling told a full room of around

120 lay Buddhists, the sound of a mantra or prayer uttered by a human may be enough to secure a better future rebirth for a nonhuman being. He explained that during his three year, three month, and three day long retreat on Kangaroo Island, south of Adelaide, he hoped that upon hearing him read the mantra of Avalokiteśvara that the kangaroos would be reborn as humans. Such, he said, is the power of prayer.

When Oyunbileg, a thirty-one-year-old urbanite with long black hair, describes her religious practice, she discusses a religious recording made by one of her family members. While none of the family members understand its contents, as it was made by a (now deceased) relative thought to be knowledgeable about religion, they play the recording for its believed benefits.

> I don't read [mantras]. I don't know very much about it even. But my grandfather . . . We have our grandfather's notebook. He's passed away, but he had written a lot of mantras . . . There was someone in my extended family, and he was a Buddhist, and he would do a lot of readings and actually we recorded his readings and some of our family members have it. So they just have the recording and they play it.

Although the meaning of these prayers is not known, they are still believed to have efficacy. In addition to a continuity of practices during the socialist period, placing one's trust in relatives may well relate to other burgeoning religiosities in the capital, and specifically to shamanism. Shamanic practices in Mongolia connect a person to their ancestors, linking them to deceased family members. As Pedersen writes, shamans in Southern Northern Asia "vertically" channel the spirits of dead ancestors, rather than focusing on "horizontal" communication with spirits embedded in the landscape as they do in Northern Northern Asia (Pedersen 2001). In Pedersen's view (2001) these differences in shamanic practice reflect dissimilarities in social organization among those living in the Mongolian cultural region and in northern Siberia. Those living in Northern Northern Asia tend to have more egalitarian social structures, while Southern Northern Asian societies are characterized by patrilineal descent and social hierarchies (Pedersen 2001). The spirits (*ongon*) with whom shamans communicate are bounded and narrativized in discrete historical periods, referencing the shaman's own ancestral genealogies (Abrahms-Kavunenko 2016; Humphrey 2007). For increasing numbers of urban Mongols that engage shamanism, kinship connections relate both to living and deceased ancestors. The family shaman channels a specifically located ancestor from several generations ago, and this deceased kin now plays a living role in the shaman's and their family's lives (Abrahms-Kavunenko 2016).

Along with her deceased relatives, Oyunbileg referred to a family friend whom she considered to be knowledgeable about Buddhism. While he is not a lama, he is a committed Buddhist, demonstrated by his and his family's devotion to Buddhist temples, his autodidactic knowledge about Buddhism, and his interest in meditation. Oyunbileg, like many other lay Buddhists, explained that her religious practice involves "just following" others. She does not consider herself to be independently knowledgeable about religious practice.

Along with this advice from family members or friends, lamas are consulted concerning important dates, and this is a key part of many lay Buddhists' religiosity. A friend who is a wedding planner told me this causes Ulaanbaatar's Wedding Palace to be very busy on auspicious days. At one of the weddings I attended, the main stairway of the Wedding Palace was consistently packed with wedding parties moving in hurried synchronization between the prescribed photo opportunities. Along with weddings, families ask lamas to tell them when they should first cut their child's hair (Empson 2011, 174–175).

In addition to receiving advice from lamas, family members, and friends, astrological dates are published in detailed Buddhist calendars that are widely available for purchase in local bookshops. These Buddhist calendars give advice about when, for example, an adult person should or should not cut their hair. As a friend, Oyuka, describes the calendar to me in 2015:

> For example today is Wednesday, sun will rise at that time and set at that time. Bad hours will be this and that. Good hours will be this and that. If you get a haircut then you will have long-lasting happiness . . . If I want to go to the hairdresser I always check that calendar. Because, when I was growing up, my parents were always doing that. It's like a superstitious thing. So we believe it and if I don't do it I feel bad. So that's why I think if something bad happens, I might think, "Oh, it is because I didn't do it that way; that's why I have this problem." It's all a mind thing.

While Oyuka believes that consulting the calendar is "superstitious," as her family members have always consulted it before carrying out certain activities, she feels that it has psychological efficacy, even if (as someone who identified as a Christian) she is ambivalent about the astrological influence of the days when one cuts one's hair.

Most lay Buddhists that I spoke to believe in the influence of astrology on auspicious days, seasons, and years. During my fieldwork it was common for people to believe that Tuesday was an inauspicious day, so people at the Buddhist center that I volunteered at would try to avoid doing too much on a Tuesday. Every year around Tsagaan Sar astrologers from various monasteries make predictions for the coming year. A number of people told me that 2016, as it was the Year of the Fire Monkey, would be a hot year. For other urbanites, like Oyuka, consulting lamas or astrological calendars for auspicious days works as a kind of insurance policy to mitigate potential untested ill effects, be they astrologically or psychologically generated.

Removing Obstacles, Gaining Energy

When asked how they feel after visiting temples or carrying out religious rituals, most replied that they feel "lighter" or "happier," that some kind of obstacle has been removed, and/or that their energy has improved. A number of people specifically referred to a light (*khöngön*) feeling or improved energy after visits to temples. When I interviewed Jargal, a forty-year-old man working in a government-run engineering firm, he responded:

> *Saskia:*   How do you feel after going to temples?
> *Jargal:*   A little bit of freedom I can say. My stress a little bit goes
>   down. Any bad things fly out of me . . . It is a little bit
>   lighter than before. Because I don't think about anything
>   else during this time. During my work, maybe, I think
>   about a lot of things which have happened or not happened,
>   and this makes me stressed.

Others said that after having prayers read for them they felt as if some kind of obstacle or blockage had been removed. Many indicated that they felt as if a kind of duty had been fulfilled and that afterward they were relieved to have carried out something that was important, though for unknown reasons.

Getting prayers read by lamas or visiting sacred sites, such as the Energy Centre (*Energiin Töv*) in the Gobi, or visiting one's own birthplace (*nutagt*) are thought to refresh (*sergeekh*) a person's *khiimori* (wind horse). The *khiimori san* is a popular prayer to have read at temples as it is meant to remove any contamination that may affect the natural movements and strength of a person's khiimori, which, as I described in the introduction, is a type of personal energy thought to circle inwardly. Some lamas explained to me that khiimori is similar to the Tibetan concept of *rlung* (see also Humphrey and Ujeed 2012, 154). Metaphorically, the concept is connected to the movement of horse riding and nomadic seasonal changes on the steppe. In urban life there are many ways in which one's khiimori can be obstructed. The city's location between mountains causes the air to stagnate in the winter months, worsening the air pollution. At the same time urban life is dominated by a lack of physical movement as many Mongols drive or catch public transport to work. If a person has become ill or is experiencing a period of bad fortune it can be attributed to a weakness of khiimori. A few people said that they regularly had the *khiimori san* read to increase their energy. This is a popular prayer to have read even if one is not experiencing difficulties. At Tsagaan Sar it is common for people to buy a prayer flag with the wind horse symbol on it in a color appropriate to their birth year. One takes this colored flag and ties it to a high pass in a particular (astrologically determined) direction to strengthen their vitality and to enable prayers and blessings for the coming year.

A few of my interlocutors joked with me about how they were too lazy to visit temples unless they had a problem. Illness is often cited as a reason that people would go to temples. One of my friends, a woman in her mid-twenties who worked as an administrator for Jampa Ling, told me that when she was younger her little sister had suffered from serious burns. The day after her mother and her had ordered prayers to be read at Gandan Khiid she went to visit her sister in the hospital. As she said:

> She was in hospital, and then that lama read some prayers for my sister and then my mum and myself came into the hospital, and I saw one girl, and then she was walking with new boots. And those shoes—actually my mum bought for my sister . . . And then I told my mother, "Oh, these shoes are the same like my sister's." And then she said, "Yes, it's the same for my . . . younger daughter." And then we looked up and it was my sister. She was running and

then the mother of her roommate was saying, "Your sister was running all day almost." Oh my gosh! That lama read very good prayers for my sister; some of them helped her. (Baaska)

Some were a little more skeptical about the efficacy of prayers. Some said that it would only help psychologically as a placebo, while others thought that it would only help if a prayer was read by a good lama (see chapter 8). Some said they liked to casually visit temples and sit during the daily sūtra readings to absorb the positive energy of the prayers. Others told me that just by visiting a temple or by carrying out activities in a certain sacred place one can purify one's karma and therefore not receive the negative reactions of the bad deeds that one may have committed.

Some of my interlocutors told me that a lama had attributed a person's illness to external contamination, either linked to interference with natural sites or the improper treatment of a religious object. Ankha, a talented young public servant in her early thirties, explained to me that a series of negative events befell a group of her classmates just after graduating from high school. Only one of the group did not have problems after interfering with a natural place that Ankha believed had caused them to become contaminated (see also Empson 2011, 157–158).

In Mongolia we have some places that are aggressive for human activity. At our graduation ceremony we went to a really beautiful place in the country-side . . . We were camping and the boys from our class collected some sediment from the bed of the river and they put it on their skin. They just wanted to show off to the girls like an Indian [Native American]. But after that one of my classmates committed suicide. And two of them became very sick. One of my friends had a red rash on his skin. Those things happened only to the people who got some clay from the river. And after this happened, one of my friends who had a big itchy patch on his skin went to the monk with his parents and the monk said, "This place is really aggressive for human activity. If you go to this kind of place, you can't touch anything . . . You can't break the trees, you can't take rocks, you can't touch the bed of the river, you can't break the grass . . . If you do something then this place will give you bad things." And the monks prayed . . . After that my friend's itchy skin went away.

In this case external contamination was believed to be responsible for a series of bad events that drastically altered the lives of those who did not receive some form of ritual help. When discussing Buddhism with Ankha I realized that her idea of contamination coexisted with the concept of karma (*üiliin ur,* literally "action-result"), which she explained in the same discussion in a slightly different way. While spiritual contamination (*buzar*) occurred after an ignorant action (in this case tampering with a powerful site and offending the local spirits), bad results in karmic narratives were the result of intentional wrongdoings. At another point in the interview she related the story above with a karmic narrative, separate from the idea of external contamination:

> The big example is the *Titanic.* They—it's really interesting that a lot of people died together. I think it's their karma coming or something like that. For example, one of my classmates, he committed suicide after our graduation ceremony in high school. But the police and his friends couldn't find out why he did this. He did this after he had a small party with his best friends. After his suicide the people that participated in this party suffered one by one. I mean, one of them became an alcoholic, one of them became a prostitute, some of them had a car accident. Maybe . . . they did something wrong to my classmate. So that . . . the karma came to them.

Ankha attributes two different causal dynamics to her classmate's suicide. Both explain the classmate's death, either due to spiritual interference or because of something his friends did. In the karmic narrative, ill intent creates bad results, whereas in the contamination narrative, all but one of the classmates, though ignorant, suffer from their unintentional contamination.

Wealth, Objects, and the Home

To navigate broader financial uncertainties, many urbanites go to Buddhist temples to ask for help with financial problems. In response lamas give advice to purchase specific prayers and objects and to carry out and attend certain rituals. The ceremonies I participated in concerning the health and wealth of the family involve both public rituals and keeping objects in the home. A popular ritual at Gandan is the prosperity (*dallaga avakh*) ceremony. This is believed to clear blockages to wealth generation and is thought to call (*duudakh*) prosperity to the home.

One sunny afternoon during a visit to Gandan I inquire from a friend Zaya about the signs advertising an upcoming prosperity ceremony. She tells me that these are "powerful rituals" that are held daily, and there will be one occurring on the following day. I express my interest in attending and order the *Altan Gerel Sūtra* for the set price of 1,000 tögrögs (about 50 cents) at the prayer shop in the southeastern temple of Gandan. The shaved-headed lama dressed in a bright yellow *deel* with blue cuffs behind the counter gives me a receipt and tells me that I need to bring this to one of the temples in the complex the following morning at 9:00 AM. Zaya tells me that I will need specific objects for the ceremony to be effective. I go with her to a local shop outside the temple complex owned by a friend, Gerelmaa. Pausing from her instructions to other laypeople carrying lists of ritual objects to acquire, she tells me about the specific objects that I need to present the following morning. First, I buy a brightly colored ritual bag with the eight auspicious symbols printed on it. This bag, she says, should be left in the home partially opened after the ceremony to call wealth and prosperity into the home. In the bag I deposit some dark grain, which she tells me enables purification, due to its dark color. As seeds grow, she explains, they will support the generation and multiplication of the other objects in the bag. She then instructs me to add a bag of colored rice (representing food), medicinal seeds (representing health), and nine precious jewels (to represent wealth). As she describes, like attracts (*tatakh*, literally "to pull") like.

The next morning I arrive with around thirty other lay Buddhists, hand my receipt to the four lamas sitting in the northwestern corner of the temple, offer sweets to the northern shrine, and patiently sit on hard wooden benches for two hours of Tibetan prayers in the cold temple. Perhaps as a reflection of the abstracted and seemingly arbitrary nature of economic fluctuations and the feelings of uneasiness around how capital unequally circulates in the city, this ritual requires a greater commitment of time and money than other ritual activities I have seen at temples. Toward the end of the long ceremony we circle incense clockwise around our bodies to enable purification and are given more dark grain. This we circle in a clockwise direction, saying, "*Khurai, khurai, khurai,*" meaning "let us gather," a common declaration at Buddhist, and other, ceremonies. We are instructed to add this ritually charged grain to our bags to purify obstacles and generate wealth. Feeling relieved that the long service is over, we each take our bags, eat a piece of food from the shrine, and leave.

Like the *bumba* ceremony carried out yearly at Amarbayasgalant Khiid (see chapter 8), an important aspect of the *dallaga avakh* ritual is to keep ritual objects in the home. The home is seen as a central place where one can generate fortune, and it is also a place where fortunes can be blocked. Some of my wealthier interlocutors tell me they regularly invite lamas to carry out ceremonies at their home. Odgerel, who is a successful businesswoman, invites lamas to her homes at auspicious times during the year. Her son, Enee, explained to me:

Enee: We called a really famous monk to our house . . . Usually
          he reads the sūtras, the readings from the gods, and he
          makes these shapes [*tormas*] and different types of food
          materials, like rice, flour, and alcoholic beverages . . . And
          this preparation lasts for about two hours. And once he is
          done he sets up everything for the Buddha, and once
          everything is ready he starts reading the script [sūtra], and
          the script I think lasts for three or four hours, and I think
          there were two or three, maybe more . . . I'm not that well
          educated in Buddhism; my mum knows much better about
          it. For me I'm just a good follower. We watch him and
          listen. As far as I know the scripts are mostly . . . The
          meaning is wishing happiness, prosperity, and health.
          So it's not really complicated, something that asks from god
          or something; it's just a wish to have health, prosperity,
          happiness, and things like that.
Saskia: And how do you feel afterward?
Enee: I don't think there is any physical difference afterward but
          you kind of feel like kind of safe. You had a responsibility
          and you already did it so you kind of feel good.

Another friend, Tuya, whose family had financial problems when she was a child, recollects her mother inviting a lama to their home to, as she put it, remove "bad things." When he arrived she remembers the lama closing the curtains to make the house dark inside before he began to read prayers. When I asked what kind of bad things he had removed, she replied: "In the corners [of the house] sometimes there are bad spirits. It's not evil or the devil, but just a bad spirit that needs to go out of your home." After the ritual her mother told her that the blockages that were causing problems for the family had been removed. This was believed to enable, like the prosperity ceremony, the free flow of wealth to once again enter their home.

Some businesses will ask a group of lamas to come to their building to read prayers thought to clear obstacles and invite success. In 2015 a realtor told me that it is common practice to have lamas read prayers to subdue any bad energy or offended spirits before laying the foundation for a new building. I also heard that some mining companies now employ salaried lamas to assist with prayer readings at exploratory mining sites and before beginning large mining projects to ensure that the employees of mining companies do not feel the ill effects of mining activities brought on by the disturbance of local spirits.

Almost all of my lay Buddhist interlocutors feel positive about their visits to temples and their interactions with lamas. The majority of them tell me that after visiting temples or carrying out religious rituals they have in some way removed blockages, improved their energy, and/or carried out an activity associated with purification. For some, visiting the temple at Tsagaan Sar creates a vague feeling that they had done something important for the coming year. For others, power is attributed to sacred texts, the meanings of which are obscured by a lack of literacy in Tibetan or Mongol *bichig*. Prayers read by lamas for individuals and families are generally thought to have positive effects. They can remove obstacles, purify one's bad karma, enliven one's vital energies, and attract wealth into the home.

Sacred objects passed down from family members or recently acquired have power even if their meanings are not well understood. For many of my interlocutors the home is still an important place central to ritual activities, whether public or private. Many homes contain the artifacts of a ritual on their northern shrine or hidden away (as is required of the *bumba* ritual). Most lay Buddhists tell me that they follow the advice of trusted friends and living or deceased family members, deferring expertise to exemplary people. In this way the domestication of religion that occurred during the socialist period continues to have an influence on contemporary Buddhist practice. The light of Buddhism is still, for many, carried within the home.

Chapter 8

TEMPLE CRITIQUES

Now everything is commercially driven. And you can't do anything about it.
In socialist times the Russians wanted to build a phosphorous plant on the
banks of Khövsgöl lake. There was one journalist who stood strongly [against
it], and he was able to reverse it. It was a very big decision because in socialist
times it was a planned economy and we were dictated to by the Russians.
They wanted phosphorous from Mongolia, and it is near this lake. And this
lake is connected to Russia, to Baikal lake. So it could harm nature. They
stopped it. That was a brave act. But today I don't think that politicians are
driven by the national interest. It is more commercial.

—OYUNA, 2015

Some lamas are not good . . . In their mind they are not a lama. In
1992 . . . I was with my child, and I stood in [the ration] line, and he came in
front of me. I told him, "You shouldn't do these things; you should stay in the
back." He told me, "I am a lama; I can do anything" . . . Many people are
afraid of them . . . In 1992 there were good lamas because in this time there
were very few lamas in Mongolia. I thought that at this time most of them
were good . . . But now there are a lot of temples, a lot of lamas who just
want money . . . Most of them I think can't read the sūtras, or they can read
but they can't understand what the words mean.

—OCHIR, 2009

I wonder sometimes, who is the real monk? You know, I think that
that is important, to be a real monk. I don't know if the number will
increase because there are not very good conditions in the monasteries . . . to
really practice and to live in your ordination and in your vows and to stay
in the monastery. I think financially all the conditions are just not there.
And that is why I don't think that the number will increase much. I really
hope that the quality of the monks will increase.

—OYUNBILEG, 2010

As the above quotations illustrate, there is a link between narratives of
moral decline, an increase in monetary interests, and the ways that religious
specialists are viewed in Ulaanbaatar. My interlocutors, though critical of

religious repressions, frequently discussed the socialist past as one that was collectively motivated and free from the fiscal imperatives that are thought to characterize the present. As a reflection of these broader anxieties, most lay Buddhists, while they report benefits after visiting temples, are critical of Mongolian Buddhist institutions. These critiques are closely connected to concerns about the interlinking issues of money, education, and morality. When I first started to do fieldwork in 2009, I was surprised to find that although Buddhist institutions were undergoing a relatively recent process of revitalization, they were, like the capitalist economy, imbued with narratives of degeneration. As this chapter will explore, these narratives are intimately connected to broader discourses and uncertainties surrounding the new market economy, moral degeneration, and the obscuration of light. When laypeople and monastics critique local trends within Mongolian Buddhism, they tend to link an aspect of the saṅgha or lay practice with dirt, corruption, and misunderstanding.

Negative opinions about the Mongolian saṅgha's education, morality, and motivations are connected to fiscal limitations and imperatives that are exacerbated by broader economic instabilities. Unlike other Buddhist, Jain, and Hindu societies, the practice of giving donations (Sans., *dāna*) in Mongolia is not believed to create merit or to act as purification for the donor. Most Mongols give money to temples as remuneration for ritual services, and it is the rituals themselves that provide purification—if purification is part of the intended result of the ritual. Like Laidlaw's (2000) discussion of *dan* in Jainism and Parry's (1986) analysis of Hindu gifts, my interview revealed how ill effects *can* be generated through gift giving. In Mongolia bad results are generated and experienced not by the donor but by the recipient. If a religious specialist's motivations are dubious, they lack education, or their moral conduct is poor, the activity of accepting money for ritual services may be thought to create bad karma, energy, and/or pollution for the specialist. This, along with a lack of visible charitable activities undertaken by temples, when compared with the conspicuous charity of Christian missionaries, leads to widespread criticisms about temples' relationships with money.

Pollution can be generated through poor motivations, as making money through other people's suffering is often thought to bring harm to religious specialists. The improper use of money is linked to dirt literally through lamas' clothing and temple facilities and metaphorically through concerns about corruption. Anti-syncretic tendencies within global Buddhist organizations and among Christian missionaries influence how Mongolian lay Buddhists and lamas perceive religious financial imperatives, monastic discipline, and education. For those affected by international understandings of monastic rectitude and religious education, discussions concerning the degeneration of Buddhism in Mongolia and the need for the "purification" of the saṅgha are common.

Donations and Mongolian Buddhism

In many Buddhist societies donation in the form of *dāna* is one of the key ways that laypeople and monastics interact. It is widely believed that if one donates freely with positive intentions to someone who devotes themselves to Buddhist practice the donor will make merit from this activity (Heim 2004). Making merit in Buddhist societies is seen as a central part of religious activities as it enables laypeople to obtain good karma, which in turn will facilitate a better rebirth. As Spiro (1982) describes the practice in Theravāda Burma, supported by the laity, monastics are able to "renounce" material concerns and devote their lives to pursuing Buddhist soteriological goals. Ideally, having accrued good merit from donations, lay Buddhists will eventually be reborn as monastics that, in turn, will be able to devote themselves to pursuing enlightenment. In his ethnographic study of Burma, Spiro noted that many laypeople are more concerned with obtaining better and wealthier rebirths, rather than aspiring to be reborn as monks. This relationship of donor and donee is reciprocal in the sense that laypeople support the soteriological pursuit for monastics and in return the monastics, by accepting the laity's offerings, enable them to make merit for better rebirths in their coming lifetimes (Spiro 1982).

As anthropologists have explored, the conditions, content, and ideas surrounding donations are highly variable throughout Buddhist and South Asian societies. In some places it is believed that in order to make merit from a donation, no reciprocity or thanks can be given from the monastic community to the laity (Cook 2010; Laidlaw 2000). Himalayan regions, such as Ladakh, that have been unaffected by socialism have temples that are funded by extensive landholdings and titles associated with reincarnation lineages (Mills 2003). In Asian Buddhist countries where the monastic community is thought to possess moral failings (Samuels 2007) or has low status due to their gender (Gutschow 2004), laypeople may give very little to the monastic community or withdraw their support altogether. *Dāna* is so highly valued in some Buddhist societies that it has been mobilized as a site of protest. During the 2007 "Saffron Revolution" in Myanmar monastics refused to accept donations from the political classes, upturning their bowls as a powerful form of protest (Gravers 2012). When gender inequalities restrict women's capacities to be able to engage in merit-making activities, this is seen by laypeople to have spiritual ramifications for future rebirths and can therefore further replicate worldly gender inequalities (Makley 2003).

In Tibetan regions and in Mongolia, where the landholdings of reincarnation lineages have been disrupted by radical changes to social organization, monasteries no longer acquire wealth from their lands and the laypeople that worked on them. As Caple writes (2010) of the Amdo region of Tibet, decades of socialist education mean that relying on financial support from the laity is seen as a "burden" on them, rather than as an opportunity for the laity to make merit. Instead of relying on donations from the laity for support, some temples make investments that provide financial returns and give out loans with interest to support their activities (Caple 2010). As Han Chinese donors have become increasingly influential in global Tibetan Buddhist economies, the nature of donations has become increasingly characterized by economies of charisma (Smyer Yü 2012), delocalized donations (Fisher 2008), and anxieties around outcome-dependent remunerative relationships (Caple 2015).

In Mongolia, during the pre-socialist period, donations were one of many ways that the laity interacted with temples and lamas. As Kaplonski writes, "most families that were able to would send a son to a monastery, and donations and offerings to monasteries and to individual monks were expected at various times of the year such as the Lunar New Year, as well as for individual services" (2014, 17).

Temples reciprocated as key places of medical assistance and through housing lamas' pursuits of education, fine arts, and religious rituals. These interactions were steeped in asymmetrical hierarchies, and the relationship between the laity and the monastic population, along with containing reciprocity, donation, and devotion, was characterized by domination (Abrahms-Kavunenko 2015; see also Sihlé 2015).

Mongolian lay Buddhists are no longer required, nor do most choose, to consistently financially support Buddhist temples. Laypeople who pay for private rituals, fortune-telling, or public prayer readings support temples or individual lamas predominantly in recognition of the ritual services that they offer. Some make larger donations for building works or other projects, such as building statues or *stūpa*s. Most Mongolian temples fund themselves from a combination of small local donations and donations from global Buddhist networks, wealthy individuals, or NGOs from overseas. While some lamas, especially those connected to wealthy businesspeople or politicians, earn a comfortable or more-than-comfortable wage, many struggle to support family members in, as one lama told me, "a globalized world where material needs are greater than they were before socialism."

As Munkhbaatar, a lama from Gandan Khiid, believed the situation to be in 2016:

> In Europe, Christian churches receive support from the government. When you receive a salary, 1 percent goes to the church[1] . . . Consciously and unconsciously they are supporting Christian churches . . . But in Mongolia it is totally different—the opposite. In Europe churches have memberships. Every month you give your support to the church. But in Mongolia we don't have any membership. So Buddhism in Mongolia gives you total freedom. If you want to come to the temple and make a donation once a year or not at all, if it is OK with you, then it is OK with us . . . At the same time we don't receive any funds from the government but we pay various kinds of taxes to the government, to the state.

Munkhbaatar said that until 2007 Gandan Khiid had to pay a tax on every donation the temple received. If someone paid for a prayer to be read at the temple, 10 percent of that donation would go to the government. In 2007 this tax on donations was scrapped, but, as Munkhbaatar told me, the temple still has to pay six kinds of taxes to the government, including a land tax and an income tax on lamas' salaries. He explained:

> We have eight hundred monks at Gandan monastery. It is the center of Mongolian Buddhism. Only three hundred monks get a so-called salary. It is not a proper salary, because a proper salary, a minimum salary level, is 190,000. This [minimum salary] was declared by the state so that you can pay social insurance and health insurance. Below that there is no social insurance. When you get older then you don't receive a pension. Most of the monks receive below 190,000.

When I asked him how lamas were able to survive on such a low salary, he told me that many were supported by their extended family.[2] Considering that most lamas live outside of the temples and support families, this income (around $95 in the middle of 2016) is very low. The cost of living in Mongolia is expensive relative to other middle-income countries due to inflation, the proportion of imported products, and Ulaanbaatar's relatively isolated location. As one friend told me in 2015, while one could afford to pay one's electricity bills on what she deemed to be a reasonable salary of 600,000 tögrögs a month, buying food and clothing is costly. On a salary of 600,000 tögrögs per month, if one needs to buy a good pair of shoes half of their salary would be gone. A 300,000 tögrög pair of shoes for a lama on a salary under 190,000 tögrögs would be more than one and a half times their monthly salary.

Many Christian churches in Mongolia ask for a tithe of 10 percent of the salaries of those that regularly attend services. These tithes, along with extensive global financial connections to wealthy nations, mean that Christian churches are able to raise significant funds for charitable activities, the construction and maintenance of buildings, and the expansion of their activities. Over the last few years there have been some attempts by the government to curtail the impact of Christian missionaries. According to a number of my interlocutors, NGOs that employ foreign staff must pay a monthly fee of over 380,000 tögrögs for each foreign worker (in mid-2016 this was around $190). This rule was apparently introduced to decrease the number of foreign missionaries living in Mongolia but has directly affected the capacity of Buddhist temples and centers to finance foreigners, including Tibetan lamas, who come to Mongolia to teach Buddhism. Given the relative percentage of the population that identify as Christians, 2.2 percent, and as Buddhists, 53 percent (National Statistical Office of Mongolia 2010), the number of Christian churches is much larger than the number of Buddhist temples. According to the 2010 Mongolian census there were 198 registered Christian churches in Mongolia with a further estimated 250 that were unregistered. In Teleki and Majer's survey only 200 Buddhist temples were documented in the country. By 2007, over half of the temples that were reinhabited and built by old lamas in the early 1990s had shut down. These closures were due mostly to the temples' difficulties in sustaining themselves financially and in retaining young lamas (Teleki 2009).

Figure 11. A man reaches into his wallet to pay for prayers
at Gandan Khiid during Tsagaan Sar.

The lack of stable funding affects how lamas are educated, their domestic lives, how they choose to make an income, and their involvement in charitable projects. As temples no longer dominate the urban landscape physically, socially, economically, or politically, the relationship that laypeople have with temples and lamas has changed dramatically. While it is certainly seen as positive to donate money to temples, particularly after a family member (Humphrey 2002) has died or at special times during the year, making merit (*buyan khiikh*) through donations to temples was not mentioned by any of my interlocutors.

The bulk of donations to temples happen at prayer shops where one orders prayers to be read on the following day. Donations are also given out during the morning prayer readings when some people walk around temples handing out banknotes to individual lamas. On auspicious days, such as Tsagaan Sar, very wealthy people pay for entire services to be read. Inside the temples the higher the pile of cushions on which a lama sits, the more senior he is considered to be. Most people I spoke to thought that the blessings received from the lamas sitting on the higher seats were more efficacious because they were more learned.[3] One of my interlocutors told me that in some temples lamas hire the best spots to sit on so that they can collect more donations.

These personal donations, unlike those centrally collected and paid for at the prayer shops, directly add to the very small salaries that most lamas receive. In addition to these activities some families pay for lamas to come to their homes or businesses to carry out specific rituals to clear obstacles that are believed to hinder health and success (see chapter 7).

Motivations, Donations and Pollution

> The gift is held to embody the sins of the donor, whom it rids of evil by transferring the dangerous and demeaning burden of death and impurity to the recipient. Nor is it without peril for the donor, for it binds him dangerously close to one who may prove unworthy. (Parry 1986, 459–460)

Based on fieldwork in Varanasi, Parry (1986) argues against Mauss's (1954) idea of reciprocity contained within the gift. He illustrates that the relationship of religious gifts between the donor and recipient within Hinduism is fraught. As donations to Brahmins are given to purify the donor's karma or spiritual pollution, these gifts carry with them the ills of the donor, thereby endangering the recipient. For the donor, gifts must be given to the religiously pious who can effectively purify the impurities contained within the gift through their religious libations (Parry 1986, 460). If they fail to carry out the appropriate purification rituals, the pollution latent in the gift remains, endangering both the donor and the donee. In Laidlaw's (2000) analysis of Parry's description of *dan*, he contends that these donations are morally compromised because they are supposed to contain no reciprocity but in reality bring further social enmeshment. Laidlaw (2000) argues that donations to Jain renunciates, carefully ritually removed from social entanglements, may be considered to be very close to a free gift.

In Mongolia the ideal of the non-reciprocated gift is not an important aspect of giving money to temples. In general Mongolian lay Buddhists expect reciprocity through ritual efficacy or the material improvement of temples when they make donations. Many people believe that pollution or bad karma can be generated through donations if the motivations or morality of the lamas is lacking. However, the donor does not pass this on to the donee (as in Parry): it is the religious specialist that generates the negativity. If a religious specialist has impure intentions, such as the desire to make money from the distress of others, they can attract negative results. Lamas, and other religious specialists, must have good morals and pure motivations in order to not be harmed from the wealth they accrue by carrying out rituals.

Many lay Buddhists complain about the price lists that are found at some temples, including at Gandan Khiid. While I have heard from lamas that these price lists are to ensure proper accountability for donations to temples (and are perhaps a consequence of their taxation), the presence of price lists and the "shop-like" ambience at temples are one of the main criticisms that lay Buddhists have of temples. As Nergui, a male friend in his mid-twenties, told me in 2009:

> It's becoming like a business now; that's what I really don't like about going to monasteries at the moment. Because I know that they are helping people and so on, going to houses and driving their own cars and everything it's just not what it's about, it doesn't feel right. It just looks like a business . . . Ideally . . . I want to see a monastery that is very, very peaceful to visit and very calm, where I can stay calm and, you know, really concentrate on what I'm trying to pray because that's what a spiritual place is all about.

This sentiment was reflected in a conversation with another friend, Enkhtur, in 2015: "I feel bad when at Gandan they ask you for a thousand [around 50 cents]. I feel bad because it's supposed to be a religious thing and you shouldn't have a price on things. When I go to Bakula Rinpoche [Betüv Khiid] and Dashchoilin they don't ask how much you give. So I feel better. At least, you know, they are not after money."

Following the end of the socialist period in Mongolia there has been an increase in concerns about corruption, particularly among public figures (see chapter 1). Depictions in the media of well-known shamans and lamas rubbing shoulders with important politicians and businesspeople have the dual effect of generating the impression that these religious specialists are spiritually powerful and that they are mixed up in the corruption of the elites. As Buyandelger (2013) has eloquently shown with her descriptions of ethnic Buryat shamans in Mongolia, religious specialists are placed in a double bind when it comes to directly asking for donations. While on the one hand wealth is equated with spiritual power, on the other, asking directly for money attracts critiques. Not all wealth is thought to be generated equally. As Højer (2012) has demonstrated in his analysis of pawnshops (*lombard*) in Ulaanbaatar, how a person makes money can lead them to be afflicted by bad energy (*muu energi*). The generation of wealth through the destruction of the natural environment, the suffering of humans, or the suffering of other-than-human beings is often thought to carry with it contamination in the form of bad karma, bad energy, and/or spiritual pollution (see also High 2013).

In spite of these views, during many Buddhist rituals money represents value and potency, and its inclusion in religious ceremonies is not generally seen as being problematic. Many public ceremonies include small and large donations of money as offerings for local spirits, temples, individuals, and Buddhist icons. For many lay Buddhists making offerings of money at temples, as with other offerings that are considered to be highly valuable (such as white foods, sweets, and vodka), is a sign of appreciation and generosity and invites prosperity.

The more expensive a ritual is and the less needy it's recipients the more it seems to attract criticism. One ritual that I heard critiqued a number of times was the *bumba* ritual at Amarbayasgalant Khiid. Many middle-class urbanites along with the urban elite visit this temple in the countryside to carry out a prosperity ceremony involving a special kind of bumba—a clay vase with sacred materials inside. A less expensive version of the bumba is used as an offering to spirits when one visits their homeland (*nutag*). Unlike other prosperity ceremonies, the bumba ceremony is secret and cannot be attended by laypeople. The ritual is associated with the worship of Dorje Shugden, a controversial icon whose adulation has been actively discouraged by the Fourteenth Dalai Lama and has caused significant conflicts among Tibetans. There is a statue and *thang ka* of Dorje Shugden at the Choijin Lama temple, indicating that it was one among many icons worshiped before the socialist period. Although this figure was the subject of a popular book sold at the Internom bookstore in 2013, none of my lay Buddhist interlocutors that irregularly visited temples seemed to be aware of the political controversies surrounding it. While I have never directly come across anyone who told me that they worship Dorje Shugden, it is the subject of heated discussion among some Mongolian lamas (Jadamba 2013). Apparently unaware of the controversy, every year thousands of urbanites travel to the temple from Ulaanbaatar and leave their bumba, which is then blessed by lamas and afterward kept hidden within the family home. The bumba is taken there for three consecutive years, and it is believed to call wealth and abundance into the home. The ritual and the bumba itself are relatively costly. It costs 25,000–35,000 tögrögs ($12.50–$17.50) for the ceremony and sometimes as much as 500,000 tögrögs ($250) to buy a bumba. This ceremony, unlike the *dallaga avakh* ceremony, which is accessible to most urbanites, is frequently criticized as an indulgence for those who already have enough and as a means for the wealthy to accumulate ever more dubious forms of power.

Morality and the Purification of the Saṅgha

As the majority of lamas and female lamas are not able to live in residential housing within temples, most live with their families and must, along with their working husbands and wives, support themselves and their family's material needs. While some lamas carry out lengthy practices that involve extended periods of disciplined meditation and *pūjā*s, for example in the preparation for Dashchoilin's annual Tsam dance or the lengthy preparations made before the now yearly Danshig Naadam, for many life as a lama is much like any other occupation. Most drive to work and arrive at the temple in the morning just as any other urban worker. Some lamas, unable to support themselves on their small lama salaries, find other forms of employment or business opportunities and only become lamas on the weekends or to carry out occasional rituals.

According to Majer and Teleki's (2008) survey, the majority of Mongolian lamas do not keep full monastic vows. A couple of Mongolian lamas told me that being married is part of the Mongolian variant of Buddhism and that this is supported by historical precedence. Before the socialist period many lamas did have families (Kaplonski 2014). Those lamas that were found to be breaking rules of celibacy by Buddhist institutions were asked to carry out *pūjā*s or to pay a fine to their temple rather than being forced to disrobe (Wallace 2018). In the early 1990s, as old lamas began to practice in public, they were already married and had families. Neither the lamas nor their lay supporters saw celibacy as a prerequisite for living life as a lama and having students. Although some lamas explained to me that being a married lama is a unique part of Mongolian Buddhism, others told me that lamas tend to get married because they have nowhere to live within the temples. Although it may appear to resemble the situation of married priests in Japan (Covell 2008), the teaching lineage that the majority of Mongolian lamas follow is the Gelugpa, whose founder, the Bogd Tsongkhapa, was well known for emphasizing the importance of strict monastic celibacy. While many lay-people and monastics see married lamas as a local variant of Buddhism, conflicting opinions mean that for most lamas their marriages are an open secret rather than an accepted custom (see Humphrey and Ujeed 2013 re-garding Inner Mongolia).

Most Mongolian families do not see a contradiction in wearing robes and being married, and I was told by many lamas and female lamas that it is common for a young man or woman after they have finished their monastic training to be placed under significant pressure by family members to get married and have children. These pressures are greatest for the few young women who decide to study in India to become nuns, as it is com-monly believed that if a woman doesn't have children she will be afflicted by serious health problems. While there are a number of high-profile female Buddhist religious specialists who are married, have long hair, and hold high status in Mongolia, celibate nuns (who have not already had children) tend to have much lower status than childless celibate lamas and non-celibate lamas. The notable exception to this status hierarchy is Ani Gyalmo, the Australian resident teacher at Shredrup Ling, who is held in high es-teem as a likeable and kind foreigner committed to helping Buddhism flourish in Mongolia. Partly this may be attributed to her age, her foreign-ness, and the fact that she had children decades before committing fully to a monastic life.

A couple of former lamas, now disrobed, who studied at monasteries in India, told me that they felt bad accepting donations as a lama when they weren't keeping all of their monastic vows. One lama, working in an impor-tant administrative role at a temple, who himself did not keep full monastic vows, told me that the acceptance of donations without living within full monastic vows created bad karma:

> When you share the benefits meant for the . . . fully ordained lamas, you end up creating bad karma. It is actually wrong to be respected and receive offer-ings like they do. You might have been observing that Mongolian lamas look like they are suffering from the effect of undue privilege, aren't they? They are really fat, suffering from sickness inside. They are psychologically affected as well. That means that karma is at work: they are suffering from the results of unearned benefits.

When he continued he explained that he thought that the lamas who kept their vows should be elevated above those that didn't rather than, as he asserted is currently the case, being lower than married lamas. As many lamas trained in India spend years overseas it becomes difficult for them to reestablish themselves when they return home as they have lost the personal connections that are often needed to succeed in the city. This is also common of the experience of other urbanites that have studied overseas.

The lack of celibacy among many members of the Mongolian saṅgha has caused controversy within international networks. According to a couple of Mongolian lamas that I spoke to, the Dalai Lama has, on a number of occasions, told those who are not celibate to discontinue wearing monastic robes. I have heard a number of different perspectives on the Dalai Lama's position. Many Mongolian lamas think it would be better if everyone could live residentially at monasteries but know that they don't have the resources. Other laypeople and lamas believe that being married is part of a unique Mongolian tradition, pointing historically to Mongolia's key historical lamas, such as Zanabazar, the Eighth Bogd Khan Javzandamba, and the Gobi Lama Danzan Ravjaa, who were well known for not being celibate.

While most of my interlocutors considered married lamas to be the norm, international ideas about vows and celibacy reinforced by visiting Tibetan lamas and Mongols who have spent time in India are affecting ideas concerning monastic vows. Some laypeople distinguish between true (*ünen*) and authentic (*jinkhene*) lamas and those who are not thought to be properly motivated and/or do not keep extensive vows. When I asked Dawaa, a multilingual young professional in her early twenties, if she thought there was enough male and female lamas in Mongolia, she said:

When I went to this ruined temple in the Khenti Aimag the museum person told us that [before the socialist period] there were three thousand lamas there regularly, and if there was any . . . celebration, then there were eight thousand lamas. Relating to this time, nowadays there are few lamas in Mongolia . . . I think that most lamas that we have today . . . they cannot be like these lamas . . . Most of them are married and they have children. I told you my dad's uncle was a real lama, and he was never married.

Here she points out the difficulties of devoting oneself to Buddhist study and practice when one also has a family, which is a common concern among my interlocutors. One lama that had studied in India told me that he had become celibate again after he realized that simultaneously having and supporting a wife and being a lama (due to the difficulties of earning a proper salary) was too difficult. At the time of the interview he was living in a house with one of his siblings who was helping to reduce the expenses of everyday life.

For many Buddhists that have been affected by global attitudes, discussions about the degeneration of the Mongolian saṅgha are common. I occasionally heard people discuss the need for the "purification" of the saṅgha that would involve all of the married lamas disrobing or wearing different robes to those keeping the full Vinaya. When I have pointed out that this disrobing would cause the number of lamas in the country to drop significantly (some lamas estimated to me that around 90 percent of the lamas are not celibate), a couple of people replied that it would be better to have fewer lamas than to have only those who were not fully ordained.

Dirt, Education, and Charity

Both lay and monastic Buddhists question whether temples properly make use of the donations they receive. Many laypeople complain about the dirty and dark physical conditions of the temples and the poor keeping of lamas' clothing. Others focus on whether the lamas are properly educated (*gegeerel*), commenting that they are unsure whether or not the lamas can understand what they are reading. Another major critique of temple spending highlights the perceived lack of charity work carried out by large Buddhist temples. This final critique often explicitly references the visible charitable works that Christian missionary organizations have been involved in since the early 1990s.

As Erdenee, a spritely meteorologist in her late thirties that irregularly visits temples, told me:

Sometimes I see that the clothes that they wear don't look so good . . . Some people will think that a person who is poor will become a lama. I think that every country, every nation has their religion. Who will believe, who will not believe, it's their right . . . Lamas don't have to wear poor clothes . . . It's our culture. The government needs to help. If they have agreed that people can have their beliefs . . . then their part is to help it to be clean, to be nice and comfortable. Why must these places be dirty?

Here Erdenee links the conditions of the temples with pride in Mongolia's Buddhist heritage. Just as artworks that predate the socialist period are predominantly Buddhist, the bulk of the pre-socialist built environment in Ulaanbaatar is comprised of older temples and the former residence of the Eighth Javzandamba. As I described in chapter 3, for many Mongols Buddhism is linked to nationalism. Most foreign visitors visit Ulaanbaatar's temples as part of their tours. To have dirty temples and unkempt lamas is, for Erdenee, a problem not only for Buddhists but also for how Mongolian culture and heritage appear to others. Some temples, such as Dashchoilin Khiid, are now heritage listed and are recognized as important parts of Mongolia's material heritage. Although most of my interlocutors did not explicitly identify the state as being responsible for the conditions of temples or indeed lama's clothing, a number of people said that they would enjoy temples more if they were more comfortable and were not dirty, cold, or dark.

Many lay Buddhists expressed concerns about both their own lack of Buddhist knowledge and that of the lamas (chapter 4). When lay Buddhists go to a temple, they enter an environment where they understand certain ritual expectations. Most people I met knew, for example, the correct direction in which to walk around sacred objects, where to pay for prayers to be read, and, in some cases, where to find a lama to ask for advice. However, the "meaning" of religious activities is obfuscated in a number of ways. First, the prayers are read in Tibetan, a religious language that not all lamas, and only a very few committed laypeople, understand. Second, religious objects, such as tantric paintings and sculptures, are enigmatic, and very few laypeople have more than a superficial understanding of them. Third, participants often tell me that they don't know where to find out about religious teachings. Meetings with lamas tend to focus on astrology and advice about which prayers to have read rather than on Buddhist philosophy.

Alternative sources of information, such as books and websites, include specialist terms that most Mongols find very difficult to understand. Many people told me that they have tried to read Buddhist literature but cannot understand the Mongolian religious language that is used. The texts that a number of lay Buddhists have tried to read were *sūtra*s, such as *Altan Gerel*, the *Sūtra of Golden Light*. These contain complicated and obscure *sādhanā*s, utilizing imagery, terms, and metaphors intended for the use of initiated religious specialists, for the carrying out of ritual practices, and for philosophical contemplation. While some texts, such as the Dalai Lama's books, were being translated into Mongolian, these texts were not widely read by the lay Buddhists that I spoke to. Even when relatively simple texts are translated into Mongolian, some of the key terms are difficult to understand. This is due to the effect of key Buddhist terms being appropriated during the socialist period and of them presently being used to describe categorically different religious concepts. This is particularly common with terms such as "enlightenment" and *burkhan*, which is commonly used to mean Buddha, a monotheistic god, multiple gods or spiritual beings, and/or some combination of these (Abrahms-Kavunenko 2012).

While many local temples and Dharma Centers do offer free or inexpensive Buddhist classes to the lay public, many lay Buddhists were not aware of these classes. Additionally, lamas who travel to India or devote themselves to religious study in Mongolia while receiving often voluminous instruction in mnemonics, Tibetan language, and Buddhist philosophy miss out on a more general education, a dearth of which can make it difficult to communicate core Buddhist ideas to secularly educated laypeople. Some start their Buddhist education as early as twelve and often more or less completely cease secular education from this point on. Lama Zorigt told me that at some point while studying in a monastery in India, he realized that he would not be able to communicate effectively with lay communities as, after almost eight years of living full-time in a monastery, he did not have a basic understanding of science or politics or the challenges that one faces as a lay person living in Ulaanbaatar. This difficulty compounds the common sentiment that Buddhist temples are not doing enough to educate themselves or the broader population. As Oyunbileg explained to me while sitting at the small kitchen table in my apartment:

> At least the *sūtra*s should be translated into Mongolian . . . for the ordinary people are able to understand what is in there . . . Even for the lamas themselves, they have to be educated about what they are reading, you know . . .

You pay for something and you get something back. But there is no such spiritual part involved in it, you know. You go to a store and you pay some money and you buy something. It's exactly the same way that you would behave in the monastery. You go there, you pay for it, and you get back something. But what is missing is there is . . . a lack of a spiritual part . . . They don't educate much . . . I think there should be at least some kind of a room where people can just go to read something. I don't know there is this public space, public sphere, missing at the monastery. It's very crowded, and there is really a special part missing . . . In a Christian church, or in a Catholic church, you can really see it. There's plenty of nice room and space and it's clean and they do a lot for the prayers and there is always something going on.

Many temples, Dharma Centers, and individuals work hard to tackle this criticism. Jampa Ling translates and prints a number of lay-friendly texts (such as the Dalai Lama's books) into Mongolian. Temples such as Gandan Khiid, the Javzandamba center, Dashchoiliin Khiid, Jampa Ling, and the FPMT's central center provide education and meditation classes for interested lay Buddhists. Some monastics now use social media, such as Twitter, as a form of education. There are also now some popular Buddhist radio shows, and Facebook (which has become a major way to communicate in Mongolia) is increasingly used to communicate about Buddhist philosophy, coming celebrations, and activities.

Influenced by global religious expectations, many Mongolian Buddhists critique the use of temple funds in relation to a lack of charity. While many Buddhist organizations and temples have started NGOs to help the poor, the visibility of Christian charities is unassailed given their relative wealth, resources, and priorities. Many Christian churches provide charity as an essential part of their core beliefs and/or as a way of encouraging new converts. Some Mongols attend Christian churches as a way of receiving financial support or education. This support varies in the degree to which it could be perceived as being a freely given donation. Attempts at conversion range from large charitable organizations, such as World Vision, strongly encouraging their employees to be Christian, to Christian organizations only giving out blankets to prisoners in Ulaanbaatar's overcrowded prisons if they convert. As Mongolia is considered to be a remote outpost for "saving souls," some of the more radically Evangelical forms of Christianity from the United States and Korea have been attracted to Mongolia to set up missionary activities.

These Christian groups often have an anti-syncretic attitude toward religious practice, and some lay Buddhists told me that they stopped going to church after they were told that they could only practice one religion (which is an unpopular idea in Mongolia, see chapter 9). The meanings of an older translation of the Bible, which was in widespread use until the release of a new translation in 2015, were so grammatically disorienting that there was a series of suicides of newly converted Christians who thought that they were going to be reborn three days after their death (Wallace 2015, 56). A number of Mongols expressed their concern to me about these suicides when discussing religion. Others were worried that if Buddhist temples did not support the poor in the same way that Christian churches did, the poor would all convert to Christianity. As Chuluun told me in a concerned voice:

> They have not got a lot of money, but they should feed the street children or those who haven't got a lot of money. There are a lot of poor people in our country. They should do things as much as possible for these children. These children will grow up and they will have only two ways. One way is to go to the jail; another way is that they become a Mormon. If they would like Mongolia to be a good Buddhist country they should make good things for those who haven't anything to live with.

This (somewhat erroneous) idea that Buddhist temples have a lot of money is reinforced by visits to bustling prayer shops at Tsagaan Sar, stories of wealthy donors giving money for the building of *stūpa*s and other building works, and pictures of top lamas spending time with politicians and businesspeople. As Sarantuya told me in the winter of 2009:

> Regarding Gandan, Mongolian people are criticizing them now because, why is Gandan not doing anything for the poor people? They are building some temple in India . . . Because all other religions, Christian people and other religions, are making food for the poor people—why is Gandan not doing this? . . . Maybe they are proud that we cannot criticize them, but in reality people are. They are doing nothing. They are earning a lot of money and where is this money? But maybe they have to build some temple in the Taj Mahal, I don't know.

Here she is referring to the building of a Mongolian Buddhist temple in Bodh Gaya. Most countries with a large enough Buddhist population have one or more temples at the holy site of Bodh Gaya as it is regarded as the holiest pilgrimage site in the Buddhist world. Sarantuya's concerns about the use of temple funds were echoed by many of my interlocutors. Interestingly these criticisms tend to be in reference to temples that contain a collective of lamas rather than being leveled at individual lamas who do rituals or provide astrological advice. This may point to some threshold past which the acknowledged and accepted transactional nature of paying for ritual efficacy opens out to some broader expectation of institutional responsibility or mutual aid.

Although the donor-recipient relationship between Buddhist temples and laypeople has historically been dominated by donations from the laity to monastics, many contemporary Buddhist institutions want to and do give out charity to the poor (reflecting broader changes within monastic-lay relationships elsewhere, Darlington 2007; Hayashi-Smith 2011; Huang and Weller 1998). Many temples, such as Dashchoilin Khiid, give to the local community when they are in need. Sadly many of the charitable works undertaken by the Dharma Centers that I worked with have been adversely affected by a stalling global economy since 2008 and, as the Mongolian economy continues to fluctuate erratically, a lack of local donations.

Because many Mongols visit temples to clear blockages, refresh their vital winds (khiimori), and create good energy, the sense that they could encounter a lama with potentially fiscal motivations, dubious morality, corrupt monetary practices, and/or a lack of education is a major concern. Most visit temples to cleanse, to revitalize, and to enlighten (in the sense of education). As a result of this the purity of religious institutions is under scrutiny both internally and externally. Most of my lay Buddhist and religious specialist interlocutors expressed concerns about how money was made at temples and how this money was used. These anxieties are not decoupled from broader narratives about moral decay and dubious fiscal motivations in the city.

The presence of these criticisms places Buddhist religious specialists and institutions in a difficult position. If a ritual is to be efficacious, a lama or female lama must be educated. To learn and understand Tibetan sūtras takes an impressive amount of study. If they are to teach others about Buddhism, it requires some general education that they may have missed during their Buddhist studies. Additionally, most Buddhist education does not focus on ritual efficacy but on learning and understanding complex Buddhist philosophy. Not recognizing this effort, most local donors expect religious specialists to be highly educated but prefer to give money as remuneration for rituals. Introductory meditation classes and philosophy classes are generally free (or near to it), which can create two classes of lamas within large temple complexes: those in which lamas study and teach and are poor, and the wealthier temples that carry out rituals. On top of these already constrictive financial constraints, temples are expected to run successful charities.

As most Mongols correlate spiritual success to material well-being, lamas and female lamas must somehow be reasonably wealthy without being fiscally motivated. Most have to live outside of the monasteries, but they must still be able to offer free or inexpensive services, look clean, and not be motivated by fiscal remuneration. They must be highly educated but are generally expected to carry out efficacious ritual services rather than use their education for religious education and/or the renunciation of worldliness and the pursuit of awakening.

Chapter 9

White Foods, Purification, and Enlightenment

In the spring of 2016 my friend Zaya tells me that she is visiting a friend who is a "fire doctor" to treat some problems that she is having with a sore ear. She explains to me that one of her ears is ringing, which is particularly worrisome as the ringing is happening in her left ear. Bad things, she tells me, enter from the northeast. If you orient yourself to look toward the south, as most Mongols do,[1] this means that problematic elements would tend to enter the body from the direction of the left ear. Her daughter too, she tells me, has always been sensitive to loud noises coming from her left. Since Zaya started receiving treatment from the fire doctor, her ear has improved. She recommends that I book a healing session, as fire is an excellent vehicle for purification.

Unsure of what to expect, my husband and I travel to Gunjee the fire doctor's apartment accompanied by Zaya and her sister on an afternoon in late May. As we make our way through an impromptu snowstorm, which follows the previous day's rather warm temperatures, we find her apartment within a Soviet-style apartment complex just to the southeast of Gandan Khiid.

Her clinic is in her home, as is common with many religious specialists, including shamans, astrologers, and healers, in Ulaanbaatar. One of the rooms of her three-bedroom apartment has been converted into a fire-healing room. The room itself, much like the rest of the apartment, is relatively unadorned. It has a simple shelf with towels, matches, and burning spirits, and it is equipped with two massage tables. Just as her daughter returns home from school, we begin the healing session. She commences the treatment with my husband, placing wet towels first on his hands and then on his head, squirting purified spirits on the towels and then setting them alight with a match. She instructs him to tell her to suffocate the flame when he can no longer take the intense heat that this causes. The sensation after the fire is extinguished is more extreme than when the towel is alight, as the heat from the towel pushes downward before it cools and ceases to radiate heat into the skin. Gunjee learned this practice in China making her the only person that I have met who told me that their religious or spiritual training occurred in mainland China.[2]

Gunjee explains that fire has special powers to purify and heal. It quickly rids the body of any pollution or blockages that are causing problems, as fire is an element characterized by its strength. Her practice incorporates ideas from Traditional Chinese Medicine about the meridians, to which non-allopathic Mongolian medical systems are related, along with ideas about chakras from India and Buddhist/Hindu notions of karma. In all of these systems, energetic blockages are believed to cause physical and mental afflictions. During the session, Gunjee points to where the flames are at their highest. Where the burning is the hottest, she says, is where the body has the greatest problems. As fire contains its own intelligence, the heat of the flames reflects the places on the body that have the greatest need for purification.

Gunjee, like the friend who recommended her, is a committed follower of the Supreme Master Ching Hai. In order to learn the Supreme Master's Quan Yin method, she eats a vegan diet and practices meditation every day. For Gunjee and other followers of the Supreme Master's method, the drive for purification is a central part of religious practice and is frequently discussed among friends and acquaintances. A person's diet is believed to purify or cause contamination, depending upon what is consumed. Eating meat is believed by the Supreme Master's followers to pollute a person physically, mentally, and spiritually, as meat carries with it the suffering of the animal that has been killed. Dairy products and eggs, likewise, due to contemporary factory-farming practices, are thought to contaminate a person as these products are connected to the suffering of the animals that produce them. By eating food that has not directly caused suffering, behaving in accordance with the Supreme Master's moral systems, and practicing her meditation method, it is believed that one can purify accidental contamination and bad karma and ultimately potentially become enlightened in this lifetime.

Gunjee's fire healing shares similarities with many of the New Religious practices that I encountered in Ulaanbaatar. First, it itself is a mixture of different religious and spiritual practices from a range of sources—in this case mostly Indian, Mongolian, and Chinese medical and religious ideas. Second, when it is enters the Mongolian context it is incorporated and interpreted into existing beliefs and practices by both Gunjee and her patients. The idea that fire can purify, as illustrated in chapter 6, exists within a set of associations already present among Mongolian Buddhists and within Buddhist ritual activities. The impetus to seek purification is a common motivation for seeking ritual efficacy in Mongolia and relates to perceived energetic or spiritual blockages, pollution, and karma (see chapters 6 and 7). When talking about her experiences with the fire doctor, Zaya refers to the spatial systems in the Mongolian context through which she interprets the ringing in her ear and the need for purification. Third, this is not the only religious/spiritual practice that Gunjee or her patients are committed to. The Supreme Master's followers, like others who participate in what can be broadly described as New Religious Movements, tend like other Mongols to be ecumenical, incorporating a range of ideas and practices into their lives. In this case Gunjee practices fire healing that she has learned in China, is a vegan, practices meditation, and follows the teachings of the Supreme Master Ching Hai.

The Supreme Master Ching Hai's followers have become visible in the capital mostly due to the presence of a range of new vegan restaurants that have appeared in the capital over the last ten years. Since 1990, a diverse range of vegetarian and nonvegetarian New Religious Movements have found followers in the capital. Visits from charismatic teachers, including the popular Hindu guru Sri Sri Ravi Shankar, and the presence of new religious teachings often written in Russian have helped to create the bubbling enthusiasm for a wide range of religious/spiritual practices, which display broad influence on how people relate to Buddhist and non-Buddhist movements in Ulaanbaatar. Just as Christianity has exerted influence on understandings about life after death and enlightenment (see chapter 6), New Religious Movements affect how my interlocutors understand enlightenment and purification.

In a city where air pollution dominates life for most of the year, vegetarian New Religious Movements promoting physical and spiritual purification have become very popular among middle-class urbanites. Half of the forty-eight people I formally interviewed during my doctoral research told me that they had been on a retreat or attended classes from a vegetarian New Religious group. Of the twenty-three of these that irregularly visited Buddhist temples, those that had learned meditation had done so with Sri Sri Ravi Shankar (frequently referred to by my interlocutors as "Sri Sri") or with the Supreme Master Ching Hai. In 2009 and 2010 during Shredrup Ling's Wednesday night meditation classes, questions about meditation practices that people had learned from Sri Sri's weeklong retreats were common. Like educational classes at Dharma Centers and local temples, vegetarian New Religious groups emphasize the possibilities for purification and enlightenment. These popular groups teach that enlightenment, rather than coming from strict observations over multiple lifetimes, is a real possibility for all people (albeit with great commitment) in this life if you follow a vegetarian or vegan diet, act in accordance with an ethic of nonviolence, and practice meditation. They emphasize purification through diet, contact with spiritual teachers and healers, and meditation and/or yoga practice.

The ways that these New Religious Movements approach purification and enlightenment elucidates some of the categorical similarities between air pollution (*agaariin bokhirdol*), spiritual pollution (*buzarlal*), and karmic systems of causality as these groups link the more ineffable aspects of religious practice to the corporeal through dietary and ritual practices. Abstaining from participating in environmental and spiritual pollution through bodily activity (in this case, abstaining from meat eating and consuming intoxicants) removes them from the collective karma and contaminants of a polluted city. By avoiding ingesting foods that are contaminated with the suffering of animals, it is believed to be easier to purify the spiritual contaminants stored within the body. Bodily interventions, like those above, can purify accidental contaminants and moral infringements. As one's body is a place where impurities exist, it is also a site for purification.

As this chapter will illustrate, although vegetarianism is very much a peripheral phenomenon, because of the popularity and coherence of their practices vegetarian New Religious groups' approaches toward purification and enlightenment have considerable influence on broader religious understandings within the capital. Both Sri Sri Ravi Shankar's group and the

Supreme Master Ching Hai share some core concepts with Buddhism. As such, they tend to broaden and reify local understandings of religious concepts that lay Buddhists infer from interactions with Buddhist temples and pilgrimage sites. These groups practice their own versions of meditation and transformative practices, discuss and enact purification, and have their own perspectives on reincarnation and karma. Their practices and teachings, while they might not wholly accord with Buddhist concepts and practices, often provide answers for religious questions that remain unanswered by lay Buddhists' limited interactions with Buddhist temples.

Through their abstinence from meat, intoxicants, and moral infringements, these groups connect themselves with existing Mongolian associations with milk and its links with environmental and spiritual purity, purification, and the maternal bond. People following vegetarian New Religious Movements attempt to purify themselves from external contaminants, both environmental and spiritual, that are thought to permeate the city. They carry out their own transformative practices and seek ritual efficacy from teachers, healers, and astrologers, among others, to assist with purification. Enlightenment in Ulaanbaatar is no longer only possible within the domain of high lamas within Buddhist institutions, nor with scholars and cadres within socialist secular educational institutions.

Purity and Vegetarianism

In September 2009, as I left to visit Russia on the Trans-Siberian Railway, families crowded onto the platform of the Ulaanbaatar railway station to wave good-bye to young students heading off to start university in Russia. Some stood in large family groups, tearful as they said good-bye to their young relatives. When it came time for the train to depart, many of those waiting behind began to throw oblations of milk onto the outsides of the train. Like the milk that is thrown on the back of a horse at the beginning of a horse race, these offerings are thought to be a way to purify obstacles, along with being a reminder of the maternal bond and a blessing for the start of a journey (Thrift 2014).

In the countryside, women make daily oblations with their morning cups of milky tea (*süütei tsai*) to local spirits, and this practice is carried out by some women from the balconies of their apartments in Ulaanbaatar. A

Figure 12. Women offer milk for purification at an ovoo near Sainshand before sunrise.

friend complained to me that it is so common to be hit by milk tea walking directly past a particular set of apartments that she avoids walking under them altogether. Dairy products, as they are seen to be sacred, are offered to shrines within temples and at pilgrimage sites. At Eej Khad (Mother Rock), a sacred rock in the countryside believed to have the power to grant wishes, people circumambulate around her in a clockwise direction throwing milk as an oblation before they whisper their three wishes underneath her arms. At Mandshir Khiid to the south of Bogd Khan Uul, the paintings of *burkhan* in the meditation caves that were built facing south from the mountains, to the north of the burned-out temple remains that were razed during the socialist period, have milk and dairy products smeared across their mouths. Milk is also used within some shamanic ceremonies. The shaman that lived in my apartment block's basement was often outside before ceremonies throwing milk to the mountains of the north, south, east, and west, priming us for the sound of arrhythmical drumming that would soon be heard ascending the building's stairs.

As nomadic pastoralism still dominates the livelihoods of those in the coun-

tryside and is linked to Mongolian national identity in the urban imagination, milk is important both symbolically and literally. Urbanites told me that
dairy foods dominate the diet for herders in the summer months (Thrift 2014).
Companies that sell dairy products in Ulaanbaatar link themselves to the purity of nomadic lifestyles through their packaging and by calling their products
names such as "good" (*Sain*), "beautiful" (*Goyo*), and "pure milk" (*Tsever Süü*).
As Thrift writes, "milk is a highly symbolic commodity representing purity,
the pastoral heritage, and maternalism. Milk, along with various other pure
white objects, is associated generally with the concept of 'purity', which en-
compasses goodness—including thoughts unadulterated by selfishness or
guile, in the sense of *tsagaan setgel* ('white mind' or 'white thought')—
and, through association with pure white milk (*ekhiin tsagaan süü*, 'the mother's
white milk'), maternalism or the mother-infant relationship" (2014, 498).

In early 2014 Mongolia was rocked by a scandal involving blurred pictures
that suggested that the popular brand of *Goyo Tarag* (Beautiful Yoghurt) was
being imported from China (Thrift 2014). The news, shared on social media
and taken up by local news outlets, shocked many urbanites, who began to
question whether the popular brand of Mongolian yoghurt was in fact an
intentionally "poisoned" milk product from China, whose food products are
widely regarded with deep suspicion (Thrift 2014, see chapter 4). As Thrift
describes, the hyperbolic tone of the Mongolian media as they discussed the
scandal reflected the sanctity of the purity of dairy foods along with pervasive fears of contamination of both national identity and Mongolian foods
(Billé 2015; Thrift 2014).

While for English speakers vegetarianism conjures up images of lettuce
and carrots, the term *tsagaan khool*, or "white food," is used to refer to vegetarian dishes in Mongolia. Before the increase in popularity of vegetarian
diets, this term was used to describe dairy foods and other white foods, such
as flour and rice, which were eaten when Mongols abstained from meat on
special Buddhist days, such as the Buddha's birthday. The Buddha's birthday is still one of the most popular days to eat vegetarian foods and is a day
when most of Ulaanbaatar's vegetarian restaurants are full. In the countryside in summer, nomadic diets are dominated by Mongolian cream and
cheese, along with fresh and dried yoghurt. Friends often speak of how eating meat-free foods, which for herders consist mostly of dairy, flour, and
rice, or "white foods" (*tsagaan khool*), clears out the digestive system from the
meat-rich foods of winter. Summertime is when the much loved fermented

horse milk, *airag*, is drunk and when many herders settle around the outskirts of the city to sell fresh *airag* to urban dwellers.[3]

When I first visited Mongolia I was surprised to see how popular vegetarian foods, *tsagaan khool*, had become—"white foods" in this context being reworked to refer to an exclusive, morally reckoned diet rather than referring to one component of seasonally shifting dietary patterns. I was told that the first vegetarian restaurants appeared in Mongolia in 2003, and in 2009 I counted around twenty in the capital. Rather than being a result of burgeoning Buddhist moralities, the appearance of vegetarian restaurants is linked to the growth of New Religious Movements, an emerging globally informed environmental consciousness, globalized religiosities that are flowing into and out of the capital, and, more recently, a growing interest in health food crazes.

The connection of purity with milk products and white food links vegetarian diets to purity and purification. More recently the term "vegan," transliterated into Cyrillic, has become common in the city, as the number of vegans in the city has increased. Even with the conspicuous use of the term "vegan," many of my interlocutors still associate vegetarian foods with purity and purification resonating with the original term *tsagaan khool*. Some of my nonvegetarian middle-class friends restrict or abstain from meat eating during the summer for health reasons. Others, including Buddhists and those interested in shamanism, follow vegetarian diets for short periods to enact ritual purification. I have heard nonvegetarians discussing problems with eating meat during summer, as this is believed to cause excessive heat and anger (and therefore arguments and fighting) in warm weather.

Although white foods are frequently associated with purity, vegetarianism has not become normalized in the city. Following a vegetarian or vegan diet requires a lot of effort in a nomadic pastoralist country. The dependence on meat for subsistence in the countryside and the love of meat-heavy Mongolian dishes means that abstaining from meat remains a highly controversial activity. When I first carried out fieldwork animals were a part of the city's landscape. Herding animals (*mal*) at this time grazed happily on the banks of the now dried up Dund River that ran through part of the city north to south and then west to meet the Tuul River. It was not uncommon in the city to come across a couple of people blow torching a dead sheep on the street or to see someone dragging a live animal up the Soviet-built apartment stairs. Occasionally I heard an animal bleating from a balcony, but this has become less common since the government enacted a ban on live animals entering the city limits sometime after 2010. Many people I spoke to associated meat eating with strength and vitality. Eating meat, I was told on a number of occasions, was why Mongols were strong (*khüchtei*). Others worried aloud that vegetarian diets would cause people to be sick, especially in Mongolia's harsh climate. Still others told me that they found it offensive to consider meat eating to be problematic as eating meat is the diet of nomadic herders and therefore an essential part of being Mongolian. As part of the culture of hospitality in the countryside is to eat foods that a person has offered you, enacting a bond of trust that the food that they offer you does not contain poison, traveling on a strict vegan diet in the countryside could cause some difficulties.

New Religious Assemblages

The most popular vegetarian New Religious groups among my interlocutors were Sri Sri and the Supreme Master Ching Hai, although other groups, such as the Ananda Marga, were also mentioned. These groups don't generally self-identify as being religions and are very ecumenical. Zaya, who practices the Supreme Master Ching Hai's Quan Yin method of meditation and is a vegan and owns a vegan restaurant, is a Buddhist. Likewise, one of the few people I interviewed who maintains a regular spiritual practice that she learned on a Sri Sri retreat is a Muslim. In 2009, the chef at the Ananda Marga vegetarian restaurant told me that she does not follow a religion even though she is planning to become a nun and study at the Ananda Marga center in Sweden. As a result, these groups tend to coexist with other religious practices and ideas and complement rather than compete with visits to Buddhist temples or other religious institutions.

Like international Buddhist organizations, these vegetarian groups all have complicated origins and are often already a mixture of different philosophical traditions before they reach Ulaanbaatar. The Vietnamese-born Supreme Master Ching Hai married a German aid worker when she was young and moved to Europe. She then traveled extensively in India, pursuing spiritual practice, and has since set up centers across the world, including the one in which she currently resides, which is located in France. Sri Sri's meditation and yogic system is firmly rooted in Hindu philosophies of nonviolence and has interacted significantly with global environmental discourses. The Ananda Marga is a Hindu-based philosophical and yogic system invented in the 1950s in Bihar, India (Ananda Marga Pracaraka Samgha 2006). Having global appeal, the Mongolian group was started by an Australian woman who also runs the Lotus Orphanage with help from foreign and local volunteers. She opened a vegetarian restaurant in Ulaanbaatar in 2006 and in 2010 also ran a yoga and meditation center.

Inside Mongolian bookstores, it is common to see the teachings of the Dalai Lama sitting alongside the global Hindu guru Osho, books written by Sri Sri Ravi Shankar, books detailing shamanic rituals, and those describing auras, energy work, and prophetic visions from the Bulgarian-born Baba Vanga. A range of spiritual and self-help books have been translated into Mongolian, and these are often on the "best-sellers" shelf. Notable examples include the bestselling book *The Secret*, written by an Australian writer, which asserts that positive thinking can alter reality (Byrne 2006). In 2009 the book *What the Bleep Do We Know!?* was very popular, claiming to combine "quantum physics" and spirituality with its proposition that words, such as "love" and "hate," can affect the shape of water molecules (Arntz, Chasse, and Vicente 2005). Some of my interlocutors referenced writings from self-help psychology gurus from Russia when talking about religion, such as Alexander Sviyash, and other international self-help books that use Mongolian themes or imagery, such as *The Horse Boy* (Isaacson 2009).

The interest in alternative religious practices has not abated since I first visited Ulaanbaatar in 2009. Vegetarian-friendly yoga studios have now cropped up in significant numbers in the center and south of Ulaanbaatar, and some carry out retreats in the countryside. In 2015 and 2016 having one's aura read by a computer had become very popular. If a person's aura is displaying imbalances, people are instructed to purchase special colored candles to burn from the aura reader or to seek out ritual efficacy from religious specialists. When one friend told the aura reader that the candles were too expensive for her to buy, she was told to ask a Buddhist lama to have *sutras* read instead. As she doesn't visit Buddhist temples but visits a family shaman, the aura reader said that she could ask her family shaman to carry out a ritual for her.

New Religious Movements and individuals that claim to assist in the generation of wealth have become prevalent as Mongols try and navigate an increasingly unstable economy. In 2015 and 2016 I noticed that there seems to have been a growth in people selling pictures and objects claiming that they can assist in the multiplication of wealth. Perhaps this impression is merely a result of my growing awareness of these practices, as when

I interviewed Gerelmaa, the owner of a religious shop in 2016; she had not noticed an increase in the sales of objects that are associated with prosperity rituals.

In this changing landscape both Sri Sri and the Supreme Master Ching Hai are enduringly well liked. The popularity of these New Religious Movements seems to have grown from an accord with local ideas of purity and the desire for purification, a growing awareness of environmental crises, and increasing access to globalized forms of religious ideas and practices. At Sri Sri's weeklong urban meditation retreats participants are instructed to eat only vegetarian food, and they participate in regular classes involving meditation and other physical exercises. They are given lectures on moral and spiritual themes, including on reincarnation and karma, the importance of keeping oneself healthy through diet and exercise, and how to look after the environment. When I asked Otgonbayar, a middle-class university student in her mid-twenties, about how she felt after doing Sri Sri's retreat, she replied:

> *Aimar* [really! frighteningly] different. Because the course is like about how people do bad things, you know, it is bad. No matter how many people do this, it is still bad and we shouldn't do that. We should protect our environment and love each other or something like that. And then after that course I felt, *aimar!* People, they don't really care about the environment, or they don't really care about other people, which is not good. And after that I knew more ways of doing things. It's good or important to do good stuff.

Much like the descriptions of the benefits of visiting temples, most urbanites talked about how they felt energized, healthier, and/or happier after doing Sri Sri's retreat. Interestingly, because of the high attendance of Sri Sri's meditation retreats, in 2009 and 2010 meditation for many of my interlocutors was associated with vegetarianism rather than with Buddhism. As visits to lamas are more likely to involve ritual efficacy rather than spiritual teachings, both meditation and vegetarianism, which is rarely a dietary habit of lamas, were associated with New Religious Movements rather than Buddhist institutions.

Although many people had participated in Sri Sri's weeklong retreats, only two people that I spoke to continue the exercises that they had learned on the retreats. One was a forty-year-old professional who continued the morning yoga practice of "salute to the sun" (Sans., *sūrya namaskāra*), saying that it had many health and spiritual benefits. The other was a young Kazakh woman, Tulpan, who was thirty and still attended regular retreats and classes. Interestingly, although as an ethnic Kazakh Tulpan said she is a Muslim, she and her parents visited Buddhist temples at least once a year. Her family also visited Buddhist temples when they faced illness or difficulties, as most Mongols do.

At the time that I interviewed her in 2010, she said there was not yet a functioning mosque in Ulaanbaatar. One was under construction, but since that time until 2016 this large construction to the west of the city has been stalled, with only the skeleton of the building completed. I have heard, however, that a number of informal mosques have popped up in the city, including in the ger district areas. Tulpan in 2010 attended Muslim community events but did not go to any Muslim public religious institutions. At the time that I interviewed her she was attending Sri Sri classes at least twice a month, did regular exercises at home, and participated in further week-long retreats. When I asked her about her thoughts on enlightenment, she replied: "I think it's possible for humans because some Buddhist lamas and Buddha are examples. We all can, if we do everything true and good and we meditate, we all could go to *gegeerel* [become enlightened]."

This idea that enlightenment was possible coexisted with her other beliefs, including that there was only one God (*burkhan*) and that after one dies they will go to heaven (*divaajin*) or hell (*tam*). In no way did she indicate that enlightenment, her visits to local temples, or her belief in karma contradicted her other ideas. Like many of my other interlocutors she incorporated Hindu concepts from a New Religious Movement into her existing Islamic and Buddhist beliefs and practices.

Like the followers of Sri Sri's group, the Supreme Master Ching Hai's followers avoid meat and practice meditation. Led by a charismatic self-proclaimed enlightened master, the group meditates using the Quan Yin (Avalokiteśvara) method. The Supreme Master Ching Hai was born to Catholic parents in Vietnam and reportedly learned about Buddhism from her Buddhist grandmother. Her website says that she studied under a number of Buddhist teachers and then found an unnamed Himalayan master who gave her the transmission for the Quan Yin method of meditation. It also states that she attained enlightenment by doing this practice in retreat in the Himalayas (Supreme Master Ching Hai International Assoc. n.d.a). She has a twenty-four-hour TV channel in Mongolia and is so popular that she visited in 2009 to air one of her international video teachings. One of her central messages is that veganism is linked to an environmental ethic. On the front cover of her international newsletter, she wears a Mongolian *deel*, and it reads, in English, "Be vege, go green, save the world. We don't have to die to save the world, just be vegan" (Supreme Master Ching Hai International Assoc. 2009).

The Supreme Master Ching Hai requires that all who wish to be initiated into the Quan Yin method take the five basic lay Buddhist precepts, which are to abstain from theft, harmful speech, sexual misconduct, intoxicants, and killing. She makes some alterations to the precept of refraining from intoxicants by including in this category excessively violent literature and films and pornography, and a substantial extension to the precept of not killing, which is that people must follow a strict vegan diet (Supreme Master Ching Hai International Assoc. n.d.b).

Purifying the Body, Becoming Enlightened

The idea that the body is a vehicle for contamination, along with containing the possibility of purification, is overtly discussed among the Supreme Master's followers. When I interviewed Dr. Bold in 2015 in a vegan restaurant he told me that while abstaining from meat used to be enough to avoid spiritual pollution, dairy products, due to the suffering of the animals that produced them, were also dirty (*bokhir*) and caused spiritual contamination (*buzarlal*). The term for dirt (*bokhir*), which Dr. Bold extends in this case to discuss the qualities of dairy, is also the term often used to describe air pollution (*agaariin bokhirdol*). As animal lovers, the Supreme Master's followers do not believe that the animals themselves are dirty or impure but rather that the meat and dairy that comes from them is sullied by their poor treatment and death. The contamination passed on through animal products causes contamination within human bodies, which in turn becomes a form of spiritual pollution that needs to be purified through changes to one's diet, meditation, and other healing practices.

Dr. Bold related that once a person commits to following the Supreme Master's teachings she is able to eliminate a person's bad karma that they have accrued from their previous lives. Just as many lay Buddhists told me (see chapter 6) one is always making karma, so a person must work to be moral in all of their activities and routinely purify any bad actions. These, after all, include negative thoughts and bad speech, which are difficult to completely avoid. Along with carrying out daily practices for purification, the Supreme Master's adherents tend to be very sensitive about environments that they consider to be polluting. Places where cigarettes are smoked and alcohol is drunk are perceived to be polluting, as are environments that are dominated by those with strong egos and selfish intentions. In spite of these concerns, the group in no way encourages people to disconnect from their family members or those that eat meat.

Zaya, a friend who runs a popular vegan restaurant in Ulaanbaatar, lived in India for six years, where she came across the Supreme Master Ching Hai's teachings and started following her practices. She said that she became a vegetarian because of her daughter, a well-known Mongolian pop star. Her daughter became interested in the Supreme Master's teachings and decided that she wanted to become vegetarian when she was fourteen. Zaya grew up in a Buddhist family and was always taught not to kill animals and insects, a common report among my interlocutors above their mid-thirties, though some told me that it was due to shamanic beliefs rather than Buddhism. Her daughter began to believe that a natural extension of the Buddhist ideal not to kill was also to avoid eating meat. Like many Mongols the most important religious figure for Zaya growing up was a member of her family, her grandmother. Many in her family believe that her daughter is a reincarnation of this grandmother. This is believed to be a common form of rebirth in Mongolia (see chapter 6), and lamas frequently predict a specific rebirth within the family (Humphrey 2002). She told me that her grandmother performed Buddhist *takhil* for the family during the socialist religious restrictions.

For Zaya being a vegan is a core part of her spiritual life. She recounted that when she first arrived in India people would ask her what her religion was, and when she told them she was a Buddhist they always looked at her with great respect and admiration. Looking back, however, she describes that at that time she was very aggressive and that this she attributes to her former meat-dominant diet. During our conversations she said that she loves talking to young people because they are not polluted by years of eating meat and consequently don't have a clouded mind. Of particular note were children who have grown up entirely vegan, whom she regularly mentioned in relation to their health, vitality, and positive mental qualities. Her religious practice is diverse, incorporating Buddhism and the teachings of the Supreme Master

Ching Hai, along with other practices. She said that her first teacher is the Dalai Lama and that her second teacher is the Supreme Master Ching Hai. Both of these figures she considers to be enlightened, and she believes that enlightenment is within the realm of possibility for every person on earth.

Among my other interlocutors the Supreme Master Ching Hai's name came up in discussions about enlightenment. One friend asked me if I thought that the Supreme Master was enlightened. This claim, she thought, was confusing because at the time of the Buddha everything was magical with lotuses blooming everywhere and nature at its most beautiful, but since that clearly wasn't the case now it seemed strange that someone else could be enlightened. When I asked her if she thought the Dalai Lama was enlightened she thought for a while and then said yes, which was followed by her thought that perhaps her ideas about enlightenment were contradictory. Because of the breadth of the Supreme Master's popularity in Ulaanbaatar and the presence of her twenty-four-hour television channel, I noticed that her group is influencing many people's ideas of enlightenment and meditation, even if there is a lot of uncertainty as to the truth of her claims. As Sarangerel told me on a freezing, smoky day in the winter of 2010:

Saskia: What is enlightenment?

Sarangerel: It's difficult. I don't have any experience about that. But sometimes I watch on the TV Supreme Master Ching Hai, who they say is enlightened . . . I only watch her speak sometimes on TV because it is in English and I use it to practice my English. Only on TV I've heard about it. Actually I don't know about that. Sometimes I don't believe that people are enlightened. What does it mean? Because I have no experience, I haven't read about that, so I don't know it very well. Sometimes I don't understand—why are people enlightened? And the Supreme Master Ching Hai always says that in your mind you're everything.

Saskia: Do you think that she is enlightened?

Sarangerel: I actually don't know. Only on TV I was told that she is enlightened. But I don't know if she is enlightened or not enlightened. Maybe when people are enlightened, in my opinion, it means that she or he doesn't think

> about money or that I have to buy expensive clothes,
> and only thinks about human things . . . And also they
> can maybe go without food for many days. Because in
> their mind maybe something happened, I think so. But
> about that I never read anything; it's only my opinion.

Here even though Sarangerel expresses skepticism about the Supreme Master's claims, she is still the first person that she recalls when asked a question about enlightenment.

According to both Sri Sri and the Supreme Master's followers, eating a vegetarian or vegan diet helps participants to attain higher spiritual states. Impurities carried through meat eating (or eating dairy) are thought to block a person's potential to become enlightened. As meat eating is connected to global warming, being a vegetarian also means that one disconnects from the creation of animal suffering and the carbon emissions that raising livestock produce. When talking about enlightenment with Enee, who had not had personal contact with vegetarian New Religious Movements, he connected enlightenment with vegetarianism, meditation, and abstaining from creating physical pollution:

> Like unconsciously you do bad things just by smoking a cigarette, by making a fire, and polluting the air. By driving a car we pollute the air and things like that. So with that, you know, I try to balance everything out. Try to do something good while I'm here. So I don't think that I will be able to get enlightened in the future, and I don't think I have the strength or the requirements for enlightenment. I've heard that you have to go through a lot of difficult stages to get enlightened. Like you cannot eat meat and you have to stay and meditate for months and years. That's not possible for me. Maybe when I grow really old.

Here he explains that generating air pollution blocks a person's capacity for enlightenment. This is contrasted to activities that he perceives as being conducive to the pursuit of enlightenment—being a vegetarian and carrying out meditation. Meditation and vegetarianism are connected to enlightenment and presented in opposition to air pollution.

During my fieldwork in 2009 and 2010 the only Buddhists I met who were vegetarians were either involved in the Supreme Master Ching Hai's group or were experimenting with regular meditation practice. Shredrup Ling ran its own vegetarian café on the ground floor until 2014, when it began to be run by the Luna Blanca, a restaurant significantly associated with the Supreme Master, but this was more a reflection of its foreign roots than its Buddhist affiliation. At the end of a Buddhist meditation class at Shredrup Ling, a participant asked Ani Gyalmo if being a vegetarian was an important part of meditation practice. Ani Gyalmo, a vegetarian herself, was very careful to stress that while it might be helpful, it wasn't necessary. What is important, she said, is that you hadn't overindulged in food before sitting down to practice. She answered in this way, I think, because of her awareness that it would be unreasonable to ask low-income Mongols to become vegetarians. Meat and flour are very cheap, and it is considerably more expensive to switch to a sufficiently nutritious vegetarian diet (though the city's vegetarian restaurants make sure that their meals are very affordable). Every Tuesday at Jampa Ling was "white food" day, but I often saw people eating meat at the center on Tuesdays and heard many hearty complaints about the food that was served on that day.

In addition to the Supreme Master Ching Hai's group and Sri Sri, the influence of smaller religious groups, such as the Ananda Marga and no doubt countless others, is difficult to track. The rapid growth and success of spiritually oriented groups suggests that urban Mongols have a voracious interest in spirituality and alternative philosophies that they yearn to satisfy, even if these pursuits, such as following the exercises learned on Sri Sri retreats, may well be short-lived. These groups, because of their philosophical similarities with Buddhist ideas about reincarnation, karma, and enlightenment, are often incorporated into individual philosophies to fill explanatory gaps about concepts such as enlightenment and the purpose of meditation that are left open by ordinary levels of contact with Buddhist institutions.

Following the end of the socialist period enlightenment is contested. Its meaning is diffuse and difficult to pin down. It is once again associated with purity, but it is no longer something found only among highly esteemed Buddhist lamas. Vegetarian New Religious Movements strengthen the associations of enlightenment with personal purification practices and, like socialist formulations, make enlightenment a real possibility. Their emphasis on personal purification makes them an attractive complement to obfuscated Buddhist rituals. Within these groups, one can purify oneself, even if one cannot necessarily influence the choking air of the city.

Conclusion

Stillness and Movement

Every morning Dr. Bold and a small group of his students gather together at the southern mountain Bogd Khan Uul to stare at the sun. He returns again at noon, when the sun is high in the sky, to practice sun meditation for another hour. Here the air is clearer. This is part of the reason that expensive new developments have been built to the south of the city in recent years, some even encroaching the base of the sacred mountain and blocking nearby water catchment areas for the Tuul River. A retired scholar specializing in steppe ecosystems with a PhD from a Russian university, Dr. Bold has been practicing sun meditation as a method of purification for four years. He received authorization from an Indian sun meditation master to teach others, which he does with those who express an interest, free of charge. He tells me that when he was working as a biologist, during and following the socialist period, he saw the health of Mongolian ecosystems diminish. He contrasts the past with the present:

People are becoming more materialistic. This hurts my mind/emotion [*setgel*] a lot. Everything was great when I was a small child. When I was young I asked my elders if their life was OK when they were children, and they replied that in their youth it was even better. I have seen the degradation of the countryside in my lifetime, and it keeps getting worse. Human minds [*oyun sanaa*] and ecosystems have both deteriorated.

Like many of my interlocutors Dr. Bold expresses a common perception of moral decline, albeit with some material improvement. He tells me that the socialist times were good for the clarity of mind but that people were poor in material terms. The present-day deterioration of the environment is a reflection of this broader moral degeneration. Selfish intentions shift how people treat what surrounds them, destroying ecosystems.

Mongols orient themselves toward the south, in the direction of the sun. The word for south is *ömnö*, the same word that refers to the past. The past that Dr. Bold describes here is one that is clear, pure, light, and unburdened. By staring at the sun rising in the southeast, Dr. Bold believes that he can purify his past actions. The sun both eliminates negative elements and imbues him with good energy. He resists the broader spiritual contamination that he sees occurring in Mongolia and avoids the air pollution's effects on the body by accessing the sun's light directly.

A committed practitioner of the Supreme Master Ching Hai, he tells me that as her student the Supreme Master is able to eradicate the bad karma from his previous lifetimes. The karma and spiritual contamination that he has accrued in this lifetime, however, he must learn to purify with her guidance and with that from other spiritual masters. Sun yoga is not something that was taught to him by the Supreme Master. It is an Indian yogic tradition that he learned from an Indian guru. This practice, he tells me, is simple and effective. The sun works to purify, specifically to burn (*shataakh*), a person's bad karma and other forms of contamination. It requires little effort on the part of the meditator. Once one passes the initial phases of the skin becoming red, a sign that the sun is eliminating surface contaminations within the body, one can stare directly at the midday sun.

The internal organs suffer from illness due to the lack of the light. Because the body feels pain, the emotional body is angry, cruel and diffident. That's why we can't connect with *burkhan* [which he describes as both polytheistic and pantheistic]. Additionally, we eat meat, which is a dirty [*bokhir*] food. When you practice meditation your body is purified and will feel pain. For instance, if the heart's chakra is opened, the heart will be in pain. There are three different glands in the brain that will be cleaned [by sun meditation] . . . You can connect to *burkhan* once all those glands are purified. Your karma will be extinguished and your body will become healthy.

The time of religion has passed, he tells me, and the time of science has come. "The saints are being reborn as scientists," he explains. Religion, he says, has become overly concerned with morality and neglects its focus on enlightenment. Science can communicate more directly with the younger generation and explain the processes of illumination. The light from the sun provides us with good energy that is accessible to everyone, he tells me; *burkhan* (in this case referring to multiple polytheistic gods) are implementing a project, proliferating the qualities of light. While we are in a period that is characterized by materialism and environmental destruction, this light is being proliferated and is freely accessible for all. Moral and environmental degeneration contain within them the seed of hope, of a luminous future.

The light of the sun for Dr. Bold and his students has the capacity to burn away negative aspects, to purify. It is the source of life on the planet, yet as our planet gets hotter, we find ourselves increasingly wishing to shield ourselves from the direct energies of the sun. One of the great ironies of burning coal is that, by literally blocking the light of the sun, it masked the effects of global warming up until the 1980s through a process called "global dimming" (Wild 2015), all the while kick-starting global warming and causing the planet to heat beneath the atmosphere, like a greenhouse. Dr. Bold channels the energies of the sun and, like many ritual practices in Mongolia, uses them to burn and purify negative elements. Fire is polyvalent. It provides illumination, heat, and energy, and in some circumstances purification, yet it also creates smoke, smog, and obscuration. So too the light of the sun can illuminate and enliven or, when trapped within a thickened atmosphere, drive a heating planet into catastrophic disequilibrium.

It's November 2016 and I am sitting in Berlin. I read in the newspaper that Delhi has become so inundated with smog that the air quality is too bad to allow the city's children to go to school. They are told to stay at home, to take refuge from the outside air that has become too toxic to breathe. I think back to three years ago when I lived in the north of India, in the town of Bodh Gaya, Bihar. In December 2013 the air quality sharply declined as the fog descended on the densely populated northern Gangetic Plains trapping the fumes from fuels burned for cooking and for warmth by local villagers. Bodh Gaya is Buddhism's most holy pilgrimage town. It is here that the Buddha is said to have attained enlightenment while sitting under the Bodhi tree. A descendant of the tree under which the historical Buddha sat now grows in the central Mahabodhi Temple (the temple of the "great awakening"). This is the sacred center, sometimes called the "navel of the earth," for Buddhists across the world (Geary 2008). It is the seat of the Buddha's enlightenment, yet persistent poverty in the town and the surrounding region and the proliferation of polluting industries mean that the air is inundated with smog through the winter months. I think back to my memories of children huddling around bonfires made out of plastic bags for warmth. And I think of how, for many street children, homeless people and villagers with their open housing, taking shelter as northern India's skies are plumped with acrid smoke is not a possibility.

Air pollution now affects 92 percent of the world's population (BBC News 2016). Outdoor air pollution is estimated to kill more people in Africa than malnutrition or dirty water (Vidal 2016). This pollution is both the symptom and cause of broader problems. Just as the food we eat sustains us, the air we breathe is a foundation for life. As pollution literally smothers light and breath, it proclaims the urgency of our situation. Poverty and inequality both cause and amplify it. And it unequally affects those who cannot hide in buildings equipped with air-filtering systems and insulation, or in wealthier countries. Inaction and lethargy exacerbate it. Corruption derails our collective responses to it—as my friend Baaska tells me in 2015:

> *Baaska:*   Somebody told me that the mines are using chemicals and
> it's polluting the water and the soil. And the animals are
> eating that. That's why the milk and other products are
> coming out with some kind of pollution. That's what we
> are eating now. That's why if there was no pollution
> everything would remain the same as before. Everyone
> could drink the water without any issues. But now it's
> getting polluted—unfortunately. Now everyone needs to
> buy a water purifier . . . Our air system . . . Oh that's
> horrible in winter. [Because the air is so polluted] I can't
> see myself. We don't have industry and factories like in
> China. They do and that is why their air is polluted. But

> our air is always like this . . . also mining . . . There aren't
> many controls. There are, but they are easily corrupted by
> money. So that's why people say it's like . . . Developing
> countries with natural resources never can become highly
> developed.

Saskia: Because of corruption?

Baaska: Yes.

Saskia: Do you think there is a lot of it in Mongolia?

Baaska: I think it is common. What about Africa? They have a lot
> of diamonds but what is happening? I think it's happening
> to Mongolia too. We do have a source [of wealth] but we
> can't manage it. We are losing it, and we are destroying
> nature at the same time. That's why there is no benefit for
> us unfortunately.

As Baaska points out, Ulaanbaatar's problem is somewhat unique. Unlike large swathes of northern China or northern India, its air problems do not blow in from vast industrial belts belching out pollution to fuel burgeoning economies. The lives of its citizens are not being harmed as a result of exports to consumers in countries such as the United States, Germany, Australia, and the emerging middle classes in Asia. In Ulaanbaatar you do not gaze from the glass windows of a shiny new shopping mall, complete with fake birdsong, at a toxic sky caused by the systems that generate the products inside (as I and countless others have done in Beijing and Shanghai). The causes of Ulaanbaatar's air-quality crisis are simply heating, energy, and light.

The history of light in Mongolia has long been associated with enlightenment and a growth in understanding, however erroneous or calculated these associations may have been. Just as Buddhist missionaries saw themselves as enlightening the dark northern lands, socialist educators proclaimed that they were bringing light to the nomads, through electricity and education. These narratives concerning light and enlightenment, in turn, have been related to ideas about purity and practices of purification.

Historically, like Latour's (1991, 11) outline of the work of purification, ideas of purification have been mobilized to encourage processes of antisyncretism, and these processes have created unintentional hybridizations. Throughout Buddhism's history in Mongolia, proselytizing the need for purification and enlightenment has accompanied Buddhist missionary activities. Similar dialogues were present during the time of Buddhism's persecution when the early socialists (some of whom were lamas) called for the purification of the saṅgha. Ideas of purification are again in play in today's resurgence. Yet in contemporary Mongolia the movements toward hybridity between religious categories are much more prevalent than the drive for purification. Religious practices tend to resist rigid classification and instead are most often characterized by improvisation and bricolage. However, the drive for purification does find strength elsewhere: in discourses surrounding Mongolian national purity and its bedfellow Sinophobia.

Nationalist narratives that emphasize purification are not directly linked to air pollution. Rather, along with religious practices and new forms of spirituality, they form a cluster of categories or assemblages, which feed each other through their collective anxieties and connected remedies. Like nationalism, religions in the capital dig deeply into shared memories, physical realities, and ritual practices. They are successful when they rise above morally framed misgivings, and can be easily tainted by the strong pull of collective and individual uncertainty. Though concerns about religious ignorance are generative of religious rituals and specialists, discussions of ignorance can besmirch the prestige of religious specialists also. Anxieties about fiscal motivations for many urbanites color interactions with the Mongolian saṅgha and make it difficult for local temples and individuals to support themselves without pursuing more financially lucrative ritual practices. In a country where having money is linked to karmic and spiritual success, religious specialists must somehow be financially stable without directly asking for money.

Mongolia's entry into a global market place, the ways that wealth flows from a problematic extraction economy, and the unequal distribution of capital have caused the light in the city to dim. Those less well-off must directly burn fuel to survive the harsh winters, causing the air to become thick with smog. Unlike the other hardships that accompany poverty in the city, both rich and poor must live with the toxicity of the seasonal winter smog. Ideas of enlightenment, as generating clarity in dimness, provide a palette for reading the vicissitudes of a city. Pollution, spilling from the air and the soil, stains the dominating fiction of modern times: far from universally fungible, money becomes bespoiled and bespoiling, to be rendered clean again through ritual or palmed as quickly as possible from one's hand. Capitalism, an uncertain economy, and growing inequalities have created the conditions that have caused the skies to be blackened with soot.

The metaphors and practices that people use to try to mitigate, disconnect from, or justify unbreathable air request of us an effort at broader understanding. What can we learn from these metaphors about chronic environmental problems in the Anthropocene and the inactions and actions that sustain them? How do religious metaphors and practices interact with other comprehensions of this increasingly, alarmingly common condition?

The acrid air instantiates broader anxieties about corruption and moral decline. Air pollution in the capital has worsened with economic changes and the growth of a new kind of political and business elite. As the skies have become fuzzy with smog, inequalities have become more visible, compounding the sense that Ulaanbaatar is imbued with spiritual and moral decline and that this decline literally hangs over the city. Corruption, through widening inequalities and skimming money from projects needed to reduce urban migration, worsens the air pollution. It is a source of inaction, blocking efforts to transform the city.

For Mongols the air that hangs thickly over the city during the winter months indicates stagnation and obscuration. Just as invisible blockages are thought to linger and obstruct one's fortune, so the city air stagnates. For some this air is caused by polluted minds and ill intentions. For others it is simply a condition of ignorance that, like the globalized economy, is something that the urban population cannot see their way around or through. For all it is a physical reality for most of the year, shortening the length and quality of the lives of those that breathe it.

The Mongolian notion of khiimori, with its connection to movement, vitality, and good fortune, is a call to arms. The energies of the steed, with its dynamism as it catches the wind, have the power to reenergize that which lies dull. Having khiimori is apparent in the movements of nomads. In an urban environment, where one no longer moves across the open steppe lands, khiimori is being reimagined. Just as urban Mongols visit temples to remove obstacles to purify, to energize, and to lighten, so might blockages to generating political will to change the trajectory of the city be removed, through vigorous movements. The blanket of air hanging thickly over the city is there because the spirit of vitality, that which moves and revives, has been dampened. The notions and practices surrounding khiimori suggest that life needs recurrent invigorating.

As urbanites struggle to make sense of their untenable seasonal condition they interact with old ideas and new challenges. Buddhist doctrine already contains a metaphorically rich lexicon describing the obscuration of light. Within its doctrine and practices Buddhist students learn to feel their interconnections through the air, highlighting their interdependence. Rituals at local temples call for obstructions to be removed. The notion of khiimori among Buddhists and non-Buddhists advocates the urgency of resisting malaise and inaction.

Alongside the image of the wind horse's unbridled energy, it is fitting to place here one of the most highly regarded images in Buddhism, that of the lotus. In Zanabazar's famous sculptural depiction of Green Tārā, found today in the Bogd Khan Winter Palace Museum, she carries in her left hand the stem of an open lotus, while her right leg is forward, grounded upon another floating lotus, indicating that she is ready for immediate compassionate action. Compassion is not a quiescent quality for Tārā, despite her serene and otherworldly demeanor compassion is the power and realization of enlightenment. This lotus is a beautiful flower that grows out of murky waters, and perhaps too in murky air.

There are many forces that divide human experience. Our breath connects us. Even in this smothering air the seed of enlightenment.

GLOSSARY

aimag: an administrative unit, or province, of Mongolia, of which there are currently twenty-one.

Avalokiteśvara (Sans.; Mon., Janraisig): the Bodhisattva of compassion.

bodhicitta (Sans.; Mong., bodi setgel): the motivation to attain enlightenment for the benefit of all beings.

Bodhisattva (Sans.; Mong., Bodsadvaa): beings that indeterminately delay complete enlightenment in order to help others to be free from suffering and the endless rebirths.

Bogd Gegeen: Eighth reincarnation of the Javzandamba lineage (see below).

Bogd Tsongkhapa (Tib., Tsong kha pa): a Tibetan teacher whose teachings led to the foundation of the Gelug school.

burkhan: can refer to the Buddha, buddhas, a monotheistic god, or polytheistic deities.

Cakravartin (Sans.): the wheel-turning king, a ruler who protects the dharma and Buddhist religious institutions.

dāna (Sans.): the act of freely giving alms within Buddhist, Jain, and Hindu philosophical systems.

deel: a piece of traditional clothing in the shape of a tunic commonly worn by both men and women.

dharma: natural law, the teachings of the Buddha.

Dharma Center: non-monastic Buddhist community centers that teach doctrinal and contemplative practices to laypeople.

ger: nomadic felt tent, frequently referred to as a "yurt" in English.

gegereel: enlightenment, a term used in the Buddhist sense and in the sense of the seventeenth-century European Enlightenment tradition. It is also used to mean educated.

gerel: light.

Green Tārā (Mong., Nogoon Dara Ekh): the Bodhisattva of immediate help and active compassion. She is often pictured as seated with one leg reaching down, symbolizing her readiness for assistance.

Javzandamba (Tib., Jetsun Dampa): a reincarnation lineage in Mongolia that follows the rebirth lineage of the seventeenth-century figure Zanabazar.

karma (Mong., üiliin ür): actions and their accompanying reactions.

khadag: a silk prayer scarf, sometimes imprinted with the eight auspicious symbols. These are generally either sky blue, yellow, white, red, or green.

Khalkha: the main ethnic group living in Mongolia.

khiid: temple.

khiimori: literally "wind horse," a type of energy that circulates inwardly but is affected by external factors.

khural: literally "meeting," including prayer meeting.

kleśa (Sans.; Mong., nisvaanis): the defilements of the mind and body that bring about suffering in the form of desire, anger, pride, ignorance, doubt, and holding wrong views in Buddhist philosophy.

Maitreya (Sans.; Mong., Maidar): the coming Buddha.

mantra: a sound or series of sounds and words that are repeated for ritual and soteriological efficacy.

Medicine Buddha (Mong., Manal): a Buddha who is considered to be a powerful antidote for physical and mental illness.

Mongol bichig: the traditional vertical Mongol script that was replaced by Cyrillic in 1941.

ovoo: sacred rock cairn.

pūjā (Sans.; Mong., takhil): ritualized offerings made in the form of food, flowers, and chanting.

Rinpoche (Mong., Khutagt; Tib., Rin po che): an honorific title meaning "Precious One" given to high-ranking lamas.

saṃsāra (Sans.; Mong., orchlon): the eternal cycles of rebirth in Buddhist and Hindu philosophical systems.

saṅgha (Sans.; Mong., khuvrag): the monastic community of robed religious specialists.

stūpa (Sans.; Mong., suvarga): a dome-shaped or mound-like built structure used for circumambulation and prayer.

sūtra (Sans.; Mong., sudar): Buddhist scriptures, prayers.

Tārā (Mong., Dara Ekh): the female Bodhisattva of compassion who is said to have been born out of the teardrops of Avalokiteśvara.

thang ka: silk painting or appliqué depicting Buddhist religious iconography.

tögrög: Mongolian currency.

Tsagaan Sar: the Mongol Lunar New Year.

Vajrapāṇi (Sans.; Mong., Ochirvaani): a ferocious-looking symbol of power within tantric Buddhism that is believed to protect the Buddhist teachings.

Vajrasattva (Mong., Ochir Cetgelt Baatar): a Bodhisattva associated with purification.

Vajrayāna Buddhism: sometimes known as the "thunderbolt school," the school of Buddhism that uses tantric and esoteric practices to blaze a "quick path" toward enlightenment.

Vinaya: monastic vows that date back to the time of the Buddha.

Zanabazar: First incarnation of the Javzandamba lineage, well known in Mongolia for his remarkable sculptures and his Soyombo script, a part of which forms the basis of the Mongolian flag.

zud: a harsh winter, which usually follows a summer drought, characterized by heavy snowfall or other conditions that make it difficult for herding animals to graze.

NOTES

Introduction

1. A harsh winter, which usually follows a summer drought, that is characterized by very heavy snowfall or other conditions that make it difficult for herding animals to graze.

2. A non-monastic Buddhist education center that teaches Buddhist philosophy and transformative practices to laypeople.

3. *Sūtra* (Sans.) or *sudar* (Mong.) are Buddhist scriptures or prayers.

4. *Saṃsāra* (Sans.) or *orchlon* (Mong.) is the term for the eternal cycles of rebirth in Buddhist and Hindu religious systems.

5. Though it too had been ushered in with the profound uncertainties that characterized the 1930s and 1940s.

6. An *aimag* is an administrative unit (or province) of Mongolia, of which there are currently twenty-one.

7. *Pūjā*s (Sans.) or *takhil* (Mong.) are ritualized offerings made in the form of food, flowers, chanting, and bowing.

Chapter 1

1. The Mongolian currency.
2. A commonly worn silk piece of clothing, shaped like a long tunic.
3. A holiday camp made up of a group of gers, and possibly also small wooden houses, rented out by herders to urbanites and foreign tourists.
4. Ninja miners are artisanal miners not employed by the mining companies, and they get their name because their appearance (carrying a green plastic bucket on their backs) resembles the Teenage Mutant Ninja Turtles.

Chapter 2

1. Tibet is still referred to as *Tövd*, literally meaning "located at the center," in Mongolian.
2. The "wheel-turning king," one who protects Buddhism and allows it to flourish.
3. Vajrapāṇi (Sans.), Ochirvaani (Mong.), and Phyag na rdo rje (Tib.) is a ferocious-looking symbol of power within tantric Buddhism that is believed to protect the Buddhist teachings.
4. This narrative has weakened. In subsequent visits to Mongolia, Buddhist lamas increasingly linked Buddhism with earlier periods and empires. In 2016 two lamas told me that Buddhism's presence in the region dated back to over two thousand years ago to the Hunnu (Ch., Xiongnu) period (see chapter 3).
5. Natural law also refers to the teachings of Buddhism.
6. The female Bodhisattva of compassion (Mong., Dara Ekh; Tib., Dölma) who is said to have been born out of the teardrops of Avalokiteśvara.
7. His image was no longer present at the site in 2016.
8. Silk painting or applique depicting Buddhist religious iconography.
9. See also Blazer 2005; Hann and Pelkmans 2009; Papkova 2008; Peyrouse 2007; Wanner 1998.
10. Tib., Sa skya Paṇḍita Kun dga' rGyal mtshan.
11. Tib., Gro mgon Chos rgyal 'Phags pa.
12. Chin., *Guoshi*.
13. Tib., bSod nams rGya mtsho.
14. The main ethnic group living in Mongolia.
15. "Outer Mongolia" is often used to distinguish the country from "Inner Mongolia," a Mongolian cultural region in China.

Chapter 3

1. See also Blazer 2005; Hann and Pelkmans 2009; Papkova 2008; Peyrouse 2007; Wanner 1998.
2. Since my first visit to Mongolia from 2009 to 2010, both Christianity and shamanism have become more popular. Many Mongols believe that shamanism is the tradi-

tional religion of Mongolia at the exclusion of Buddhism (though these religions are by no means necessarily exclusive). Other reasons I heard for not taking on a Buddhist identity include membership to another religious group or ethnicity, strong opposition to the doctrine of karma, scepticism about the values of Buddhist lamas, and a belief that Buddhist doctrine leads to nihilism.

3. A museum that contains many of Zanabazar's famous Buddhist sculptures.

4. This statue is rumored to have later appeared in the center of a nightclub called Ismuus.

5. Tsongkhapa (Tib., *Tsong kha pa*) is the founder of the Gelug lineage. *Bogd* in Mongolian means "holy," "sacred," or "divine."

6. *Saṅgha* (Mong., *khuvrag*) is the monastic community of Buddhist monks/lamas and nuns/female lamas.

7. See chapter 9 and Thrift 2014, regarding fears of Chinese milk imports.

8. For a discussion of the use of exemplars in Mongolian morality, see Humphrey 1997.

Chapter 4

1. The Medicine Buddha (Mong., Manal; Tib., Sanjai Manla) is often depicted as an azure blue, seated figure with a medicine bowl in the left hand. This Buddha is frequently referred to as the "child's *burkhan*." This is probably a historical consequence of formerly high rates of infant mortality, as reading the mantra of the Medicine Buddha is believed to help oneself and others with mental and physical health problems.

Chapter 5

1. The temple that once housed Mongolia's state oracle. It was kept (and remains) as a museum during the socialist period.

2. Maitreya (Mong., Maidar) is the future Buddha who will teach Buddhism when the teachings of Buddha Śākyamuni, the current Buddha, have been forgotten. Historically, statues depicting Maitreya have been linked with state-making activities and Gelugpa dominance in the Mongolian cultural region (Tsultemin 2015).

3. And other religions: see also Luhrman 2012; Mahmood 2011; 2013.

4. Here she is probably referring to Mongolia's own secret police.

5. Bodhicitta (Mong., *bodi setgel*) is the motivation to attain enlightenment for the benefit of all sentient beings.

6. Green Tārā is the Bodhisattva of immediate help and active compassion. She is often pictured as seated with one leg reaching down, symbolizing her readiness for assistance.

Chapter 6

1. Excepting the instantiated reverence of Chinggis Khan and the many *ovoos* that have adorned the city's adjacent mountaintops since the early 1990s.

2. Practices involving Vajrasattva (Mong., Ochir Cetgelt Baatar; Tib., rDo rje Sems dpa') are associated with purification.

3. Descriptions of karma in Mongolia tend to use agricultural metaphors of seeds, of ripening, and of fruit, as a result of translations of texts from Sanskrit.

Chapter 7

1. An *ochir* (Mong.) (Sans., *vajra*) is a ritual object representing a thunderbolt and adamantine insight.

Chapter 8

1. This idea that European countries give a tithe to churches that is collected as tax revenue from the populace probably comes from Mongolia's ties with Germany, where a portion of a person's taxes (if they identity as Christian) are paid to support the Christian church.

2. I have heard that it is common for friends and family members to financially assist shamans, so they can pay for expensive rituals, and some also provide them with direct support so that they can spend more time channeling the family's ancestral spirits.

3. This is an interesting contrast to some Thai Theravāda lay Buddhists who prefer to give to young lamas who have not yet been exposed to corrupt practices (see Cook 2010).

Chapter 9

1. See chapter 5 regarding the south-facing orientations of temples and gers.

2. This is probably due to the general atmosphere of Sinophobia that pervades the country (see chapter 3).

3. This quite literally does clear the digestive system if drunk in large quantities.

REFERENCES

Abrahms-Kavunenko, Saskia. 2016. "Spiritually Enmeshed, Socially Enmeshed: Shamanism and Belonging in Ulaanbaatar." *Social Analysis* 60 (3): 1–16.

———. 2015. "Paying for Prayers: Perspectives on Giving in Postsocialist Ulaanbaatar." *Religion, State and Society* 43 (4): 327–341.

———. 2012. "Religious 'Revival' after Socialism? Eclecticism and Globalisation amongst Lay Buddhists in Ulaanbaatar." *Inner Asia* 14 (2): 279–297.

Ahmed, Saiyada. 2003. "Carya Nrtya of Nepal: When 'Becoming the Character' in Asian Performance Is Nonduality in 'Quintessence of Void.'" *The Drama Review* 47 (3): 159–182.

Ananda Marga Pracaraka Samgha. 2006. "History of Ananda Marga." Accessed April 30, 2011: http://www.anandamarga.org/history.htm.

Anderson, Benedict. 1983. *Imagined Communities: Reflections on the Origins and Spread of Nationalism*. London: Verso.

Amogolonova, Darima. 2015. "A Symbolic Person of Buddhist Revival in Buryatia." *Inner Asia* 17:225–242.

Appadurai, Arjun. 1996. *Modernity at Large: Cultural Dimensions of Globalization*. Minneapolis: University of Minnesota.

———. 1988. "Introduction: Commodities and the Politics of Value." In *The Social Life of Things: Commodities in Cultural Perspective*, edited by Arjun Appadurai, 3–63. Cambridge: Cambridge University Press.

Arntz, William, Betsy Chasse, and Mark Vicente. 2005. *What the Bleep Do We Know!? Discovering the Endless Possibilities for Altering Your Everyday Reality.* Deerfield Beach, FL: Health Communications.

Atwood, Christopher. 1996. "Buddhism and Popular Ritual in Mongolian Religion: A Reexamination of the Fire Cult." *History of Religions* 36 (2): 112–139.

Balzer, Majorie. 2005. "Whose Steeple Is Higher? Religious Competition in Siberia." *Religion, State and Society* 33 (1): 57–69.

Batbayar, Tsendendamba. 2002. "Geopolitics and Mongolia's Search for Post-Soviet Identity." *Eurasia Geography and Economics* 43 (4): 323–335.

Bautista, Julia., ed. 2012. *The Spirit of Things: Materiality and Religious Diversity in Southeast Asia.* Ithaca, NY: Cornell University Press.

Bawden, Charles. 1997. *Mongolia-English Dictionary.* London: Kegan Paul International.

———. 1968. *The Modern History of Mongolia.* London: Weidenfeld and Nicolson.

BBC News. 2016. "Polluted Air Affects 92% of the World's Population, Says WHO." Accessed October 3, 2016: http://www.bbc.com/news/health-37483616.

Benwell, Anne. F. 2013. "Making Migration Meaningful: Achievements through Separation in Mongolia." *Norwegian Journal of Geography* 67 (4): 239–248.

Berliner, David. 2005. "An 'Impossible' Transmission: Youth Religious Memories in Guinea-Conakry." *American Ethnologist* 32 (4): 576–592.

Bernstein, Anya. 2013. *Religious Bodies Politic: Rituals of Sovereignty in Buryat Buddhism.* Chicago: University of Chicago Press.

Billé, Franck. 2015. *Sinophobia: Anxiety, Violence and the Making of Mongolian Identity.* Honolulu: University of Hawai'i Press.

Bonilla, Lauren. 2016. "Internalizing External Debt." *UCL Emerging Subjects Blog*, February 24. Accessed July 1, 2016: http://blogs.ucl.ac.uk/mongolian-economy/2016/02/24/internalizing-external-debt/.

Bourdieu, Pierre. 1977. *Outline of a Theory of Practice.* Cambridge: Cambridge University Press.

Bulag, Uradyn E. 1998. *Nationalism and Hybridity in Mongolia.* Oxford: Clarendon Press.

Buyandelger, Manduhai. 2013. *Tragic Spirits: Shamanism, Memory, and Gender in Contemporary Mongolia.* Chicago: University of Chicago Press

———. 2008. "Post-Post-Transition Theories: Walking on Multiple Paths." *Annual Review of Anthropology* 37:235–250.

———. 2007. "Dealing with Uncertainty: Shamans, Marginal Capitalism and the Remaking of History in Postsocialist Mongolia." *American Ethnologist* 34 (1): 127–147.

Bruun, Ole, and Li Narangoa. 2006. "A New Moment in Mongolian History: The Rise of the Cosmopolitan City." In *Mongols from Country to City: Floating Boundaries, Pastoralism and City Life in the Mongol Lands*, edited by Ole Bruun and Li Narangoa, 1–20. Copenhagen: NIAS Press.

Byrne, Rhonda. 2006. *The Secret.* London: Atria Books.

Campi, Alicia. 2012. "The Dalai Lama Card Reappears in Sino-Mongolian Relations." *China Brief Volume* 12 (5): 5–8.

——. 2006. "The Rise of Cities in Nomadic Mongolia." In *Mongols from Country to City: Floating Boundaries, Pastoralism and City Life in the Mongol Lands*, edited by Ole Bruun and Li Narangoa, 21–59. Copenhagen: NIAS Press.

Caple, Jane. 2015. "Faith, Generosity, Knowledge and the Buddhist Gift: Moral Discourses on Chinese Patronage of Tibetan Buddhist Monasteries." *Religion Compass* 9 (11): 462–482.

——. 2010. "Monastic Economic Reform at Rong-bo Monastery: Towards an Understanding of Contemporary Tibetan Monastic Revival and Development in A-mdo." *Buddhist Studies Review* 27 (2): 197–219.

Carlisle, Steven. 2008. "Synchronizing Karma: The Internalisation and Externalisation of a Shared Personal Belief." *Ethos* 36 (2): 194–219.

Carrithers, Michael. 2000. "On Polytropy; or, the Natural Condition of Spiritual Cosmopolitanism in India: The Digambar Jain Case." *Modern Asian Studies* 34 (4): 831–861.

Cassaniti, Julia. 2006. "Toward a Cultural Psychology of Impermanence in Thailand." *Ethnos* 34 (1): 58–88.

Chien-Yu, Julia, and Robert Weller. 1998. "Merit and Mothering: Women and Social Welfare in Taiwanese Buddhism." *The Journal of Asian Studies* 57 (2): 379–396.

Chuluundorj, Khashchuluun, and Danzanbaljir Enkhjargal. 2014. "Financing Mongolia's Mineral Growth." *Inner Asia* 16 (2): 275–300.

Cook, Joanna. 2010. *Meditation in Modern Buddhism: Renunciation and Change in Thai Monastic Life*. Cambridge: Cambridge University Press.

Covell, Steven. 2008. *Japanese Temple Buddhism: Worldliness in a Religion of Renunciation*. Honolulu: University of Hawai'i Press.

Dalby, Simon. 2016. "Framing the Anthropocene: The Good, the Bad and the Ugly." *The Anthropocene Review* 3 (1): 33–51.

Damba, Galsandorj. 2014. "Mongolian Mineral Products and Issues of International Trade." *Inner Asia* 16 (2): 301–313.

Darlington, Susan. 2007. "The Good Buddha and the Fierce Spirits: Protecting the Northern Thai Forest." *Contemporary Buddhism* 8 (2): 169–185.

DeLanda, Manuel. 2016. *Assemblage Theory*. Edinburgh: Edinburgh University Press.

Delaplace, Gregory. 2012. "Parasitic Chinese, Vengeful Russians: Ghosts, Strangers and Reciprocity in Mongolia." *Journal of the Royal Anthropological Institute* 18 (S1): 131–144.

——. 2010. "Chinese Ghosts in Mongolia." *Inner Asia* 12 (1): 127–141.

Dragadze, Tamara. 1993. "The Domestication of Religion under Soviet Communism." In *Socialism: Ideals, Ideologies and Local Practice*, edited by Chris Hann, 141–151. London: Routledge.

Durkheim, Émile. [1912] 1957. *The Elementary Forms of Religious Life*. London: Allen & Unwin.

Elverskog, Johan. 2008. *Our Great Qing: The Mongols, Buddhism and the State in Late Imperial China*. Honolulu: University of Hawai'i Press.

——. 2007. "Tibetocentrism, Religious Conversion and the Study of Mongolian Buddhism." In *The Mongolia-Tibet Interface: Opening New Research Terrains in*

Inner Asia, edited by Uradyn Bulag and Hildergard Diemberger, 59–80. Leiden, UK: Brill.

———. 2000. *Buddhism, History and Power: The Jewel Translucent Sutra and the Formation of Mongol Identity*. PhD diss., Department of Central Eurasian Studies, Indiana University.

Empson, Rebecca. 2016a. "Chains of Debt: Accessing 'Ready Cash' through 'Material Loans." *Emerging Subjects Blog*, January 13. Accessed July 23, 2016: http://blogs.ucl.ac.uk/mongolian-economy/2016/01/13/chains-of-debt-accessing-ready-cash-through-material-loans/.

———. 2016b. "Archive for the 'Tsagaan Sar Gift Index' Category." *Emerging Subjects Blog*. Accessed August 15, 2017: http://blogs.ucl.ac.uk/mongolian-economy/category/blog-series/tsagaan-sar-gift-index/.

———. 2012. "The Dangers of Excess: Accumulating and Dispersing Fortune in Mongolia." *Social Analysis* 56 (1): 117–132.

———. 2011. *Harnessing Fortune: Personhood, Memory and Place in Mongolia*. Oxford: Oxford University Press.

Enkhmaa, D., N. Warburton, B. Javzandulam, J. Uyanga, Y. Khishigsuren, S. Lodoysamba, S. Enkhtur, and D. Warburton. 2014. "Seasonal Ambient Air Pollution Correlates Strongly with Spontaneous Abortion in Mongolia." *BMC Pregnancy and Childbirth* 14 (1): 146–152.

Evans-Pritchard, E. E. 1937. *Witchcraft, Oracles and Magic among the Azande*. Oxford: Clarendon Press.

Even, Marie-Dominique. 2012. "Ritual Efficacy or Spiritual Quest? Buddhism and Modernity in Post-Communist Mongolia." In *Revisiting Rituals in a Changing Tibetan World*, edited by Katia Buffetrille, 241–271. Leiden, UK: Brill.

———. 2011. "Ups and Downs of the Divine: Religion and Revolution in 20th Century Mongolia." In *Proceedings of the Third International Symposium "The Book. Romania. Europa,"* edited by A. Berciu, R. Pop, and J. Rotaru, 627–644. Bucharest: Bibliothèque Métropolitaine de Bucarest.

Fisher, Gareth. 2008. "The Spiritual Land Rush: Merit and Morality in New Chinese Buddhist Temple Construction." *The Journal of Asian Studies* 67 (1): 143–170.

Flora, Jane. 2012. "'I Don't Know Why He Did It. It Just Happened by Itself': Causality and Suicide in Northwest Greenland." In *The Anthropology of Ignorance: An Ethnographic Approach*, edited by Casey High, Ann Kelly, and Jonathan Mair, 137–161. New York: Palgrave Macmillan.

Foucault, Michel. 1978. *The History of Sexuality, Volume 1*. London: Penguin Books.

Froese, Paul. 2001. "Hungary for Religion: A Supply-Side Interpretation of the Hungarian Religious Revival." *Journal for the Scientific Study of Religion* 40 (2): 251–268.

Fukuda, Chisato. 2017. "A Fight to Breathe." *Medical Anthropology Quarterly*, March 29. Accessed December 3, 2017: http://medanthroquarterly.org/2017/03/29/a-fight-to-breathe/.

Geary, David. 2008. "Destination Enlightenment: Branding Buddhism and Spiritual Tourism in Bodhgaya, Bihar." *Anthropology Today* 24 (3): 11–14.

Gershon, I., and D. Raj. 2000. "Introduction: The Symbolic Capital of Ignorance." *Social Analysis* 44 (2): 3–14.

Goluboff, Sascha. 2001. "Fistfights at the Moscow Choral Synagogue: Ethnicity and Ritual in Post-Soviet Russia." *Anthropological Quarterly* 74 (2): 55–71.

Gombrich, Richard. 1971. "'Merit Transference' in Sinhalese Buddhism: A Case Study of the Interaction between Doctrine and Practice." *History of Religions* 11 (2): 203–219.

Gombrich, Richard, and Gananath Obeyesekere. 1988. *Buddhism Transformed: Religious Change in Sri Lanka*. Princeton, NJ: Princeton University Press.

Gravers, Michael. 2012. "Monks, Morality and Military: The Struggle for Moral Power in Burma—and Buddhism's Uneasy Relationship with Lay Power." *Contemporary Buddhism: An Interdisciplinary Journal* 13 (1): 1–33.

Gutschow, Kim. 2004. *Being a Buddhist Nun: The Struggle for Enlightenment in the Himalayas*. Cambridge, MA: Harvard University Press.

Guttikunda, Sarath, Sereeter Lodoysamba, Baldorg Bulgansaikhan, and Batdorj Dashdondog. 2013. "Particulate Pollution in Ulaanbaatar, Mongolia." *Air Quality, Atmosphere and Health* 6 (3): 589–601.

Guyer, Jane. 1995. "The Currency Interface and Its Dynamics." In *Money Matters: Instability, Values and Social Payments in the Modern History of West African Communities*, edited by Jane Guyer, 1–33. Portsmouth, NH: Heinemann.

Hamilton, Kitty. 2011. "Coal Stoves Coat Mongolian Capital in Smog." *UB Post*, February 8.

Hann, Chris, and Matthijs Pelkmans. 2009. "Realigning Religion and Power in Central Asia: Islam, Nation-State and (Post)Socialism." *Europe-Asia Studies* 61 (9): 1517–1541.

Haraway, Donna. 2016. *Staying with the Trouble: Making Kin in the Chthulucene*. London: Duke University Press.

Havnevik, Hanna. 2015. "Female Temple Founders, Ritualists, and Clairvoyants in Post-Socialist Mongolian Buddhism." *Revue d'Etudes Tibétaines* 34:35–52.

Havnevik, H., B. Ragchaa, and A. Bareja-Starzynska. 2007 "Some Practices of the Buddhist Red Tradition in Contemporary Mongolia." In *The Mongolia-Tibet Interface: Opening New Research Terrains in Inner Asia*, edited by U. Bulag and H. Diemberger, 223–237. Leiden, UK: Brill.

Hayashi-Smith, M. 2011. "Contesting Buddhisms on Conflicted Land: Sarvodaya Shramadana and Buddhist Peacemaking." *Journal of Sociology and Social Welfare* 38 (2): 159–180.

Heim, Maria. 2004. *Theories of the Gift in South Asia: Hindu, Buddhist, and Jain Reflections on Dāna*. New York: Routledge.

———. 2003. "The Aesthetics of Excess." *Journal of the American Academy of Religion* 71 (3): 531–554.

Heissig, Walther. 1980. *The Religions of Mongolia*. London: Routledge & Keegan Paul.

Henare, Amiria, Martin Holbraad, and Sari Wastell, eds. 2007. *Thinking Through Things: Theorising Artefacts Ethnographically*. New York: Routledge.

High, Casey. 2012. "Between Knowing and Being: Ignorance in Anthropology and Amazonian Shamanism." In *The Anthropology of Ignorance: An Ethnographic Approach*, edited by Casey High, Ann Kelly, and Jonathan Mair, 119–135. New York: Palgrave Macmillan.

High, Casey, Ann Kelly, and Jonathan Mair. 2012. "Introduction: Making Ignorance an Ethnographic Object." In *The Anthropology of Ignorance: An Ethnographic Approach*, edited by Casey High, Ann Kelly, and Jonathan Mair, 1–32. New York: Palgrave Macmillan.

High, Mette. 2013. "Polluted Money, Polluted Wealth: Emerging Regimes of Value in the Mongolian Gold Rush." *American Ethnologist* 40 (4): 676–688.

High, Mette, and Jonathan Schlesinger. 2010. "Rulers and Rascals: The Politics of Gold in Mongolian Qing History." *Central Asian Survey* 29 (3): 289–304.

Hobsbawm, E. J. 1990. *Nations and Nationalism since 1780: Programme, Myth and Reality.* Cambridge: Cambridge University Press.

Højbjerg, Christian. 2002. "Inner Iconoclasm: Forms of Reflexivity in Loma Rituals of Sacrifice." *Social Anthropology* 10 (1): 57–75.

Højer, Lars. 2012. "The Spirit of Business: Pawnshops in Ulaanbaatar." *Social Anthropology* 20 (1): 34–49.

———. 2009. "Absent Powers: Magic and Loss in Post-Socialist Mongolia." *Journal of the Royal Anthropological Institute* 15:575–591.

Højer, Lars, and Morton Pedersen. 2008. "Lost in Transition: Fuzzy Property and Leaky Selves in Ulaanbaatar." *Ethnos* 73 (1): 73–96.

Huang, C-Y., and R. Weller. 1998. "Merit and Mothering: Women and Social Welfare in Taiwanese Buddhism." *The Journal of Asian Studies* 57 (2): 379–396.

Humphrey, Caroline. 2007. "Inside and outside the Mirror: Mongolian Shamans' Mirrors as Instruments of Perspectivism." *Inner Asia* 9 (2): 173–196.

———. 2002. "Rituals of Death as a Context for Understanding Personal Property in Socialist Mongolia." *Royal Anthropological Institute* 8:65–87.

———. 1997. "Exemplars and Rules: Aspects of the Discourse of Moralities in Mongolia." In *Ethnography of Moralities*, edited by Signe Howell, 25–48. London: Routledge.

———. 1993. "Avgai Khad: Theft and Social Trust in Post-Communist Mongolia." *Anthropology Today* 9 (6): 13–16.

———. 1992. "The Moral Authority of the Past in Post-Socialist Mongolia." *Religion, State and Society* 20 (3): 375–389.

Humphrey, Caroline, and Hürelbaatar Ujeed. 2013. *A Monastery in Time: The Making of Mongolian Buddhism.* Chicago: University of Chicago Press.

———. 2012. "Fortune in the Wind: An Impersonal Subjectivity." *Social Analysis* 56 (2): 152–167.

Hurcha, N. 1999. "Attempts to Buddhicise the Cult of Chinggis Khan." *Inner Asia* 1:45–57.

Ignacio Cabezón, José. 2006. "Tibetan Buddhist Society." In *The Oxford Handbook of Global Religions*, edited by Mark Juergensmeyer, 91–107. Oxford: Oxford University Press.

IPCC. 2014. *Climate Change 2014: Synthesis Report; Contribution of Working Groups I, II and III to the Fifth Assessment Report of the Intergovernmental Panel on Climate Change.* Edited by R. K. Pachauri and L. A. Meyer. Geneva: IPCC.

Isaacson, Rupert. 2009. *The Horse Boy: A Father's Quest to Heal His Son.* New York: Little Brown.

Jackson, Sarah. 2015. "Dusty Roads and Disconnections: Perceptions of Dust from Unpaved Mining Roads in Mongolia's South Gobi Province." *Geoform* 66: 94–105.

Jacob, P. 2011. "Ulaanbaatar Air Pollution Linked to Public Health Crisis." *UB Post*, March 22.

Jadamba, Lhavgademchig. 2018. "Double Headed Mongolian Buddhism." *CESS Blog*, February 28. Accessed March 27, 2018: http://thecessblog.com/2018/02/28/double -headed-mongolian-buddhism-by-lhagvademchig-j-shastri-visiting-researcher -university-of-shiga-prefecture/.

———. 2013. "Mongolian Buddhism: Identity, Practice and Politics." In *The Mongolian Collection: Retracing Hans Leder*, edited by M. Lang and S. Bauer, 25–35. Vienna: Austrian Academy of Sciences Press.

Jadamba, Lkhagvademchig, and Bernard Schittich. 2010. "Negotiating Self and Other: Transnational Cultural Flows and the Reinvention of Mongolian Buddhism." *Internationales Asienforum* 41 (1–2): 83–102.

Jampa Ling Tibetan Buddhist Centre, n.d. "Rinpoche: Venerable Panchen Ötrul Rinpoche." Accessed on April 23, 2012: http://www.jampaling.org/rinpoche.html.

Janes, Craig, and Oyuntsetseg Chuluundorj. 2015. *Making Disasters: Climate Change, Neoliberal Governance and Livelihood Insecurity on the Mongolian Steppe*. Sante Fe, NM: School for Advanced Research Press.

Jerryson, Michael. 2007. *Mongolian Buddhism: The Rise and Fall of the Sangha*. Chiang Mai, Thailand: Silkworm Books.

Kaplonski, Christopher. 2014. *The Lama Question: Violence, Sovereignty and Exception in Early Socialist Mongolia*. Honolulu: University of Hawai'i Press.

———. 2012. "Resorting to Violence: Technologies of Exception, Contingent States and the Repression of Buddhist Lamas in 1930s Mongolia." *Ethnos* 77 (1): 72–92.

———. 2008. "Neither Truth nor Reconciliation: Political Violence and the Singularity of Memory in Post-Socialist Mongolia." *Totalitarian Movements and Political Religions* 9 (2–3): 371–388.

———. 2004. *Truth, History and Politics in Mongolia: The Memories of Heroes*. London: RoutledgeCurzon.

Kollmar-Paulenz, Karénina. 2014. "The 'Light of the Dharma' against the 'Fog of Darkness': Tibetan Perceptions of the Mongolians and the Formation of a New Mongolian Buddhist Identity in the Early 17th Century." In *Religion and Ethnicity in Mongolian Societies: Historical and Contemporary Perspectives*, edited by Karénina Kollmar-Paulenz, S. Reinhardt, and T. Skrynnikova, 47–60. Wiesbaden: Harrassowitz Verlag.

Laidlaw, James. 2000. "A Free Gift Makes No Friends." *The Journal of the Royal Anthropological Institute* 6 (4): 617–634.

Latour, Bruno. 2014. "Agency at the Time of the Anthropocene." *New Literary History* 45 (1): 1–18.

———. 1991. *We Have Never Been Modern*. Cambridge, MA: Harvard University Press.

Lattimore, Owen. 1962. *Nomads and Commissars: Mongolia Revisited*. New York: Oxford University Press.

Lattimore, Owen, and F. Isono. 1982. *The Diluv Khutagt: Memoirs and Autobiography of a Mongol Buddhist Reincarnation in Religion and Revolution*. Wiesbaden: Otto Harrassowitz.

Lkhagvadorj, D., M. Hauck, C. Dulamsuren, and J. Tsogtbaatar. 2013. "Pastoral Nomadism in the Forest-Steppe of the Mongolian Altai under a Changing Economy and a Warming Climate." *Journal of Arid Environments* 88:82–89.

Lopez Jr., Donald. 1996. "'Lamaism' and the Disappearance of Tibet." *Comparative Studies in Society and History* 38 (1): 3–25.

Luhrmann, Tanya. 2012. *When God Talks Back: Understanding the American Evangelical Relationship with God.* New York: Vintage Books.

Mahmood, Saba. 2003. "Ethical Formation and Politics of Individual Autonomy in Contemporary Egypt." *Social Research* 70 (3): 837–866.

———. 2001. "Rehearsed Spontaneity and the Conventionality of Ritual: Disciplines of 'Salāt.'" *American Ethnologist* 28 (4): 827–853.

Mair, Jonathan. 2007. *Faith, Knowledge and Ignorance in Contemporary Inner Mongolian Buddhism.* PhD diss., Department of Social Anthropology, Cambridge University.

Majer, Zsuzsa. 2009. "Continuation or Disjuncture with the Past and the Tibetan Buddhist Tradition." *The Silk Road* 7 (Autumn): 52–63.

Majer, Zsuzsa, and Krisztina Teleki. 2009. "Buddhism in Mongolia Today: Introduction." *Silk Road* 7 (Autumn): 51.

———. 2008. "Survey of Active Temples in Ulaanbaatar in 2005–2006, with Some Annotations in 2007." Accessed October 16, 2010: http://www.mongoliantemples.net/en/index.php?option=com_content&view=article&id=50&Itemid=59.

Makley, Charlene. 2003. "Gendered Boundaries in Motion: Space and Identity on the Sino-Tibetan Frontier." *American Ethnologist* 30 (4): 597–619.

MARCC. 2009. *Mongolia: Assessment Report on Climate Change.* Published by the Ministry of Environment, Nature and Tourism, Mongolia, United Nations Environment Program and United Nations Development Program.

Marsh, Peter. 2009. *The Horse-Head Fiddle and the Cosmopolitan Reimagination of Tradition in Mongolia.* New York: Routledge.

Mauss, Marcel. 1954. *The Gift: Forms and Functions of Exchange in Archaic Societies.* Glencoe, IL: Free Press.

McGlade, C., and P. Ekins. 2015. "The Geographical Distribution of Fossil Fuels Unused When Limiting Global Warming to 2°C." *Nature* 517:187–190.

Miller, Daniel. 2005. "Materiality: An Introduction." In *Materiality*, edited by Daniel Miller, 1–50. Durham, NC: Duke University Press.

Mills, Martin. 2012. "Ritual as History in Tibetan Divine Kingship: Notes on the Myth of the Khotanese Monks." *History of Religions* 51 (3): 219–238.

———. 2003. *Identity, Ritual and State in Tibetan Buddhism: The Foundations of Authority in Gelukpa Monasticism.* London: RoutledgeCurzon.

Morton, Timothy. 2013. *Hyperobjects: Philosophy and Ecology after the End of the World.* Minneapolis: University of Minnesota Press.

Moses, Larry. 1977. *The Political Role of Mongolian Buddhism.* Bloomington, IN: Asia Studies Research Institute, Indiana University.

National Statistical Office of Mongolia. 2010. *Main Results of the 2010 Population and Housing Census of Mongolia.* Accessed May 27, 2012: http:www.toollog02010.mn/doc/Main%20results_20110615_to%20EZBH_for%20print.pdf.

Obeyesekere, Gananath. 2006. "Thinking Globally about Buddhism." In *The Oxford Handbook of Global Religions*, edited by Mark Juergensmeyer, 69–82. Oxford: Oxford University Press.

Odling-Smee, F. John, K. Laland, and M. Feldman. 2003. *Niche Construction: The Neglected Process in Evolution*. Princeton, NJ: Princeton University Press.

Olsen, Bjørnar, and Thora Pétursdóttir. 2016. "Unruly Heritage: Tracing Legacies in the Anthropocene." *Arkæologisk Forum* 35:38–45.

Papkova, Irina. 2008. "The Freezing of Historical Memory? The Post-Soviet Russian Orthodox Church and the Council of 1917." In *Religion, Morality, and Community in Post-Soviet Societies*, edited by Mark Steinberg and Catherine Wanner, 55–84. Bloomington: Indiana University Press.

Parry, Jonathan. 1986. "The Gift, the Indian Gift and the 'Indian Gift.'" *Man* 21 (3): 453–473.

Pedersen, Morton. 2016. "Debt as an Urban Chronotope in Mongolia." *Ethnos*. Accessed October 1, 2016: http://dx.doi.org/10.1080/00141844.2016.1192213.

——. 2012. "A Day in the Cadillac: The Work of Hope in Urban Mongolia." *Social Analysis* 56 (2): 136–151.

——. 2011. *Not Quite Shamans: Spirit Worlds and Political Lives in Northern Mongolia*. Ithaca, NY: Cornell University Press.

——. 2001. "Totemism, Animism and North Asian Indigenous Ontologies." *Journal of the Royal Anthropological Institute* 7 (3): 411–427.

Pedersen, Morton, and Mikkel Bunkenborg. 2012. "Roads That Separate: Sino-Mongolian Relations in the Inner Asian Desert." *Mobilities* 7 (4): 555–569.

Perl, Jeffrey. 2011. "Introduction: 'Abominable Clearness.'" *Common Knowledge* 17 (3): 441–449.

Peyrouse, Sébastien. 2007. "Islam in Central Asia: National Specificities and Postsoviet Globalisation." *Religion, State and Society* 35 (3): 245–260.

Pozdneyev, A. M. 1892. *Mongolia and the Mongols*. Bloomington: Indiana University Publications.

Pranke, Patrick. 2010. "On Saints and Wizards: Ideals of Human Perfection and Power in Contemporary Burmese Buddhism." *Journal of the International Association for Buddhist Studies* 33 (1–2): 453–488.

Proctor, Robert. 2008. "Agnotology: A Missing Term to Describe the Cultural Production of Ignorance (and Its Study)." In *Agnotology: The Making and Unmaking of Ignorance*, edited by Robert Proctor and Londa Schiebinger, 1–36. Stanford, CA: Stanford University Press.

Reeves, Jeffrey. 2011. "Resources, Sovereignty and Governance: Can Mongolia Avoid the 'Resource Curse'?" *Asian Journal of Political Science* 19 (2): 170–185.

Reynolds, G. 2016. "Tugrik Slump 22-Day Slump to Record Low Marks Crisis: Chart." *Bloomburg Markets*. Accessed November 22, 2017: https://www.bloomberg.com/news/articles/2016-08-16/tugrik-s-22-day-slump-to-record-low-marks-mongolia-crisis-chart.

Rosaldo, Michelle. 1980. *Knowledge and Passion: Ilongot Notions of Self and Social Life*. Cambridge: Cambridge University Press.

Rossabi, Morris. 2005. *Modern Mongolia: From Khans to Commissars to Capitalists*. Berkeley: University of California Press.

——. 1988. *Khubilai Khan: His Life and Times*. Berkeley: University of California Press.

Ryan, A., E. Gombojav, B. Baldorj, B. Tsogtbaatar, L. Oyuntogos, A. Ofer, T. Takaro, and C. Janes. 2013. "An Assessment of Air Pollution and Its Attributable Mortality in Ulaanbaatar, Mongolia." *Air Qual Atmos Health* 6:137–150.

Safi, Michael. 2016. "Indian Government Declares Delhi Air Pollution an Emergency." *The Guardian*. Accessed March 13, 2017: https://www.theguardian.com/world/2016/nov/06/delhi-air-pollution-closes-schools-for-three-days.

Sagaster, Klaus. 2007. "The History of Buddhism among the Mongols." In *The Spread of Buddhism*, edited by Ann Heirman and Stephan Bumbacher, 379–432. Boston: Brill.

Samuels, Jeffrey. 2007. "Monastic Patronage and Temple Building in Contemporary Sri Lanka: Caste, Ritual, Performance, and Merit." *Modern Asian Studies* 41 (4): 769–795.

Śāntideva. 1997. *A Guide to the Bodhisattva Way of Life (Bodhicaryāvatāra)*. New York: Snow Lion Publications.

Sihlé, Nicholas. 2015. "Towards a Comparative Anthropology of the Buddhist Gift (and Other Transfers)." *Religion Compass* 9 (11): 352–385.

Smyer Yü, Dan. 2012. *The Spread of Tibetan Buddhism in China: Charisma, Money and Enlightenment*. New York: Routledge.

Sneath, David. 2014. "Nationalising Civilisational Resources: Sacred Mountains and Cosmopolitical Ritual in Mongolia." *Asian Ethnicity* 15 (4): 458–472.

——. 2009. "Reading the Signs by Lenin's Light: Development, Divination and Metonymic Fields in Mongolia." *Ethnos* 74 (1): 72–90.

——. 2006. "Transacting and Enacting: Corruption, Obligation and the Use of Monies in Mongolia." *Ethnos* 71 (1): 89–112.

——. 2002. "Mongolia in the 'Age of the Market': Pastoral Land-Use and the Development Discourse." In *Markets and Moralities: Ethnographies of Postsocialism*, edited by Ruth Mandel Caroline Humphrey, 191–210. Oxford: Berg.

——. 1998. "State Policy and Pasture Degradation in Inner Asia." *Science* 281 (5380): 1147–1148.

——. 1994. "The Impact of the Cultural Revolution in China on the Mongolians of Inner Mongolia." *Modern Asian Studies* 28 (2): 409–430.

Southwold, Martin. 1978. "Buddhism and the Definition of Religion." *Man* 13 (3): 362–379.

Spiro, M. 1982. *Buddhism and Society: A Great Tradition and Its Burmese Vicissitudes*. Berkeley: University of California Press.

Supreme Master Ching Hai International Association. 2009. *News no. 202*. Accessed April 5, 2011: http://www.godsdirectcontact.org.tw/eng/news/202/.

——. n.d.a. *A Brief Biography of the Supreme Master Ching Hai*. Accessed April 3, 2011: http://www.godsdirectcontact.org/eng/article/chinghai.html.

——. n.d.b. *The Quan Yin Method*. Accessed April 3, 2011: http://www.godsdirectcontact.org/eng/quanyin.html.

Swancutt, Katherine. 2012. *The Fortune and the Cursed: The Sliding Scale of Time and Mongolian Divination*. New York and Oxford: Berghahn Books.

Tambiah, Stanley. 1970. *Buddhism and the Spirit Cults in North-East Thailand*. London: Cambridge University Press.

Teleki, Krisztina. 2009. "Building on Ruins, Memories and Persistence: Revival and Survival of Buddhism in the Mongolian Countryside." *The Silk Road* 7 (Autumn): 64–73.

Thrift, E. 2014. "'Pure Milk': Dairy Production and the Discourse of Purity in Mongolia." *Asian Ethnicity* 15 (4): 492–513.

Tiezzi, S. 2015. "Red Alert: Beijing Warns of Heavy Air Pollution." *The Diplomat*, December 8. Accessed August 15, 2016: http://thediplomat.com/2015/12/red-alert -beijing-warns-of-heavy-air-pollution/.

Tsong-kha-pa. 2000. *The Great Treatise on the Stages of the Path to Enlightenment: Lam Rim Chen Mo*, vol. 1, translated by the Lam Rim Chenmo Translation Committee. Ithaca, NY: Snow Lion Publications.

Tsultemin, Uranchimeg. 2015. "The Power and Authority of Maitreya in Mongolia Examined Through Mongolian Art." In *Buddhism in Mongolian History, Culture and Society*, edited by Vesna Wallace, 137–159. Oxford: Oxford University Press.

Tumursukh, Undarya. 2001. "Fighting Over the Reinterpretation of the Mongolian Woman in Mongolia's Post-Socialist Identity Construction Discourse." *East Asia: An International Quarterly* 19 (3): 119–146.

Ujeed, Uranchimeg. 2011. "Persecuted Practice: Neichi Toyin's Way of Conducting Missionary Work." *Inner Asia* 13:265–277.

UNDP Mongolia. 2016. "About Mongolia." Accessed on May 2, 2016: http://www.mn .undp.org/content/mongolia/en/home/countryinfo/.

——. 2010. *New Horizons: The Newsletter of the United Nations in Mongolia.* Accessed June 5, 2010: http://www.un-mongolia.mn.

——. 2009. *Third National Report Summary: The Millennium Development Goals Implementation.* Ulaanbaatar: National Development and Innovation Committee.

Vanchikova, T. 2014. "The Modern Religious Situation in Mongolia: Tradition and Innovation Processes." In *Religion and Ethnicity in Mongolian Societies: Historical and Contemporary Perspectives*, edited by K. Kollmar-Paulenz, S. Reinhardt, and T. Skrynnikova, 167–176. Wiesbaden: Harrassowitz Verlag.

Vidal, J. 2016. "Air Pollution in Africa More Deadly Than Malnutrition or Water, Study Warns." *The Guardian*. Accessed November 15, 2016: https://www.theguardian.com /global-development/2016/oct/20/air-pollution-deadlier-africa-than-dirty-water-or -malnutrition-oecd.

Wallace, Vesna. 2018. "The Interface of Mongolian Nomadic Culture, Law and Monastic Sexual Morality." *Buddhism, Law, and Society* 2:57–75.

——. 2015. "Competing Religious Conversions and Re-conversions in Contemporary Mongolia." In *Conversion in Late Antiquity: Christianity, Islam, and Beyond*, edited by A. Papaconstantinou, N. McLynn, and D. Schwartz, 49–65. London: Routledge.

Wanner, Catherine. 1998. *Burden of Dreams: History and Identity in Post-Soviet Ukraine.* Pennsylvania: Pennsylvania State University Press.

Wild, Martin. 2016. "Decadal Changes in Radiative Fluxes at Land and Ocean Surfaces and Their Consequences for Global Warming." *Wiley Interdisciplinary Reviews: Climate Change* 7 (1): 91–107.

Williams, Jerry, Dorothy Albright, Anja A. Hoffman, Andrey Eritsov, Peter F. Moore, Jose Carlos Mendes de Morais, Michael Leonard, Jesus San Miguel-Ayanz, Gavriil

Xanthopoulos, and Pieter van Lierop. 2011. "Findings and Implications from a Coarse-Scale Global Assessment of Recent Selected Mega-Fires." *Fifth International Wildland Fire Conference*. Sun City, South Africa.

Willsher, Kim. 2017. "Paris Vehicle Sticker Scheme Comes into Force." *The Guardian*, January 16. Accessed March 13, 2017: https://www.theguardian.com/world/2017/jan/16/paris-vehicle-pollution-sticker-scheme-comes-into-force.

World Bank. 2015. *Land Administration and Management in Ulaanbaatar, Mongolia*. Washington, DC: World Bank.

Wylie, Turrell. 2003. "The First Mongol Conquest of Tibet Reinterpreted." In *The History of Tibet: The Medieval Period, c. 850–1895: The Development of Buddhist Paramountcy*, edited by Alex McKay, 317–337. London: RoutledgeCurzon.

Zoljargal, M. 2015. "Mayor Apologizes for Attack against Inner Mongolian Tourists." *UB Post*, April 5, 2015. http://ubpost.mongolnews.mn/?p=14023.

INDEX

CPSIA information can be obtained
at www.ICGtesting.com
Printed in the USA
FFHW020609100519
52386747-57777FF